A Pennington Pepys

EXTRACTS FROM THE COMMONPLACE
JOURNALS AND DIARIES OF
WILLIAM FLEMING (1770 - 1829)

BOOK ONE (1800 - 1808)

Edited and Annotated By John Graeme Livingstone

VIMIERA PUBLISHING

Published in 2019 by
VIMIERA PUBLISHING

© Copyright VIMIERA PUBLISHING

ISBN: 978-1-9160217-9-2

Book & Cover Design by Russell Holden

Pixel Tweaks Publications
SELF-PUBLISHING MADE SIMPLE

www.pixeltweakspublications.com

A Catalogue record for this book is available from the British Library.

Printed in the UK by INGRAM

CONTENTS

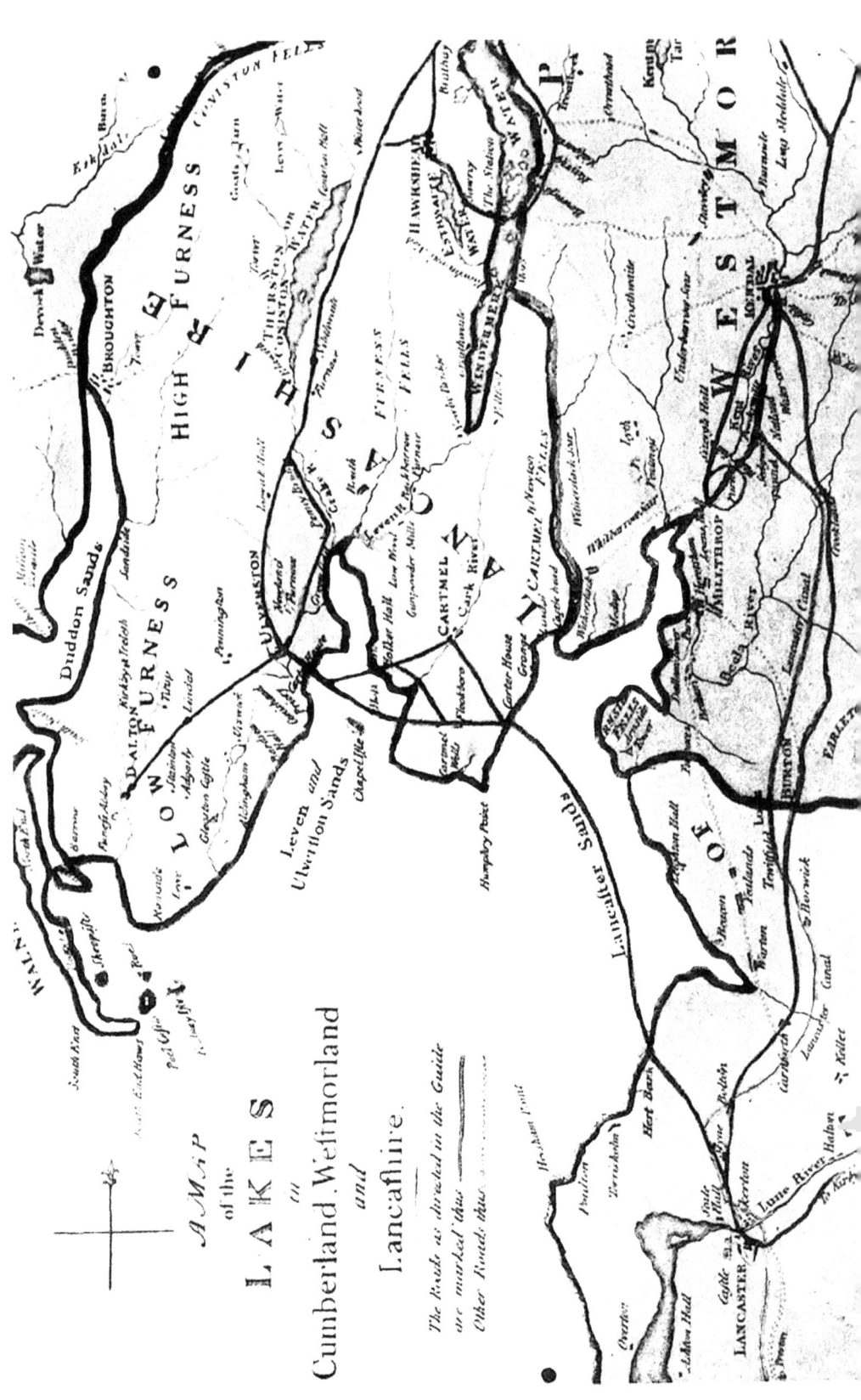

A MAP
of the
LAKES
in
Cumberland, Westmorland
and
Lancashire.

The Route as directed in the Guide
are marked thus ————
Other Roads thus ·····················

INTRODUCTION

I first came across the name of William Fleming nearly four years ago, when, after a successful performance by Flookburgh Amateur Operatic Society of my musical play, *The Adventures of Tom Dixon – Just A Little War* (A tale of a Flookburgh soldier during the Napoleonic wars), I ventured down to Cumbria Archives at Barrow-in-Furness, to try to find more about life in the Furness area during the late 18th – early 19th century.

I was immediately guided to the journals, known as the Diaries and Common-Place Books of William Fleming. These were acquired in 2009 by Cumbria Archive Services. However, it would appear that some of the work of William Fleming was known as early as 1958, when extracts were published in *'The Countryman'* magazine, by the late Mr. Frank Warriner of Millom. It was these articles that attracted the attention of the late Dr. Bill Rollinson of Barrow-in-Furness, who, three years later, whilst studying for his M.A. at the University of Manchester, managed to trace the owners, a Mr. and Mrs. Hodson of Ulpha, who kindly allowed him to see the diaries.

Dr. Rollinson states that at that time, there were ten leather-bound volumes, but since then, three have been lost. The remaining seven were microfilmed and are held by the University of Liverpool, University of Lancaster and Barrow Library.

To update this, I can reveal that there are now a total of twelve volumes, with only the first volume missing (See the list in the Appendices section at the end). These diaries record local social history, facts and observations on country life, farming, natural history, theatre, travel, the weather and the activities of Fleming's neighbours – including the clergy!

Sometimes sarcastic, often witty, Fleming always had an eye for detail and a thirst for accuracy; he catalogued facts and figures in a manner which ensures that his diaries are an invaluable source of material for local social, economic and agricultural historians.

A Pennington Pepys

The phrase was coined by Bill Rollinson, the acclaimed Barrow born lecturer, a founding member and former President of the Barrow Civic and Local History Society, using this title when lecturing on the subject of these diaries and was clearly intended to be a tribute to William Fleming, comparing him with that great 17th century diarist, Samuel Pepys.

Much of Bill's material background on William Fleming was taken from a book called *Old Lakeland, Some Cumbrian Social History* by J.D. Marshall. Bill (as he simply liked to be known) delivered, with passion and with flair, readings from Fleming's diaries with his observations, entertaining school children and local history societies alike.

Taking the title, 'A Pennington Pepys', a one-man play was written, I believe, by the late Norah Seddon of Ulverston and was produced by Renaissance Theatre Trust in 1977. The part of William Fleming was played by Barrow actor, the late David Marcus. It was re-written the following year, taking the form of a Victorian actor-manager visiting a local club, theatre or school. Once again produced by Renaissance Theatre Trust, the play was directed by Raymond Platt.

So, just who was William Fleming?

He was born on 11th June 1770 at the Row or Rowe Head, Pennington near Ulverston, then in Lancashire, now Cumbria. The family of Flemings have long been established in the Furness area and are mentioned sixty-eight times in the Parish Registers of Pennington between 1613 and 1701.

William was educated at the old Grammar School or Free School (founded in 1585 – now a private house) at Little Urswick, where he received a good grounding in the classics and literature.

The early volumes of his journal contain many facts. Lists of the Kings of Egypt and Babylon, the tribes of Israel, Roman emperors, scientific names of plants, as well as verses in both Latin and French (See Appendices at the end of this book for samples).

He had a personal library containing works by classical authors such as Horace, Cicero and Tacitus, as well as English writers like Alexander Pope. His literary leanings lead him to become a member of both the Dalton and Ulverston Book Clubs. (Dalton Book Club is the oldest in the world, having been founded in 1764 - See Appendices for website). He was also an avid reader of newspapers, particularly the Lancaster Gazette.

William Fleming's main occupation was that of a Yeoman Farmer (though technically he was a landowner and rented his land to other farmers, whilst employing one James Huddleston to farm for him). In addition to this, he was also a local historian, socialite, raconteur and a man of property. As well as the family home at Rowe, he owned a tenanted farm at Greenmoor House Pennington, another at Langthwaite near Millom and a third, possibly at High Carley. He also acquired, upon his marriage, a townhouse in Ulverston (Tarnside).

This enabled he and his family, in common with other Furness gentry, to reside during the autumn and winter months for the social season of theatre, assemblies and card parties. In Georgian times, Ulverston was referred to as the *London of Furness*, a scaled-down version of Britain's capital.

Although, at times, he was not afraid of dirtying his hands performing small tasks, William Fleming was generally a man of leisure. Often, he would go up on the moors or down to the woods to shoot game birds.

He was a church sidesman or warden at Pennington church. He was also appointed, at various times, to be Surveyor of the Highways and Overseer of the Poor. Clearly, he was a man who held many responsibilities and was generally respected. So, we may ascertain that William Fleming aspired to that of a Georgian gentleman.

He married Sarah Hodgson, from Tarnside, Ulverston on 28th April 1805 at St.Mary's Church, Ulverston. Strangely, his marriage certificate gives his occupation as a schoolmaster, but, as yet, there is no evidence of this. The Flemings' had five children - John, Richard, William, Mary and Sarah.

William Fleming died in September 1829, at the relatively young age of 59. He is buried in the churchyard of St. Michael and the Holy Angels Church, Pennington (though the exact site is unknown). His wife died the following year and she is buried there also.

A few years after his father's death, William Fleming Jnr. continued the work of Fleming, Snr. by keeping his own journal (More of that in a future book).

So, welcome to the world of William Fleming. A glimpse into a world long gone. A world without trains, planes and automobiles. No cinema or television. No photography, only the timeless expressions of painting and sketching. Certainly a world without computers and smartphones!

Medical science still in its infancy. No vote for the common man or woman. Sadly, as now, Fleming often speaks of a world of tears, a world at war... but sometimes there is time for laughter, and always there is a time for hope.

It will give any reader an insight into the economic and social life in Great Britain during the late Georgian and Regency period, but, for me, a whole new aspect on life in those times in my home town of Ulverston, the Furness Peninsula and beyond.

If local readers, today, despair of the decline of Ulverston Market, or perhaps, the number of people going to church, then nothing is new! Even Christmas was facing a lingering death in Fleming's day!

Finally, may I remind the reader that these diaries were kept purely for the writer's own purpose. Unlike authors of the time, such as Byron and Austen, they were never intended for publication, so I shall leave Mr Fleming, a far more eloquent writer than I, to explain as to why he kept them ...

When I began to write these Journals it was not merely
as a Source of Amusement and Relaxation from
Reading and other Employments but with a View of
their affording me pleasure at some future period, by
bringing to my Remembrance many little particulars
which would undoubtedly have escaped my memory,
and which, though little deserving of Notice, and on no
other Account worthy of being recorded, may delight
me, when I am reminded of them.

How very different many Objects appear to me now,
to what they did when I was a Boy: most things then
appeared to me in a pleasing View; but the fairy Visions
of Youth re seldom realised they are flattering and
delusive, and bring little but Disappointment, excepting
the delightful Impressions which the Contemplation of
the picturesque Beauties of Nature made upon me, and
these continue till the present time with undiminished
Effect.

There is an exquisite pleasure in the Recollection of the
Scenes of Youth, and doubtless old Age will be equally
gratified in reviewing the Actions of Manhood, and
calling to Mind the kindness of Friends long since gone
to their everlasting Homes.

I wish not the distinguishing Characters of some of my
Acquaintance to sink with them in the Grave and be
forgotten by me, especially of the good: let the Deeds of
the Wicked die with them, but the Virtuous and their
Actions should not be suffered to sink in Oblivion.

(William Fleming)

GUIDE TO EDITOR'S NOTES

In editing this, the first book on the journals of William Fleming, I am duty-bound to give the reader some afsiftance (sorry, assistance!) in reading his daily entries.

In the interests of authenticity, the grammar, including spelling, people and place names are taken exactly as written by Fleming in his own handwriting. In fact, ALL of the entries have been faithfully reproduced. Most of the daily entries not only have the calendar date but also the day of the week (though this is not always the case).

Notes and any corrections to the spellings, by myself, are in square brackets. For the most part, I have let Fleming speak for himself, only adding my jottings to explain the historical background or expanding on a character or place.

In general, I have omitted the many weather reports that fill his journals (some examples are to be found in the Appendices) but have left these in should they be essential to the narrative of that particular entry.

I have decided to include the entries of the various markets Fleming attends, showing the prices of food and goods over 200 years ago (Ale at 3d per pint!).

Finally, the text of William Fleming indicates the shift in spelling from Georgian times to the present. The word 'favour' for example, sometimes spelt as 'favor'.

How Ulverston or Ulverstone is spelt, has always been debatable amongst Ulverstonians. Mr Fleming uses both!

I hope you enjoy the journey

JGL

CHAPTER 1

THE CHILDREN DANCED
TOLERABLY WELL
1800-1801

As stated in my introduction, Volume One of the Fleming diaries has still not been found (as at time of going to press) and much of Volume Two contains various lists of Latin and French verse, lists of various dates, people and places in history and a lengthy list of the scientific names of plants. Some of these facts may be found in the Appendices at the end of this book.

So, let us begin with the second volume and the first of his 'social life' entries.

NOVEMBER [1800]

21st (Friday) - Attended Mr Benson's Ball at Little Urswick, the children danced tolerably well - Mr Benson danced a minuet for which I think him blameable as he could gain nothing by the Specimen, but might probably be a looser [loser ?].

22nd (Saturday) - The Market which has been re – established at Dalton....was well attended and afforded a good quantity of grain which was sold ......Oats - 17/- per bushel , Barley - 25/- per bushel Wheat - 42/- per bushel ....

This evening went to the Theatre at Ulverston where was represented the Tragedy of Barnwell: two or three of the characters were tolerably, but the others miserably, supported. A Lady in the Boxes (Mrs B-rton) *[Probably Burton]* was the only person I saw affected so much as to shed tears, and from certain circumstances in her behaviour this evening, I am induced to suspect them rather the effect of Brandy than the sympathetic proofs of sensibility. The Entertainment of the Jew and the Doctor is not destitute of humour and something worthy of remembrance might be gleaned from it by an attentive spectator.

[Most likely the theatre referred to by Fleming is one of the older theatres in Ulverston, possibly the White Hart Barn. A new theatre was opened in 1801, later called the Theatre Royal. What remains of this building is now an auction room and beauty salon]

27th (Thursday) - Read the first Vol . Of Van Braam's Ambassador of the Dutch Embafsy *[Embassy]* to China; but found little in it either instructive or entertaining ----

The first account we have of the Aurora Borealis was the 14th November 1574, from that time no mention is made of those lights till their remarkable appearance in March 1716, viz on the 6th, 7th , 8th and 9th, at which time they were seen in England, Ireland, Poland, Russia and other countries. A few beams of Aurora Borealis appeared this evening, shooting from the North but with less lively colours than usual.

DECEMBER [1800]

9th (Tuesday) - Where could a soldier have met death more honorably than under the Command of Leonidas at the Battle of Thermopylae. This is a memorable instance of the valour with which men fight for their liberty and their Country, and I doubt not but my own Country men would show the same desperate valour and determined resolution either to defend their Country and Freedom, or to meet a glorious death in the struggle, should the French ever dare to set a hostile foot in this land of liberty.

[The above entry is a reference to the French Revolutionary War, which was raging at this time and the potential threat of invasion]

12th (Friday) - Mr Tyson's Ball was ill conducted and the Man himself behaved in the most rude manner to the Parents of his Scholars and the rest of the Company. In a Dancing Master one is apt to look for Plitenes *[Politeness?]* and Gobal *[Global?]* Manners; and parents who have children under his care expect civility at least; but to be called Forls *[Fools?]* and ridiculed publicly at the Ball by the Master himself who ought to set the example of nice behaviour and good manners to his Scholars, is, in my opinion, the most effectual method he can take to loose *[lose?]* his credit (if he ever had any) as a Master, and destory *[destroy?]* any future prospect of a School in the same place. The Man is allowed to have good feet, but surely there must be a deficiency in his head.........

14th (Sunday) - Dined with Mr Postlethwaite at Dalton, who, in the Course of the Afternoon, introduced a Mr.

Hanson, Swedish Consul, resident at Liverpool. From
the little I saw of him, think him of an open cheerful
Disposition; he speaks the English Language tolerably,
but has something in his pronunciation similar to
the Inhabitants of the Town of Newcastle upon Tyne
and the Neighbourhood, called the Bur *[?-Word
unintelligible]*

On Friday 12th. Cuthbert Atkinson, Steward to Ld.
[Lord] Muncaster called a Court at the Kiln House
within the Manor of Pennington, having previously
summoned only four of the Tenants to serve as a jury,
to find Matthew Denney Tenant of an Estate at Lowfield
House. As it has from Time immemorial been the
Custom within this Manor to have a Jury of at least 12
of the tenants, the proceedings of the Steward were
opposed, and he *[was?]* accused of an attempt to break
thro' the Customs of the Manor (which he has in fact
broke thro ' before * as may be seen in the 1st volume
page 170*) ……....*[this is in the missing Volume One]* of
Consequence nothing was done, and the Steward
departed not too well pleased at the opposition he met
with ---------

31st (Wednesday) - So ends the year
1800 in which every article of food
has been at an exorbitant price and
yet continues to rise in the Markets.

Oats – 25/-, Barley – 30 /- (The
Carlisle Bushel) Wheat - £4/10s per
load of 1 and a half bushels, potatoes
at 10d per hoop; Butter 11d per
pound – Cheese 10d per pound, Malt
38/- per bushel.

1801

JANUARY [1801]

12th (Monday) - Went on a visit to Ch. *[Charles?]* Hobson Esq. of Bootle and spent the week there most pleasantly and returned on the 17th.

13th (Tuesday) - Took a cup of tea with Jos. *[Joseph?]* Benn of Middleton Place.

14th (Wednesday) - Dined with John Herbank of Beckside Esq and spent the evening with William Herbank of Beckside Esq both of which are very friendly gentlemen.

25th (Sunday) - Thomas Robinson of Newbarns was buried this evening, Mr Bradley and self desired to attend the Funeral.

FEBRUARY [1801]

26th (Thursday) - Oats at Ulverston Market sold at 28/- per bushel, Butter at 14d per pound: Potatoes at 12d per hoop. Beef and Mutton 8d per pound.

MARCH [1801]

24th (Tuesday) - William Nicholson buried this afternoon.

APRIL [1801]

14th (Sunday) - Spent the Afternoon at Mr. J. Ashburner's

16th (Thursday) - Saw a swallow skimming over the
water at Goosegreen.

MAY [1801]

15th (Friday) - A Cooper *[Copper]* Mine was discovered
this Spring on Poaks near Marton and is now opened
but does not promise abundance of ore as yet.

24th (Sunday) - Went this evening to Lancaster for
the purpose of seeing the Celebrated Mrs Siddons in
Macbeth. From what I had read and heard of her before,
my expectations were raised too high, of consequence I
was greatly disappointed, for she did not exert herself
even as much as to be distinctly heard in the upper
Boxes of this small theatre.

*[Sarah Siddons was a Welsh
actress, born in 1755. She
specialized in tragic characters
and was most famous for her
portrayal of Lady Macbeth.
She retired from the stage in
1812 and died in 1831. In
Fleming's day, this theatre
was simply known as The
Theatre, Lancaster, but is now
called The Grand Theatre.
Mrs Siddons often performed
there as her brother was the
manager]*

Sarah Siddons – Actress

JUNE [1801]

11th (Thursday) - Found about 2 pound coal upon Goosegreen, Dalton, at the lower end.........which burned extremely well.

JULY [1801]

28th (Tuesday) - …..............About 100 yards to the West of Urswick Church in Furness, in a field called Kirkfalt *[Kirk Flatt]* adjoining the Highway, stands a rough piece of unknown limestone, which the inhabitants of Urswick were accustomed to dress as a figure of Priapus on Midsummer Day, by smearing it with Sheep Salue, Tar or Butter and covering it with rags of various dyes, the head ornated with flowers.

[The Priapus Stone is some kind of fertlity symbol or votive offering. Almost certainly it pre-dates Christianity and it still exists. It is a block of unhewn limestone which measures 7 foot long by 2 feet 7 inches wide and 1 foot thick. Originally it used to stand upright in the field on the other side of the wall till around 1920, but is now built into the base of the limestone wall near Holme Bank Farm close to Urswick vicarage. It is supposed to look like male genitalia! See 'The Journal Of Antiquities' for further information]

AUGUST [1801]

1st (Saturday) - The Annual Fair at Broughton held this day was not over Stocked with Cattle which were bought up at very high prices – but the number of Beggars and their Saucinefs *[Sauciness]* especially towards the Evening was insupportable, for you must either give them Money or bear their Abusive Language which they were by no means sparing of, and highly merited to be whipt *[whipped]* thro' the Town for I am sure the most sverve *[severe]* Flagellation could not exceed what was due to them.

10th (Monday) - This evening was visited by a Mr Blakeney from Whitehaven, a polite, sensible, well informed Man, quick with Quotations to support his Arguments, ready with the Bonmot *[Bon Mot–clever remarks]*, and elegant in his Efufsion *[Effusion]*. Tho' not at present blefsed *[blessed]* with that Share of good Health which invigorates the Mind, he was cheerful and facotious *[facetious?]* and would frequently indulge in those little Flights of Fancy which in certain Bounds are so pleasing.

11th (Tuesday) - At a Dinner given by Ldp...*[Lord Pennington?]* on the Event of a Duel, which after a Fire or two was amicably terminated, Mr Wedderburn was present amongst many Gentlemen & Ladies of Rank and Fashion – Mr Wedderburn was called upon by Lord p..... for a Toast, whilst he was earnestly discufsing *[discussing]* a Law point with a Gentleman near him, and unfortunately forgetting the presence of the Ladies, who had not yet retired gave, 'The Beggars Benison' and immediately resumed the Conversation. This Caus'd a general Smile, which the Limb of the Law being too deep immers'd in Conversation to notice, a Gentleman at the other End of the Table call'd out............

'Mr Wedderburn , Lady...... *[Name left blank]* requests an Explanation of your Toast' ; Mr W. immediately recollected himself and addrefsing Ld...........

'If Lady........ desires it, I will most assuredly explain it.'
My Lord,'May you enjoy the Beggar's Blifs *[Bliss]*
And Jove himself be Bail
Your Cock and Lock may never mifs *[miss]*
And purse may never fail ---------'

[The Beggars Benison is a poem or song based on a Scottish Gentlemens' club in the 18th century devoted to the convivial celebration of male sexuality!]

16th (Sunday) - Reapers at Dalton this Day were as high as 7s 6d per Day and Meat, the highest ever known, owing to the Grain in Furnefs *[Furness]* being almost totally fit for the Sickle the ensuing Week, which is a fortnight earlier than usual.

18th (Tuesday) - The hottest day experienced here for some years.

19th (Wednesday) -The Heat this day is intollerable and the Reapers, who are *[on?]* account of the extravagant wages, are compelled to labour extremely hard and long hours, sink under it. At Gleaston Castle, one (a Scot) died this morning, and another is expected before the night to breathe his last.

20th (Thursday) - Yesterday Evening, William Harrison of St. Hellen's *[St.Helens?]*, a hired Reaper at E Slaters Park, died from the heat and too great excertion in the Harvest Field: he was reaping and in good spirits at 4 o'clock and dead at 8 o'clock.

23rd (Sunday) - Reapers this day were generally hired at 7s 6 d per day but a few at 10s 6d.

SEPTEMBER [1801]

1st (Tuesday) - Baldwin, Rev Dr. Rector of Aldingham and Preb, of Carlisle died 28th August.

8th (Tuesday) - Oats at Ulverston Market sold at 8s to 10s 6d per Bush: and Wheat at 42 s. per load: Potatoes 3d per hoop of 6 quarts. Barley at 21s per Bush:

12th (Saturday) - To Make Turnip Bread *[See ' FOOD AND DRINK RECIPES ' in the Appendices]*

OCTOBER [1801]

5th (Monday) - The Preliminaries of a Treaty of Peace with France, signed on Thursday Evening the 1st. of this Inst. October by Ld. *[Lord]* Hawkesbury on the Part of Great Britain and Monsr. *[Monsieur]* Otto for the French Republic arrived in the Gazette this day and was the Cause of great Joy, which was demonstrated by the Ringing of Bells, Bonefires Etc ------

[News of this preliminary peace, which eventually would lead to the Treaty Of Amiens, March 1802, was greeted with great excitement in Britain. People hoped it would lead to the withdrawal of Income Tax imposed by Prime Minister William Pitt to fund the war, a reduction in the price of grain, and a revival in the fortune of the markets. Witness the following account of the celebrations in Dalton]

In the Evening a Party of Gentlemen afsembled *[assembled]* at the Cock in Dalton, where a Number of loyal Toasts were drank ------ The good Lanlady *[Landlady]*, on hearing the News, had entered so heartily into the Spirit of Rejoicing, that when the Gentlemen met, they found the good Woman's Legs were grown separatory, and wou'd not obey their Mistress; when she wd. *[would]* have directed her Steps to the Cellar, they carried her to the Foot of the Stairs in a Zigzag Course, and here, thinking she placed her Dependance more on the Door than on them, these obstinate Members entirely withdrew their Support, so down the old Lady dump'd on the Floor, and her bare Posteriors were brought into Contact with the dirty Flags ------------

Of the Gentlemen who met at the Cock this Evening the Revd. Mr. C.......*[Cowperthwaite]* Vicar of D....... *[Dalton]* was one. His Reverence, who takes his Glass pretty freely, and is blest with an excellent Appetite which he seldom fails to gratify when an Opportunity offers, had a Funeral today, at which he had laid in too great a Store of good things, I mean, more than the Receptacle cou'd retain with Ease when about three Pints of Hollands and water were added to the Stock.

Now whether all these good Things taking it ill to be confined in such a narrow Compafs *[Compass]*, quarrelled among themselves, the Stronger attempting to drive out the Weaker, or whatever was the Cause, it so happened that no small Part of the confined were forced to return by the Way they entered, and not giving us any previous Notice of their Coming, we were unprepared for their Reception, yet Mr. ----- had the Luck to receive them in his Lap: Whilst these were removing, a rumbling Noise from below gave us Notice that another Part were escaping by the Postern Gate; this most probably was the Cowardly part, which began the Fray, and being afraid of the Fall they wou'd get if driven out at the Attic Story, took the Opportunity while the Rest were marching up his Throat, to steal out at the Back Door and conceal themselves in the Parson's Breeches.

But the place of their Concealment cou 'd not long be
kept a Secret, for those who sat near him soon smelt it
out & the Lawyer first rais'd the Hue and Cry.

[The Peace Treaty celebrations continue]

14th (Wednesday) - In Consequence of the Confirmation
of the Treaty of peace made with the French Republic;
an account of which arrived Yesterday Morning,
Ulverston was splendidly illuminated and many
appropriate Emblems display'd especially by the Revd.
Everard the Roman Catholic Clergyman and Mr Brooks
an active Magistrate in the Town: Fireworks were play'd
off and Ale given to the Populace.

*[Dr. Patrick Everard came from Fethard, County Tipperary.
He was educated at the University of Salamanca in Spain,
a refugee of the French Revolution and a friend of the
philosopher, Edmund Burke. He built a large house with
chapel and stables in Fountain Street, Ulverston and founded
a Lay Academy, purchased from the Jesuits. He also owned
land in the town, including Gill Banks and Ratten Row
Meadows. In 1810 he was invited to become President of the
famous Maynooth College. His health became poor and he
returned to Ulverston on a number of occasions. In 1820 he
became Archbishop of Cashel, but died there in 1821]*

16th (Friday) - Set out on a Tour to
Whitehaven................

Before I set out on my Tour, I resolved, to look for
Objects of Instruction and Amusement only, and to
be pleas'd with every Thing, that I wou'd only look
at the bright & more pleasing Side of every Object
and of Consequence be amused according as it made
Imprefsion on my Mind.

Thus determined that nothing which presented itself to me in a pleasing Form shou'd escape me, I set out in great Spirits, indulging every pleasing Idea, and banishing every tormenting Intruder which I supposed cou'd bring a Cloud over the Sunshine of Pleasure or produce Melancholy Reflections.

My first thought, as I mounted the Hill to Pennington Castle, were, that I was about to travel thro' a Part of the Country which many curious and learned Men had journeyed before me, some of which had published their Remarks, and disagreed in Opinion concerning the same objects. Now, said I to myself, suppose any one shou'd ask my Opinion of the same Things, which may probably be the Case in some part of my Journey, shall I give it according to my own Judgement or be biased by those who have gone before me?

After duly considering this very weighty Point, I resolved to give an Opinion of my own, whether right or wrong, independent of those who have trod the Path before me; for thought I, the Perusal of this Sketch may perhaps amuse me at some future Period, and shou'd it even fail in that I care not, for the only Object of my Tour is my present Amusem. *[Amusement]* and I am not inclined Servily to follow the Steps of any Man upon Earth; no, I disdain to tread the beaten Track when a pleasanter Road presents itself to me, but strike out in search of fresh, Beauties of Nature or Art, the majestic Remains of Antiquity or the Embelishments of modern Architecture, which, alas, will one Day be view'd a Heap of Ruins.

Pennington Castle, situated on an Eminence abt.*[about]* Half a Mile to the NW of the Church at a place called Castle Haw or Castle Law, is mouldered into Ruin.

It has been a Fortrefs *[Fortress]* of very great Antiquity, and, if one may judge from the Situation, impregnable, whilst our Ancestors were ignorant of the Use of Gunpowder.

Tradition informs us this was once the Habitation of the Penningtons, tho' at a remote Period, for I have been told by the present Ld. Muncaster, that his Ancestors removed from Pennington to Muncaster about Forty years before the Conquest. Little now remains of this once important Fortrefs.

The devouring Tooth or the levelling Hand of Time (for I can't positively say which has done the Deed) has reduced it to a humble State filled up a great part of the Ditch which surrounded it and despoil'd it of every Beauty; but the Prospect from it is extensive and Charming. Yet perhaps neither the Tooth nor Hand of Time alone brought it to it's present State, but the Depridations of these Neighbours might in some Measure afsist *[assist]*, tho' none of the Materials are to be distinguished in the Habitations around it. The Rampart and Ditch will remain, but very little Mason Work is now visible; and it has more the Appearance of having been one of the strongholds of the Britons or Saxons than any thing else.

From hence I crofsed *[crossed]* the Moors to Kirkby where is an ancient Church dedicated to St. Cuthbert; and proceeded to Braaighton *[Broughton]* --------

Broughton is a clean little Town, with a good Market place; it has no Trade, and none of the Inhabitants can be called rich, but they are posfs'd *[possessed]* of Pride in a superlative Degree: yet as the Superstructure of Pride is raised on the Basis of Poverty, it perhaps may not be durable.

Just above the Town to the East stands Broughton Towers a Beautiful Seat of the Lord of the Manor of Broughton, at present only inhabited by the Gardener and his Wife, who readily admitted me to see the Rooms which were open; I found a few locked up, and there I was informed contained the best Family Pictures and more valuable Part of the Furniture. The Building is falling rapidly to decay.

Scarcely had I arrived at the Inn from visiting the Tower, and was sat down to scribble over the Few Lines above when a Gentleman entered the Parlour, and without much Apology drew a Chair to the opposite Side of the Fire. After making some observations on the Weather, and fixing his Eyes steadfastly on me for some Time

'I think Sir' says he: ' I recollect your Face - I replied, ' probably, Sir you may – Yet your Name does not occur to my Memory. Pray Sir, are you married ? - 'I am not, sir; I do not yet enjoy the Happinefs *[Happiness]* of a married State – And yet perhaps you are happy for all that. - Perhaps not perfectly so. - Then I presume you think Matrimony and Happinefs near allied, as most young People do. - Yes, Sir, I look upon Matrimony as instituted for social Happinefs and mutual Comfort.

When Man was alone, formed out of the Immensity of Matter and thrown upon the World to live unconnected with any other Creature, in the Midst of Animals unendowed with the Reason or Speech, from among which it was impossible for him to select one Friend which cou'd be made Sensible of his Wants, or to which he cou'd communicate his Thoughts so as to be understood, he must have found himself unhappy, destitute of almost every Comfort which Life affords, and without the least Assistance in Sicknefs Danger and Difficulty he might perish as a Dog in the Desart *[Desert]* without any Creature being sensible of the Lofs *[Loss]*. But to soften the Miseries and alleviate the Troubles of human Nature, Woman was made at the Fiat *[a Decree]* of the Almighty and became his Wife.

Then they mutually contribute to each others' Happinefs *[Happiness]* studied to relieve each others Wants and were ready to administer Consolation either of them. 'Twas then that Man had the first Taste of Happinefs, and enjoyed these Pleasures which ....

[The following note is inserted by Fleming himself]:

'I thought this long Speech wd *[would]* silence the Gent.m *[Gentleman]*, I was mistaken.' .... are unknown in a solitary State - But yet, Sir, replied he, Happinefs does not always prove the Consequence of a matrimonial Connection.

The promised Pleasures which amuse the Imagination often vanish when the indissoluble Knot is tied and the irrevocable Sentence pronounced. Many little things occur which produce uneasinefs *[uneasiness]*, put them out of Humour, and diminish that Affection which shou'd insure Happinefs -

But, Sir, I shou'd imagine many of those little domestic Quarrels and Bickerings might be avoided, if the married Couple wd. Make a firm Resolution to substitute Cheerfulness & Goodnature for Opposition and Railery [*Raillery?*], when either of them was in a fretful Humour, for illnature can answer no good Purpose, and instead of removing the Uneasiness, may blow up the hidden Spark into a Flame, which shou'd be carefully extinguished at it's first Appearance.

Mirth kept within due Bounds, join'd to modest Goodnature has Charms which few can resist; it is contagious and communicates itself to most of those who come within its influence.

We find Persons posefsed [*possessed*] of this happy Temper constantly sought after as the most agreeable Companions, undoubtedly for the Pleasure their Company affords and the Cheerfulnefs [*cheerfulness*] which is by their Means diffused over the rest. Sudden Flights of Fancy & unexpected Sallies of Wit may for the Time please and amuse, but are far short of that steady uninterupted Cheerfulnefs which all admire.

A Cheerful goodnatured well informed Man must be the most desirable Companion in Life.

His Cheerfulness dispels that Gloom and melancholy which will sometimes come over the Mind:

His Goodnature kindness every Dispute which Contradiction and Illnature can Invent to spoil the Pleasures of Society, for I should imagine that Illnature itself can find no Gratification in Contradiction and Dispute where it finds no Opposition. ---

Well, Sir, returned he, I find you are a strong Advocate for Matrimony. But where will you find a married Pair of the Disposition you speak of?

If even one of them was blessed with it, I am persuaded he wou'd not often find himself inclined to meet his Wife, in the Height of her Peevishness and ill Humour, with Cheerfulness nor to answer her ill Nature with a Smile, except it was the Smile of Contentment. His calm Goodnature can't but be ruffled by the Storm of her impetuous pafsions *[passions]*, which he is no more able to restrain, than the Mariner on the troubled Ocean is able to smooth the rolling Surges when tempetuous Boreas *[Greek god of the North Wind]* distends his swelling Cheeks.

Now perhaps Sir, in selecting a Wife out of the numerous Tribe of Ladies wanting Husbands, you wou'd look for Money in the First Place, if you thought that an independent Fortune alone cou'd insure Happinefs *[happiness]*;

or, dispising Riches, you might only seek for Youth and Beauty, if theses were judged the only Requisites in a Wife, or perhaps you would only regard the Endowments of the Mind and sweetnefs of Temper, and when these were found wou'd not reject even a plain Face, because Beauty had no part in your prospects of Happinefs ; but take my Word for it, to whatever point your Views of Happinefs are directed, or on whatever Endowments or good Qualities in the Lady it depends , you will find yourself not a little disappointed.

Ladies before Marriage are nothing but Artiface, *[Artifice?]* and continually contriving to impose upon the Men, they conceal every Defect whether in their Mind Body or Fortune.

In whatever Light you view an unmarried Lady, she will fall greatly in your Estimation when the connubial Ties had made you better acquainted when you are placed in a Situation from which you cannot recede, may if not all those Endowments and good Qualities from which you had calculated a certain Degree of Happiness wou'd arise, will be found wanting.

Where then must we look for it? Must we expect it to ifsue *[issue]* from every hidden Source?

There is no Source in a Wife from which Happiness can spring, & whatever Ideas you may have of it whilst she is your Mistrefs *[Mistress]* they are all a Vision which will never be realised. ' Varium et mutabile semper femina ' *[Woman is ever fickle and changeable]* said Virgil & he spoke the Truth. Shou'd I be required, continued he to delineate a Lady in Character both before and after Marriage, and had Abilities to execute it; the former should be a Venus on the Margin of some smooth Lake described in Romance; the latter shou'd be, the Devil in a Tempest. How strange the Contrast, but how perfect the Resemblance - Truly, Sir, return'd I, you are extremely severe upon the Sex; I hope this is not intended for a general character.

This Sir, answer'd he, I know from Observation and Experience to be their general Character.

I have liv'd a few years more than you in the World, and have had many Opportunities of being convinced of the Truth of it: and, Sir, if you live only to my Age, and shall have been as many years a Husband; I say when that Period shall arrive; if you are not of my Opinion, and find not the Character a true one, I will forfeit the soundest of my fore Teeth which wou'd be a Lofs *[Loss]* all the women in the World could not repair.

23rd – The number of cattle at Dalton Fair greater than usual this season , but sold lower than other fairs.

NOVEMBER [1801]

3rd (Tuesday) - In a Meadow near Park, call'd Chapel Meadow, which the Farmers are now draining, the Groundwork of a Building was yesterday discovered, this Building has probably been a Chapel, and situated in the most boggy and soft part the Foundation is well secured with Oak Piles which are now as sound as the Day they were driven into the Earth tho' they have undoubtebly laid there Hundreds of Years.

5th (Thursday) - In proceeding with the Drains at Park, mentioned on the 3rd. Inst; at a little Distance from the Foundation of the Building a lead Pipe of about 1 and one half inches Diameter was discovered, the Direction of which they pursued and have taken up about 40 Yards of it, some of which is still perfect and leads directly to a Spring at some Distance, there still remain in the Ground several small lateral Pipes which at certain Distances were inserted into the main Pipe, and are not esteemed worth the Labour of taking up, & Curiosity does not induce them to do it.

12th (Thursday) - Oats from 8s to 11s per Bush [Bushel] - Wheat 40s per Load – Butter 8d & 9d per lb -

21st (Saturday) - Was visited by Lieut. Hodgson who so bravely took the Enemy's Fleet & the Island of Coricoa *[Curacao]*. *[Lieutenant Hodgson, of the Royal Navy,*

*an Ulverston man and a relative of William Fleming, by
marriage. Further details will be revealed in the next chapter]*

DECEMBER [1801]

[Only weather reports for this month]

CHAPTER 2

HE HAD BEEN OF GREAT SERVICE IN ANNOYING THE FRENCH
1802

JANUARY [1802]

7th - Pork at Ulverston – 7d per lb. Beef – 5.5d and 6d.

14th - Oats – 9s 6d per bush. Wheat – 48s per load. Butter 1s per lb. Beef – 7d. Mutton – 6d. Pork – 7.5d per lb. Potatoes – 3d per hoop.

FEBRUARY [1802]

[Fleming writes down the lyrics of various songs of times past, including 'Sirre Martynne and His Manne']

MARCH [1802]

1st - *[Fleming writes letters in Latin]*

3rd - *[Fleming lists in his journal names and dates of battles , societies etc.]*

APRIL [1802]

[Further weather reports]

MAY [1802]

13th (Thursday) - The frost so severe as to destroy all
the early potatoes.

31st (Monday) - Fruit Trees in general this Spring have
produced abundance of Blossom which is now entirely
Destroy'd by the Frosts & E. Winds or by Insects.
Last night's Frost has again kill 'd most of the Tops of
Potatoes which had sprung up again since the 20th Inst

JUNE [1802]

29th (Tuesday) – *[Fleming receives a long letter from a
friend – W . Ashburner]*

JULY [1802]

6th (Tuesday) - *[Fleming quotes more Latin]*

7th (Wednesday) - *[Fleming replies to Ashburner]*

AUGUST [1802]

9th (Monday) - To Make Currant Wine *[See ' FOOD
AND DRINK RECIPES ' in the Appendices]*

SEPTEMBER [1802]

4th -19th - Reapers – 2/6d - 6/6d per day.

26th - Harvest finished. Extremely hot.

OCTOBER [1802]

25th (Monday) - Ulverston Hunt began today.

NOVEMBER [1802]

4th (Thursday) - The first evening performance this season at the Ulverston Theatre.

[Most likely this is the new theatre, later Theatre Royal]

19th (Friday) - Mrs. Jane Branthwaite Relict of Dr. Branthwaite late of Ulverston was this Morning inter'd at Pennington. NB This is the second Funeral only which has been in the Morning, at the Parish Church of Pennington, in my Remembrance -

21st (Sunday) - This Evening about 6 o'clock Richard Fleming of Greenmoor House died; he only began to find himself ill yesterday Morning – His Age was 55 Years -

[Richard Fleming was William Fleming's uncle]

28th (Sunday) - Curacao, Ile *[Isle]* of taken by Leut. Jas. *[Lieutenant James]* Hodgson of Ulverston Sept. 1800

[Extract from *Chronological History Of The West Indies* by Thomas Southey - Captain Watkins says in his letter to Lord Hugh Seymour, I have now the satisfaction to inform your Lordship, that the English colours are flying in this island, and I have entered this harbour in consequence of the total evacuation of French forces last night.

I have received with great faith, and will do my utmost in establishing the security of the principal fortress till I receive your lordship's answer for my farther conduct.

Lieutenant James Hodgson was appointed to command the fortress; he had been of great service in annoying the French from a new – erected battery which was the principal cause of their retreat.]

DECEMBER [1802]

5th - (Sunday) - Jno. *[John]* Dodshon, Thos. Nicholson & I went to Greenmoor House to inspect the Furniture.

I took the Desk which belonged to my late Grandfather Wm. Fleming at Jno. Dodshon's Valuation: 20s –

I also brought away my late Uncle Rd. Fleming's Picture and one of his Walking Sticks a Supple Jack;

[A Supple Jack is a cane or walking stick]

Mr. T. Nicholson took another of the same kind but stronger – Five silver Teaspoons not to be found, also two Do. *[Ditto]* Table spoons wanting.

8th - (Wednesday) - Went with T. Nicholson to Greenmoor House to meet Jno. Dodshon who came to repair the Furniture preparatory to the Sale of them on Saturday next; I brought away one of the Desks valued at 20s. - At 12 o'clock went to Mill House to meet Cuthbert Atkinson, Steward to Ld. Muncaster and Jno. Robinson Atty. *[Attorney]* at Law on the subject of enclosing and dividing the Commons & waste Grounds laying within the Manor and belonging to the Parish of Pennington where Mr Robinson opened the Businefs *[Business]* by reading his Lordship's Proposals, which were that his Ld.ship should have allotted him 1st.

One eighth part of the Commons for his Lordship. Or Manor of Pennington; 2nd – one tenth part of the Remainder of the said Commons for his one tenth of the Taxes which he has paid from Time immemorial, which one eighth and one tenth wou'd be equal to about one fifth of the whole, which is certainly too great a part for his Lordsp. to have; other Lords of Manors in the Neighbourhood where the Commons have been enclosed, were allow'd only one sixteenth for the Manor, whereas Ld. Muncaster would have two sixteenths – he proposed to pay one sixth part of the Costs of enclosing and all incidental Expences – the Commifsioners for the same to be three in number, vz. *[viz]* one to be chosen by Ld. Muncaster and another by the Tenants of Pennington and these two to chose the third – the Expenses of procuring the Act of Parliament were estimated at about 300£ - the Comons to be proportioned to each Estate according to the Landtax bill, which was calculated to amount to about one acre of the Comons for every 6d paid by each Estate in the said bill, therefore my proportion would be about 36 acres for Rowe Estate the Land Tax being 18s –

It was proposed, had Lord Muncaster's Terms met with the Approbation of the Tenants, that no part of the Commons should be sold to defray the Expenses of enclosing , but the whole to be paid by a Rate upon the several Tenants according to the Landtax Bill , by which all the parish Rates are laid – Ld. Muncaster retain'd to himself all Mines Minerals, Slate and Game within the said Comons – the public Roads to be set out 30 feet wide-

11th (Saturday) - This Afternoon, sold the Furniture of my late Uncle Rich'd. Fleming at Greenmoor House, where many things were wanting. I brought away 5 square Case Bottles – Liquor at the sale; 1 Gal. Rum – Half Barrel of Ale -

Anecdote:

The Revd. W. Bifsell *[Bissell]* late Vicar of Pennington coming once to visit his Parish, lodged at the Sun Inn at Ulverston: there happened to be a Meeting of the Justices there at the same time; one of them having the Occasion to go into another Room, chanced to enter the Chamber of the Revd. Vicar who used a Trumpet to supply the Defect of Hearing. 'Pray, Sir' said the Gentleman addrefsing *[addressing]* himself to the half deaf Priest ,'is there a Pot there?' His Reverence immediately applied his Trumpet to his Ear, when the Justice repeated the Question, ' Pray, Sir, is there a Pot there?'

'Yes' replied the Parson, lifting up the Valance and drawing out the half replete Member Mug from under the Bed;

'Yes' said he, 'and if you want it you shall have it'; at the same Time discharging the Contents on the astonished Peacemaker who hasten'd from his Presence dripping like Thetis new risen from the Realms of Neptune.

17th (Friday) - This Evening Mr. Gardner of Dendron let a part of his Estate in parcels for 6 years Rent abt. [*about*] 160£ per anm. [*annum*].

[Fleming concludes his second volume listing scientific names of a great many plants and includes sketches on some pages. He categorises them and separates them into different classes]

18th (Saturday) - Invited to Newbarns to celebrate the birthday of Mr James Robinson and his son Richard Robinson.

24th (Friday) - Prices: Beef – 7d – best Mutton – 7and
a half d – Veal 6d per lb – Butter 12d – Eggs 1d doz. -
Currants & Raisons – 10d per lb – Geese alive 6d per lb
– Tallow – 8s per stone – Candles 10 per lb.

31st (Friday) - The Allotment of men to serve in the
Old Militia took place at Ulverston on 22nd instant.
when Jno. *[John]* Brunskill the Miller was allotted for the
Township of Pennington. -

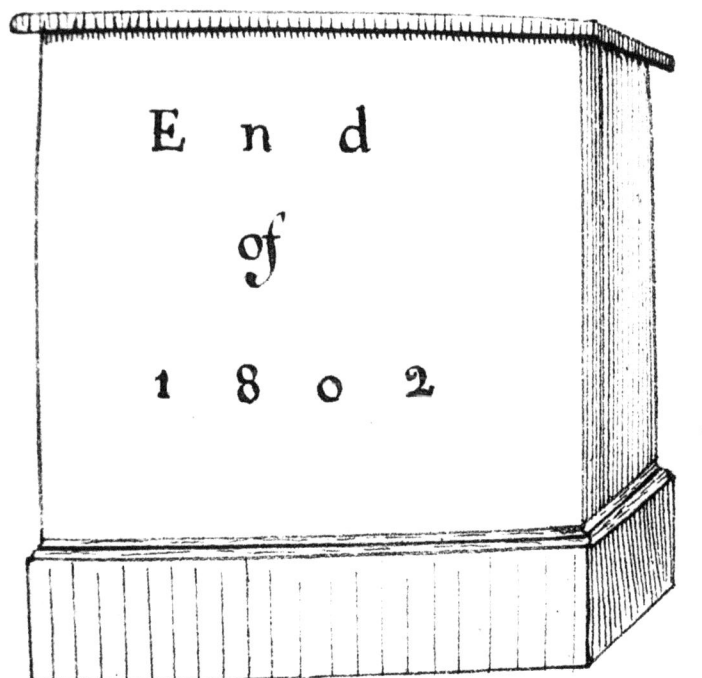

CHAPTER 3

WISE MAN OF PENNINGTON
1803

JANUARY

[Fleming writes daily reports on the weather and lists names of characters , battles , events etc. in history]

27th (Thursday) - This Evening on my Return from Ulverston I was pursued and illtriated *[illtreated]* by three men in Liquor, who abused me with ill names and much incessent language. I found them to be John Hartley, Farmer at Holibigrow, John Brunskill, Miller and Thos. Eccles of old Gill, Pitman ....

[The first of several threats of abuse on Mr Fleming]

Brewery, new one at Gill in Ulverston erected by Yarker and Co. in 1801. Began to brew 1802.

Furnesian Poetry By the Rhimning Quaker *[Rhyming Quaker]*

God made priests, Doctors but the Devil made Attorneys and plac'd them at Uston and Broughton in Furnefs. But all the Rapscallions and Rogues he made else He drove them o'er Penny Bridge to Furnefs *[Furness]* Fells.

A Person in Walney desired this Quaker to speak
in his Favour to a Woman in the Neighbourhood of
Aldingham whom he wish'd to marry & promised him
a Lobster for his Pains; but as he did not receive the
Lobster he said nothing to the Woman; at which, when
the Lover exprefs'd his Surprize, he got from him these
Lines.

'Whenever I receive the Lobster
I presently will do the Job, Sir,
But till that Time my Tongue I'll bridle,
Working for nothing makes Folks idle.'

This Rhimning *[Rhyming]* old Fellow once took a parcel
to the Rector of Aldingham, where he waited for some
Time and gave many broad Hints for a drink of the
parson's Ale which at last was brought him, but the pot
contain'd little but Foam, when he spoke these lines to
the Rector........

'To bring me Drink you're very loth *[loathe]*
And when it comes it's naught but Froth.'

*[Fleming starts to quote from ' A Fragment ' by the 'Rhiming
Quaker', however he ends with the words the rest torn off - so
it is not the full work]*

FEBRUARY 1803

*[Fleming quotes further Latin and continues to write daily
weather reports]*

8th (Tuesday) - On Monday Evening died Frances
Robinson of Newbarns in the 85th Year of her Age.

I to attend the Funeral.

10th (Thursday) - Geo. Romney Esq. was born at high
Cocken near Dalton in Furness *[He was actually born at
Beckside, Dalton in Furness and lived at High Cocken as a
boy and young man]* and for some Time wrought with
his Father who was a House – carpenter, but disliking
the Businefs he threw aside the Adze *[A tool similar to an
axe]* and Chissel for the Pallet and Brush and became a
distinguished painter in his Day. His Genius rais'd him
to the highest Clafs *[Class]* of his profefsion *[profession]*
by which he acquir'd an ample Fortune.

Some of his Productions in his best manner, may be
seen at Font *[Fonthill]* in Wilts, viz, A portrait of Wm.
Beckford Esq. An Indian Woman, Mary & Susan E.
Beckford.

At Slyne, Lancs – Thos. Greene, Esq. This is said to be
his best P. *[Portrait]*

At Trentham Hall – Marquis of Stafford, large as Life.

Verses inscrib'd to Geo. Romney Esq. By Mr Cowper.

'Romney! Expert infallibly to trace,
On Chart or Canvass not the Form alone
And Semblance; but however faintly shewn
The Mind's Imprefsion too on every Face,
With Strokes that Time ought never to erase!

Thou hast so pencill'd mine, that tho I own The Subject worthless,

I have never known The Artist shining with Superior Grace;

But this I mark – that Sympton none of Woe.

In thine incomparable Work appear;

Well! I am satisfied it shou'd be so,

Since on maturer Thought the Cause is clear,

For in my Looks what sorrow cou'dst thou see

When I was Hayley's Guest and sat to thee.'

Mr. Romney died at Kendall and was interred at the parish Church of Dalton 19 Nov . 1802

[George Romney, English portrait painter - 26th December 1734 - 15th November 1802 – is too well known for further comment here. The Mr Cowper that Fleming refers to is William Cowper, English poet - 26th November 1731 - 25th April 1800]

11th (Friday) - *[Fleming continues to write daily weather reports and lists further facts and figures - including measurements and weights]*

24th (Thursday) - *[Fleming lists a Copy of Pennington Articles and Custom Articles of Agreement and a Copy of the Channonhouse Articles]*

[An entry by Fleming on prices at Ulverston Market]

28th (Monday) - Oatmeal 15s. Per cwt – Best Flower [Flour] 22/- per cwt – Beef 7d – Mutton 7d – Veal 6d –

Pork 6d per ib Butter – 16d Eggs 6d per dozen – Apples 3s per Hoop of 6 Quarts – Cockles 1d per Quart Muscles [Mussels] 1d per Quart – Barley 9s 6d per Bushel Malt 19s. per Do. [Ditto] Pudding Peas 3s 6d per Hoop deal Timber 2s 8d per Foot – Potatoes – 5d per Hoop Onion Seed – 9d per oz. Cabb [*Cabbage*]) plants 3d per score Oats – 8s 6d per lb.

Ale – 3d per pint, wine – measure – Rum 15d per Gall Brandy – 22/- Holland and Gin – 16s per Gall.

House Carpenters wages – 3/- per Day – Labourers in Husbandry 2s / 6d per day.

Passage by the Stage Coach from Ulverston to Lancaster – 5s per person.

MARCH [1803]

[Further daily reports on the weather followed by lists of abbeys, priories and historical characters (e.g. Wm. Cowper, Esq. Eng: Poet died 25th April 1800]

Ulverston Market Place as William Fleming would have known it.

31st (Thursday) - Prices: Best Flower [Flour] 24/-
Seconds – 20/- Oatmeal 16s. Per cwt . Beef – 7d Mutton
– 7 and a half pence Veal -6d Pork - 5 and a half pence
per lb. Eggs – 8d per score. Butter – 12 and a halfpence
lb. Apples – 3/- per Hoop Muscles – 4 and a halfpence
per Hoop. Cows, good - £18. Peats – 4/- per cart.

Ale – 18d per Gall .Writing paper – 16d per Quire Coals
– 25/- per Ton of about 16 cwt. Seed oats – 12s. per lb.

APRIL [1803]

[No entries of any note]

MAY [1803]

1st (Sunday) - Jonathan Hodgson, generally known by
the Names of Hermit or Wise Man of Pennington died
this evening at Loppergarth. About 20 years ago he was
taken up for a Conjuror and underwent an Examination
before Wilson Braddyll Esq. of Conishead Priory who
finding him to be an inoffensive Harmlefs [*Harmless*]
Fellow dismifsd [*dismissed*] him with an Injunction
never to use the Bible & the Key or the Sieve and Shears
[*A method of divination, sometimes called Coscinomancy, for
the future*]

He was pofefs'd [*possessed*] of a Memory wonderfully
inventive and would if desired repeat Stories from the
Arabian Nights Entertainment, Baron Munchausen and
others which inclined to the marvellous with much of
his own genuine Humour.

He would frequently amuse a Company of Neighbours
on the Winter Evenings by telling their Fortunes

repeating Anecdotes which were generally original
and such other little things as afford Entertainment
to the young. With the older he would talk of Events
which he had heard mentioned by his Father who was
very old, and frequently he wd. attempt to explain the
Scriptures being ready with Quotations in Support of
his Arguments which were chiefly correct. I have seen
him once impose himself upon a Clergyman, who was
a Stranger to him, as a Man of Learning & even beat
him at his own Weapons. This Clergyman was one of
my Acquaintance who had received an Academical
Education and in his Coll: (J.C.Camb.) *[Jesus College
Cambridge]* was one of those few who were at his Time
distingushed by the Name of Litterate.

Having heard this Person mention'd in a Company at
Ulvn. *[Ulverston]* as a Man of an astonishing Memory
etc. etc. he became very desirous of seeing him and
wished me to introduce him to this wonderful Man,
which I accordingly did, and giving Jonathan his Cue I
had nothing more to do but to enjoy the Interview.

So he began with, 'I apprehend Sir, you are a
Clergyman.' -

'Yes Sir.' - 'I have a very great Regard for the Cloth; I
was brought up for the Church myself; I scan'd over
the Tyutu patual *[Latin]* of Virgil & attended his pious
Aneas *[A hero in Virgil's Aeneid and Homer's Iliad]* for
the Trojan War; but when I came to engage the blind
Grecian with his *[? -Words are possibly ancient Greek]* and
his d..d *[dead?]* Dialect, and could not find the Measure
of the first line of his Writings, I threw aside my Books
in a pafsion *[passion]* went Home and prevailed upon
my Father to bind me Apprentice to a Tailor. I then
studied the Science of Astrology and on casting my

Nativity *[A horoscope at the time of a persons' birth]* I found I was born to be a great Man: but in all my Studies nothing has puzzled me more than to find out whether St.Mark the Evangelist and John were the same or Different Persons.

I applied to the parson of our parish here to solve the Question but without Succefs *[Success]* ; indeed he confefsed *[confessed]* to me he had never heard that there was a Suspicion of their being the Same, so I still remain in Doubt, but I hope that you will determine it and set me right.

[Johnathan Hodgson was buried on the 12th May 1803 in St.Michael and the Holy Angels Churchyard at Pennington. Aged 49 years]

15th (Sunday) - The Weather has been so cold and dry for some Time past, that it has entirely put a Stop to the Vegetation & is injuring Fruit Tree Blossom which is abundant and promised a most plentiful Crop. The pasture Grounds have not for many Yrs. Been known to be so thin of Grafs *[Grass]* at this Time of Spring -

Gardner Jno.*[John]* Of Dendron married to Eliz: *[Elizabeth]* Coward of Gleaston 11th Inst.

31st (Tuesday) - Oatmeal – 18/- per cwt. Potatoes – 6d per Hoop – Beef, Mutton & Lamb 7d per lb. - Veal 5d per lb. Oats, best – 11s 6d per Bushel – Barley 12/- Coals 25s per Ton -

JUNE [1803]

[Fleming continues to document the weather and lists historical events and names of Kings, Lord Mayors of London etc.]

12th (Sunday) - Jno. Fell of Ulverston, Surgeon, who died on Wednesday last was this Morning interr'd in the Friends' Burying ground adjoining to their meeting house on Swarthmoor.

30th - Prices: Wheat 35/- per Load – Oats 9/- per Bush. - Potatoes old 7 and a half pence per Hoop.

New Potatoes 3-4 d. Beef 7d per lb Mutton 7d Lamb 6 and a half pence per lb. Veal 5d per lb Butter 10 per lb

Eggs 1/8d per score Peats 2/6 per Do. Coals 27/- per Ton – Young Ducks 14d each. Chickens 1/- - Salmon 10d per lb. - Salmon Trout 7d per lb. Rum 18s. Per Gall. Brandy 22s. Hollands 20s. Common Gin 8s. Maidstone Gin 11s. British Brandy 12s. Per Gall. Ale 20d per Gall.

JULY [1803]

[Fleming continues his weather reports and his historical lists - ie. Archbishops of Canterbury, Abbots of Furness Popes of Rome etc.]

6th (Wednesday) - Hay Harvest in Furnefs, began this Week. Crop abundant.

27th (Wednesday) - The great preparations for War made by Bonaparte, Chief Consul in France and his threatened Invasion of England have aroused the

English to unparalleled Exertions for the Defence of the United Kingdoms. In Furness this secluded Corner of Britain, the Inhabitants capable of bearing Arms have in general enrolled themselves for the Defence of their Country.

In Ulverston a Corps of Volunteers consisting of 4 companies are raising & the Officers for each were this Evening thus shabbily elected.

The Election was conducted as follows; This Day 27 July public Notice was given thro' the Town for the Volunteers who had already entered their Names to afsemble [assemble] at an appointed Time and place this Evening for the purpose of electing Officers to command the said Volunteers; of Consequence a Number of them attend in the Afsembly [Assembly] Rooms at the Hour fix'd upon: Soon after about 8 or 10 Gentlemen came from an adjoining Room and after a short Conversation on the Subject of the meeting the Question was put whether the Officers shou'd be elected this Evening or not till the whole Corps were enrolled; when the House being divided there appeared a Majority of 5 against the Election this Evening. The Businefs [Business] now seem'd finished and many of the Volunteers returned Home; but soon after a Barrel of Ale appeared & was given to the remaining Electors. When the Barrel was exhausted, to the Astonishment of many present, the same Question was again put, and now carried, for an immediate Election by a majority, and immediately they proceeded

Ulverston Volunteer
Light Infantryman by
Mrs Cowper – 1805

to elect the following officers, who chiefly proposed themselves & were at the Expence of bribing the two or three poor Fellows with a skinfull of Ale, as the only means to accomplish their Purpose.

Thus they took away from the major part of the Corps the Privilege of Election: but how far their Proceedings will give Satisfaction and what Method they will take to justify their Conduct if enquired into, Time must shew

OFFICERS: COMMANDER – IN - CHIEF - Thomas Sunderland, Esq.

CAPTAINS - Henry Morritt, Joseph Yarker – a collector of the Customs at Ulverston, Thomas Tolmin – lately a very poor Negro driver in the West Indies, who by some Means fingured a handsome Fortune there in about a year & Half & is now a Brandy spinner in Ulverston, Miles Burton – a poor Clergyman's son, put out some years ago, an apprentice to Mr Robt. Fell, a linen draper in Ulverston, by a charitable Society and at the Expiration of his Apprenticeship became in some Degree a partner in the House.

LIEUTENANTS – Daniel Dickinson, a pettifogging Attorney – Richd. Shaw, another of the same honest Tribe – Wm. Wilkinson, a partner in Yarker's Brewery – Robert Briggs, an apprentice to a West India Merchant and now maintained by the Creditors of a person who had the Misfortune to fail in a Trade.

ENSIGNS – Edmund Petty, a partner in Yarker *[Bros?]* Brewery – Richard Towers, a straddling Pettifogger – Tyson Addison, an Ironmonger and Geo. Coward, a Tallow Chandler & Grocer – such are the Gentlemen elected to command the Volunteer Corps at Ulverston.

[So, a scathing attack on the Ulverston Volunteers with this opening salvo! Just how Fleming comes by this information isn't clear. Perhaps a friend, or one of the volunteers themselves divulged this information, though it is certain that Fleming himself knew many of the men involved, George Coward being an old school acquaintence. I have done a great deal of research into their calling, seen the battalion's orderly book as kept by their commander-in-chief, Thomas Sunderland and studied their behaviour throughout the three years of their fellowship, from well kept records.

At every turn they were monitored and frequently inspected by a colonel of the regular army, the UV's being militia. They were finally pronounced 'fit to act with Regiments of the Line' by Lt. Col. Tomlinson in June, 1806.

However, as the reader will see in the ensuing entries of Fleming's journal, he does bestow some praise on them in later accounts! The Assembly Rooms mentioned in this entry were above the Theatre Royal, as previously mentioned]

31st (Sunday) - Prices: Beef – 7d – Mutton – 7d - Lamb – 6d - Veal -5d – Salmon – 8d . Salmon trout – 6d per lb. Butter – 12d per lb. Eggs 6d per Score. Cheshire Cheese – 8 and a half pence . Lancaster Do. - 7 and a half pence. Gloucester Do. 8d – Chickens 1s. Young Ducks – 14d. Bacon – 9d per lb. - New Potatoes – 10d. Old Do. 8d per Hoop. Pease – 8d per Hoop.

Shot – 4 and a half pence per lb. - Powder – 4s. Game License - £3- 4s.- 0d. Game – Dog Tax – 10s. Per year.

AUGUST [1803]

[Fleming continues his weather Reports]

11th (Thursday) - This Morning my Sister and I attended the Funeral of Mrs. Ireland at Dalton; she was inter'd in the Grave of her Mother, Mrs. Chapman, who was one of the Daughters of *[blank space]* Matson, Esq. Of Titup Hall near Dalton.

14th (Sunday) - The Harvest is commenced on the Shores of Furness and there were Reapers to hire at Dalton today, the first this Season. Their Wages were 1/6d per Day & Meat -

22nd (Monday) - Reapers Wages this Week 2/6 per Day & Meat.

[A piece that shows that Fleming did not care too much for some of the clergy]

26th (Friday) - POEM BY W . FLEMING

Those Revd. Sinners first shou'd feel the Rod Who live for Beelzebub but preach for G-----------
The Rev'd Kelly always will be poor Whilst there's a public house so near his Door;
Kelly, whose wit as much exceeds his Sense, As Love of Liquor off exceeds his pence,
And makes his poor ragg'd Family be fed, With very little Tea and far lefs Bread.

An aged Mother sure shou'd not intreat Her Son to let her have sufficient Meat;

A poor old Mother who with Care at first Hippin'd his Breech and at her Bosom nurst,

That Bosom where he hid his infant Nose And calmly suck'd himself into repose.

[Fleming keeps a detailed list of Births, Marriages & Deaths at Pennington]

30th (Tuesday) - The Ulverston Loyal Volunteers, in Consequence of their offered Service being accepted by Government, were Yesterday Evening drawn up in the Market Place and formed into Four Companies, each consisting of *[blank space]* Men commanded by their proper Officers: at the same time Drill Sergeants and non Commissioned offecers were appointed for each Company and their Muster Rolls drawn out.

The Reapers Wages this week are 3/- a Day and Victuals.

Prices: New Wheat 37s. Per Load Apples 2/3 per Hoop.

SEPTEMBER [1803]

30th (Saturday) - Wheat 38/- per Load. Oats 8/- per Bushel. Potatoes 4d per Hoop.

Manks *[Manx]* Herrings fish 1d each. Turbot – 7d per lb. Oatmeal 18/- per cwt. Best Flower (Flour) 22/- per Do. - Apples 3/- per Hoop

OCTOBER [1803]

24th (Monday) - At Dalton Fair this Day there was a good Shew of Cattle both fat and lean; of the latter many were sold at moderate prices.

An Epigram on Wm. Nicholson of Row End, a Quarrelsome Neighbour.

'Will Nicholson, who all his Life
Has fill'd his Neighbourhood with Strife
And become more wicked than old Nick cou'd make him,
May give this Reason why his Breath
Has not been stopt long since his Death;
G-------. will not, and the D----------. dare not take him.

31st (Monday) - Prices: Oats 8s per Bush: - Wheat 35/- per load – oatmeal 18s - best flour 24s. Per cwt. Potatoes 7/6 per Bushel: Onions 16d per Stone – Butter 13d per lb. - Eggs – 16d per Doz. - Beef 6d – Mutton 6d – Lamb 5d – Pork 5d per lb. - Nuts 3s 6d per Hoop.

NOVEMBER [1803]

3rd (Thursday) - This Evening William Nicholson of Rowend died. - This Man has lived in the World 40 Years before I was born, consequently I could have no Knowledge of the former Part of his Life except from Report, which is not always to be credited, for the Stories she circulates frequently exceed the Truth.

His Acquirements in Literature, his Stock of wit, and his good Breeding, he attain'd of the School Master of his Parish at the Rate of one Shilling per Quarter.

This Master was transported to America for stealing a

Bible.--------When I sit down to draw a Sketch I don't
consider it a Matter of any Consequence whether
the Original be worth the Trouble or not, my only
Case is that the Outlines of it be faithfully deliniated
(delineated): & when any Part of a Character is in my
Opinion unfit for the Eye of the Public, I can be silent,
yet I wou'd conceal nothing that cou'd with propriety
appear.

Whilst I am drawing this Sketch I cannot help heaving a
Sigh that so atrocious a Character ever existed.

The Imprefsion *[Impression]*, which bad Example in
his early Years made upon his Mind, cou'd never be
erased. And the predudices of his Infancy were not to
be corrected, but increased with his Years to the very
perfection of Vice.

It greatly becomes parents, Who have a Regard for the
future Character of their Children, at the early Season
of Life, to sow in their young Minds the Seeds of Virtue
which fail not to produce an abundant Crop of future
Happiness under proper Cultivation …...........

*[Fleming's criticism of William Nicholson is a VERY lengthy
one, running for several pages and has been curtailed by the
Editor!]*

[Yet more from Fleming on the Ulverston Volunteers]

18th (Friday) - The Ulverston Volunteers have received
their Arms and also are ordered to be prepared to march
at an Hours Warning. they also have sealed orders
delivered to the Lt. Colonel Sunderland which are not to
be opened till they have marched 10 Miles out of Town.

A Promotion of the officers took place last week when Morritt the first Captain was made Major & Yarker made first Captn. which has caus'd a Disagreement among the Officers and Tolmin has resigned in Consequence. Such is the pride of these small Gentry that none of them know who is to be the greatest Man.

20th (Sunday) - Thos. Fell snr. Of Holebigrow [*Holebiggarah*] died this morning............

23rd (Wednesday) - Thomas Fell Senior of Holebigrow buried this Evening –

[*An amusing account of the above mentioned Thomas Fell, a Pennington man involved in the militia during an earlier war. This time, the Jacobite Rising of 1745, also known as the Forty-five Rebellion*]

When a good natured friendly Man makes his Exit, his Neighbours and Acquaintances drop the Tear of Sorrow at his Funeral and heave a Sigh for his Lofs [*Loss*]. The Memory of a worthy Man is dear to his Friends.

Thomas Fell was born about the yr 1719 and received his Education in the West End of the parish Church of Pennington at a small Expence but his Learning was in [*Proportion ?*] to it. From thence he was taken to afsist [*assist*] his Father in [selling?] his Estate at Holebigrow, where he liv'd untainted with Vices.

In the year 1745 when Scotland rebelled and raising an Army marched into England he was balloted to serve in the Militia and the undisciplined and ignorant of the Use of Arms, he with many others like himself had Muskets put into their hands and were ordered out to oppose them. Thomas and his Fellow Soldiers had followed the rebel Army to below Preston, when they heard that the Scots were retreating towards Scotland and would presently meet them: upon this the valiant Commander of this little Company ordered his Men to [shift?] for themselves & fled: whereupon Thos. and his Comrades hid their Muskets in a muddy Waterfence and having no Uniform kept out of the Rout of the Rebels till they were past the place, then dragging out their Arms from amongst the Mud, they made the best of their Way for their own Homes.

Oft have I heard him repeat the Circumstances of this Expedition with much Humour and without omitting many Parts of the Story which were so little to their Honor that many wou'd have been ashamed to have told them, also how he strutted thro' Ulverston on his Return and up the dirty Roads of his Parish, big with the Idea he suppos'd his Neighbours wou'd have of his Valour and at the Foot of the Lane leading up to his Home, he fired his Musket for the first Time since it was put into his Hands. But, alas! Poor Thos. *[Thomas]*

These Days are past and gone; the Heart which then beat with Joy at the safe Return to his native Cottage is now hush'd forever and the Tongue which used to repeat the Tale with so much Humour must be forever silent; but such is the Fate of Mortals and sooner or later to it we all must Yield.

[Fleming lists names from the Burial Register of Pennington]

DECEMBER [1803]

[Fleming continues weather observations]

12th (Monday) - Yesterday one of the Ulverston Volunteers was interr'd at Ulverston Church with Martial Honors: he was the first of the Corps who died since its Establishment.

[The volunteer is not named]

31st (Saturday) - Prices:

Wheat 31s/- Barley – 10/- Oats 10/- Flour – 24 /- Oatmeal – 19/- per cwt.
Potatoes 5/- per Bushel. Apples 3/6 per Hoop – Beef 7d - Mutton 7d - Pork 4 and a half pence - Veal – 6/- per lb.
Butter – 11d - Candles - 11d - Malt – 22/- Fowls – 1/3d Egg- 7d
Raw Hides – 6 and a half pence per lb. Timber pitch pine – 2/11.
Labourers in Husbandry – 2/6 per Day. Masons – 2/6 - Wrights – 2/6 per Day without Meat and 1/6d per day with Meat. Taylors – 14d per Day & Meat.
Rum – 17/- Hollands Gin - 20/- Common Ditto 7/- Brandy 21/- per Gallon. Port Wine - 12/6.
[Fleming adds an observation]

What an Alteration since about 1556 in the Reign of Philip and Mary, when Wheat was sold at 1/- per bushel – Mutton & Veal – 3 farthings and Beef and pork at a Halfpenny per pound.

CHAPTER 4

FROM THE PALACE
TO THE COTTAGE
1804

JANUARY

[Weather Reports]

FEBRUARY [1804]

[Weather Reports]

21st (Tuesday) - This Morning the Colors were
presented to the Ulverston Volunteers by Mifs [Miss]
Sunderland of Ulverston [Mary Sunderland, the middle
daughter of Thomas Sunderland of Littlecroft] who made a
Speech no doubt proper for the Occasion but in so low a
Tone that it could not be heard.

Her Father, Col. Sunderland next addrefsed [addressed]
the Volunteers in a very long Speech, at the Conclusion
of which the Corps was marched from before the
Platform into the Field where the Colors were
consecrated by the Revd. Mr Sunderland, Chaplain
to the Corps, after which they fired three Rounds, the
band play'd God save the King, with three Times three
Cheers; then they marched to Church where an excellent
Sermon was Delivered by Revd. Mr. Sunderland. The
rest of the Day was spent in Rejoicing.

[The Sunderland family home was 'Littlecroft' or 'Little Croft' and used to stand on the site which is presently occupied by the Coronation Hall and Post Office.

Littlecroft – April 1821 – North Lonsdale Magazine

The following entry appears in the Lancaster Gazette, Saturday 25th February, 1804 -

The Officers dined with Colonel Sunderland; and in the evening concluded with a Ball at the Assembly Room, which was numerously attended by the ladies and gentlemen of the town and neighbourhood.

On Wednesday, the Ulverston Volunteers were reviewed by Colonel Tomlinson, and went through their evolutions with much credit.

[See Fleming's entry in June for Miss Sunderland's and part of Lt. Col. Sunderland's speech]

MARCH [1804]

[Weather Reports & Historcal lists of Bishops]

31st (Saturday) - Prices: Oats – 9 s. - Wheat 34s/- - Barley – 10/- per bushel. Butter 13d. Per lb. - Beef & Mutton – 5 and a half pence. - Veal - 5d per lb. Eggs – 4 and a half pence per Doz. - Potatoes – 4d per Hoop.

APRIL [1804]

[Weather Reports & list of the Bishops of Carlisle]

MAY [1804]

[Weather Reports]

21st (Monday) - The friendly Societies at Ulverston, this Day held their anniversary as usual and heard a Sermon, which was read to them from a pulpit erected in the Church porch, the people standing in the Church Yard, the Rain was heavy during the whole Time.

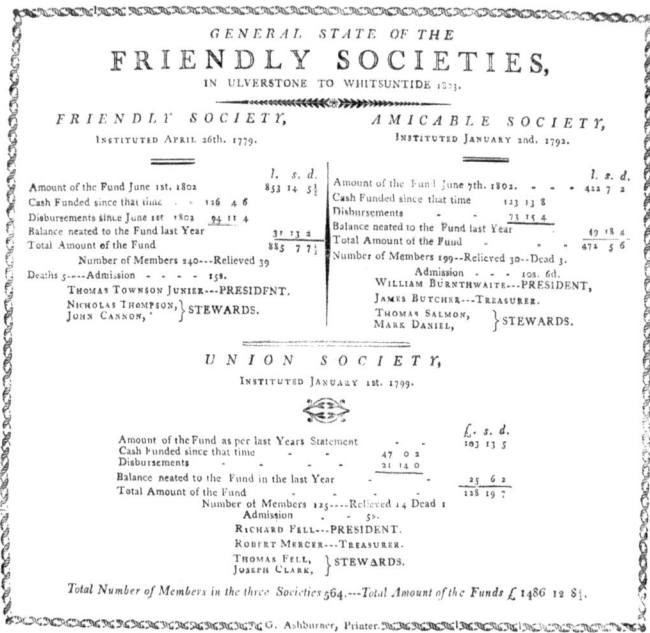

Friendly Societies – From The Soulby Collection

JUNE [1804]

[Daily weather Reports and Latin quotes]

24th (Sunday) - [Fleming quotes from the the various speeches made on 21st February 1804 at the Presentation of Colours to the Ulverston Volunteers. The speeches were first published in the Lancaster Gazette on Saturday 25th February, 1804. However Fleming seems to have decided to alter some words from the original publication]

[Miss Mary Sunderland's Speech at the Presentation of Colours to the Ulverston Volunteers] -

Gentn. It is with the deepest Regret my Mother is compelled to relinquish the Gratification of personally presenting to you these Colours. Indisposition depriving her of that Satisfaction, she has deputed me to place them under your protection; and requests you to honor her by the Acceptance of them as a Token of the high Respect and lively Interest she feels towards every Individual of the Corps, whose Conduct merits her warmest Approbation, In which Sentiments I beg Leave to assure you, Gentlemen, I most heartily concour.

[Part of Lt. Col. Sunderland's lengthy speech to the assembly]

In addressing you on this solemn and to me, most interesting Occasion, I fear my Language will fail to express the Sentiments of my Heart as strongly as they are felt; but I will make an Attempt, with the firm belief that you will favourably receive the Intention. When I look upon my Townsmen and Neighbours arrayed in Arms to oppose their Country's Wrongs, the Sight invigorates my ebbing Blood; I look with Admiration on their Ranks and confess I am proud of the honorable Situation, which, at my Age, with my Habits of Life and want of military knowledge, I thought myself unqualified to undertake; but the Time, the Occassion and your Choice superceeded every other Consideration and I became your Leader.

I will discharge my Duty to the utmost of my power and come what may you, my brave Comrades shall always find me ready to share your Toils and Dangers as more than six months Experience of your conduct added to the recent and most decided Proof of your Attachment binds me to you by the Ties of Gratitude and Affection; your spirited and generous Support on that Occasion will never be obliterated from my Mind; and it has fixed

You are too well acquainted with the Cause which associates us together in Arms, for me to engage much of your Attention on that Subject; yet I cannot help wishing it to be deeply impress'd upon your Minds, that the Stake we fight for is the All of Britain; All that becomes a Man and makes Life valuable to him.

That our Enemy vows utter Desolation to this envied Island; and from the Palace to the Cottage one general Mass of Ruin would mark his successful Footsteps.

And be it remembered, that this Enemy hath dared to proclaim us another Carthage; a degenerate Nation of Merchants and Shopkeepers, devoted but to Gain and no Match for Frenchmen of the New Creation, who vaunting by compare their France to warlike Rome: Insolent assertions!

Miserably deceived Frenchmen! ....

So vast a Burst of patriotism stands unrivalled in the page of History; and to the Credit of this little Town, with pride I speak it, this noble, Ardour has, in no Quarter of the Kingdom, shone with brighter Lustre; for here our whole Strength stepped forth, a voluntary Band, to the full Extent required..................

I must give equal praise to the Men of Bardsey *[Bardsea]* and those in the Ranks from other neighbouring Townships.

The presentation of this Day places under your protection the Nation's Honour and our own.

Those Banners moved into our Line confirm our Faith plighted to our King, our Country and to one another and which I am confident will never be departed from. They will be our rallying point in the Hour of Hazard and I am also sure they will be maintained with Valour.

Gentlemen Ensigns: Into your Care I now commit these pledges of our Loyalty. In your Hands, I am persuaded they will never be tarnished or living be wrested, from you.

JULY [1804]

[Daily Weather Reports]

AUGUST [1804]

[Daily weather reports]

8th (Wednesday) - This Evening attended a Sale of Land at Gleaston which belonged to the late *[(blank space]* Fell of Kendall, Surgeon, consisting of about 16 and a half Acres, which was sold in parcels at about 145 pounds per Acre; the whole came to 2327 £ besides the Valuation of the Timber which was growing in the Hedges; it is certainly a most extravagant price.

19th (Sunday) - Harvest begun; the first Day for hiring Reapers at Dalton, their Wages 2/6 per Day & Meat.

26th (Sunday) - The Harvest astonishlingly forward since the last Week ; the Crops, take off lighter than was expected; Grain and Malt took a Considerable rise in our Markets last Week; Reapers' Wages this week 3/6 per Day and Meat.

SEPTEMBER [1804]

[Weather Reports]

14th (Friday) - The late fine Weather has been remarkably favorable for the Farmers, who have been very busy getting their Grain into their Barns, so that a great part of the Fields are cleared and the Corn well got; Grain fell a little in the Markets last week. Apples are not abundant this Year, but hazel Nuts are extremely plentiful.

16th (Sunday) - The Harvest nearly finished. No Hiring of Reapers at Dalton today - 8 Parts: (Partridges) kill'd yesterday.

30th (Sunday) - The Weather has been so long dry that the Farmers cannot get their Crop of Wheat into the Ground.

31st (Monday) - W. Mashiter let his Estate at Row 18 Acres, for £72 per Ac. and the Farmer to pay all Taxes. What a Rent. This Estate was purchased by him about 14 Years ago for 700 pounds.

OCTOBER [1804]

14th (Sunday) - *[Lists of Orders of Knighthoods etc.]*

FRAGMENTS .....ON THE ULVERSTON
VOLUNTEERS BEING MARCHED TO CARTMEL

How chang'd is each Face In this sweet little Place
Which erst look'd so cheerful so merry and gay ;
Here's nothing but moaning Lamenting and groaning
Since the brave Volunteers were all marched away.
How hush'd is each Tongue Which so charmingly sung
And lilted and carol'd the Length of the Day;
How dull are those Eyes Which were bright as the Skies
Ere the brave Volunteers were all marched away.
No more on the Gad Each Girl meets her Lad
To enliven their Walk at the Close of the Day
The Time now seems dreary For want of her deary
Since the brave Volunteers are all marched away.
But each Volunteer so gay did appear,
They all seem'd in Full Glee and quite Strangers to
Sorrow:
May their Absence be spent In Mirth and Content
Quite free from those Ills which may happen Tomorrow.
Should it e'er be the Case That the Foe they must face,
May they all act , with Judgement & Courage their Parts
And bravely defend Their possessions and Friends

And win Battles as easy as they can win Hearts.
[No clues or whereabouts as to the origin of this song. Tune not known]

NOVEMBER [1804]

[Weather Reports]

Prices: Wheat 46/- Oats 11/- Barley 16/- Beans 18/- per Bushel.

DECEMBER [1804]

1804 – VOLUNTEERS SONG
(Ulverston – Never Published)
If Gallias' Sons our Land invade
And George his loyal Britons call,
We'll quick unsheath each shining Blade
And march to meet them, one and all.
Our Wives, our Children, all that's dear,
Each sacred and each social Tie.
Will Ulverston's brave Volunteers
Urge on to conquer or to die.
Where War , the Scourge of man, shall cease,
And ev'ry true born Briton hail
The Blessings of returning Peace
With pleasure each shall tell the Tale:
How he , to aid the common Cause
His Friends and Property defend,
Protect his Country , King and Laws
And be each loyal Briton's Friend.
Enrolled himself, resolv'd to try,

To save his Country, if all he can;
But if not, in the [attempt?] Cause to die
And so serve his Country like an Honest Man .
[Weather Reports]

[List of Poet Laureats]

CHAPTER 5

THE MANKILLING PROFESSION
1805

JANUARY [1805]

12th (Saturday) - The Christmas Dinner at the Dalton Book Club was this Day attended by 30 of the Members – 4/6 per person.....6..15..0 *[£6 – 15s – 6d]*

24th (Thursday) - Pork in great Abundance at Market price 3 and a half to 4 and a half per lb.

31st (Thursday) - Prices. Flour 3s. Wheat 50s. Per load – Oatmeal – 20 /- per Cwt. Oats – 10/- per Bushel. Barley – 16/- per Do. Beans 17/- per Do. Malt 3s. Per Bushel. Potatoes 3 and a half pence. Apples 2/6. Cockles 6d – Muscles 4d – Nuts 3/- per Hoop of 6 Quarts . Beef-6d – Mutton 5 and a half pence – Pork 4d – Veal – 5d Codfish – 2d per lb. Pudding Peas 2/6 per Hoop.

Tea, common 8s. - Coffee 5s per lb.

Ale – 22d per Gall. Rum 10s. Per Do. Holland Gin 21s. Brandy 24s.

FEBRUARY [1805]

[Latin Verse and Poem by ' Horace '. Further weather reports]

20th (Thursday) - Prices: Wheat 3£ per Load . Oats 11/- Barley – 16/- per Bush. Butter 12d . Hams 6d Pork – 4 and a half pence - Beef 5 and a half pence Mutton 6d Veal 4d per lb. Potatoes – 3 and a half – boiling peas 2/- Apples 3/6 per Hoop Eggs 13 for 6d.

MARCH [1805]

[Weather Reports]

APRIL [1805]

14th (Sunday) - The Blossom on plumbtrees beginning to burst, Little Grass.

19th (Friday) - Many of the Farmers in Low Furness who have finished the sowing of Oats are forward with their Barley.

21st (Sunday) - Very Hot & Sultry. Planted a Clump of Firs scotch and Larches upon the Bank. Got the plants from Bootle. Weak ones.

28th (Sunday) - Severe Frost. The Ground covered with Snow this Morning.

[William Fleming's wedding day] Was married to Sarah, only Daughter of the late Samuel Hodgson Esquire of Tarnside, Ulverston, (Age 20) at Ulverston Church, by Revd. Jno. *[John]* Sunderland -

29th (Monday) - Frost, the Early Potatoes destroy'd -

MAY 1805

[Weather Reports]

JUNE 1805

2nd (Sunday) - Fine and exceeding dry: the Grain is in want of Rain; none yet putting out Beards; much Blossom on Fruit trees, but the Insects are got into the Trees and appear as if they wou'd destroy it.

9th (Sunday) - Owing to the late dry Weather Grass is very thin and appears as if the Hay crop wou'd be light.

29th (Saturday) - William Nicholson of Lowgreaves, formerly a Coachman in London, but for many Years a Resident and posessing [possessing] an Estate at Low Greaves lef *[left]* him by James Greaves, died this Morning in the Eightieth Year of his Age, having an only Son, Jas. Nicholson by his late Wife Agnes Daughter of Thomas Brockbank of Walthwaite.

JULY 1805

31st (Wednesday) - Prices: Butter 12d per lb. Beef – 7d per lb. Mutton – 7d per lb. Lamb – 6 and a half pence per lb. Veal – 6d per lb. Eggs – 13 for 6d. Potatoes 6d per Hoop. Peas – 6d Do. Oats 13s. Per Bush. Wheat 62s. Per Load. - Cattle Slow

AUGUST[1804]

[Weather Reports . Lists of Baptisms and Marriages from 1600s and 1700s]

Ranz des Vaches

Quand reverrai – je en un jour
When will I see you again one day?

Tous les Objets de mon Amour;
All the objects of my love

Nos claires ruisseaux
Our clear streams

Nos Coleaux
Our hillsides

Nos Hanieaux
Our hamlets / cottages

Nos Montagnes
Our mountains

Et C'ornerment *[Couronnement -?]* de nos Montagnes
The crowing - ? of our Mountains

La si gentille Isabeau
The so gentle Isabelle

A Chombre d'un ormeau
The room of elm or walnut

Quand reverrai – je en un jour?
When will I see you again – one day?

Tous les Objets de mon Armour;
All the objects of my love

Mon Pere Mes Agneaux
My father My Lambs

Ma Mere Mes Troupeaux
My mother My Flock

Mon Frere Ma Bergere?
My brother My Shepherdess

Ma Soeur
My Sister

Quand reverrai – je en un jour?
When will I see you again – one day?

Tous les Objets de mon Armour?
All the objects of my love

[Re - the above translations - William Fleming's French not perfect, or maybe in an older style]

NOVEMBER [1805]

[Fleming records the celebrations in Furness of the Battle Of Trafalgar, 21st October 1805]

10th (Sunday) - Yesterday Evening the Towns of Ulverston and Dalton were spendidly illuminated in consequence of a victory gained by Lord Nelson over the combined fleets of France and Spain; in this battle, the brave Lord Nelson lost his life.

20th (Wednesday) - Yesterday Evening, the Estates following the property of Charles Gibson of Quernmore Esq. were sold in Public Sale at the Sun Inn, Ulverston. Sum total - £44 , 670.

29th (Friday) - This Evening an Estate at Great Urswick was sold in parcels. The whole Estate computed at 44 acres - £3,310.

30th (Saturday) -Prices:

Food: Barley – 18s. Per 3 Winchester Bushels. Beef – 5.5d. Cockles – 9.5 d. Codfish - 2d per lb. Ducks – 15d.

Fowls – 14d. Geese – 5d per lb. Hares – 3/- . Hare Skins
– 1/- . Lime – 16d per bushel. Muscles (Mussels) - 6d per
Hoop. Mutton – 5d. Nuts – 2/6 per Hoop of quarts. Oats
10/6 per 3 Winchester Bushels. Potatoes – 3d. Rabbits –
2/9d per couple. Salt – 4/6d per Stone. Veal - 5d per lb.
Wheat 50s. Per 3 Winchester Bushels. Woodcocks – 2/6

Drink: Brandy - 23s. Hollands Geneva – 20s. Port – 16s.
Rum – 16/- per gallon. Sherry – 18s.

Goods: Best Hats – £7-10s. Birch Brooms – 9d per
doz. Brick Brooms – 9d per doz. Candles – 10.5d.
Coals – 23/- per 16 cwt. Mens' Shoes – 10/6d per pair.
Newspapers - 6d.

Best Gunpowder – 3/6d. Gunflints – 9d per doz. Shot –
5d per lb.

Licenses : Licence to kill game - £3-3s. Per annum.
Licence to use armorial Bearings 10/6 per ann.

Licence to wear Hairpowder £1-1s. per ann.

DECEMBER [1805]

*[Fleming now comments on William Close. This is only a
brief biography as Fleming himself expands on this. William
Close was born near Cartmel in 1775. His father was a farmer
and the family moved to Walney. Between 1790 and 1796
he was apprenticed to a surgeon called Roger Parkinson
at Burton-in-Kendal and attended lectures at Edinburgh
University, gaining his diploma and beginning to practice
medicine in 1797.*

In 1799 he introduced vaccination against smallpox at Rampside, only a few years after Dr. Jenner's original experiments. In 1803, he married Isabel Charnock at St. Mary's Parish Church in Dalton. They had a son and a daughter. Amongst his other talents; he was a musician, an inventor and a writer, updating and expanding West's 'Antiquities of Furness'. William Close died of tuberculosis in 1813, aged 38. He is buried in an unmarked grave in Walney churchyard]

A Biographical Sketch of William Close

The Editor of West's Antiquities of Furness, was the Son of a Mole catcher for some time employ'd in Cartmel and afterwards in Furness, where by his Industry he acquired sufficient to allow his Son a liberal Education, suitable for the mankilling Profession of Surgeon and Apothecary.

In the 13 years he was at School, the Son gained almost as much Wisdom and Knowledge as the sapient Dr. Solomon himself, to whose publications and Nostrums the Inhabitants of this favour'd Isle are so much indebted. As Men of Genius scorn to wag on in the beaten Track of their Ancestors, so this Youth disdain'd to follow the Rules of Orthography *[A set of conventions for writing a language]* and Syntax *[The arrangement of words and phrases to create well formed sentences in a language]*, and in his Themes which he wrote at the End of each Week wou'd express his eccentric Ideas with unintelligible Sublimity which exceeded even the Comprehension of his Masters. Yet his Improvement was far from gratifying the Expectations of his Father, who was determined the Boy should pursue Fortune in the Line he had marked out for him whether his Learning and Abilities fitted him for the Profession or not.

He was, of course, taken from School and put an Apprentice to a Surgeon and Apothecary with whom he gained but little Knowledge of the Profession, his Genius directing him to the Study of Music, in which delightful Science he employ'd much of his Time and before the Expiration of his Aprenticeship had begun to construct a barrel Organ which he afterwards completed. The Interval between having his Masters Counter and his Removal to Edinburg was devated [*deviated?*] chiefly to his Improvement in Music and all Study omitted which cou'd contribute to perfect him in the surgical Profession.

He strove to equal Amphion [*A character in Greek Mythology*] more tham Asculepius [*Hero and God of Medicine in Greek Mythology*] but his melodious Strains had contrary Effect for the enchanting Notes of the Son of Jupiter and Antiope [*An Amazon in Greek Mythology*] attracted the Attention even of the wild Beasts, but the discordant Sounds of Master William's improved

No.2 Castle Street Dalton - Former home of William Close
Barrow-in-Furness Civic and Local History Society

Bugle horn scared them away, and more over caused such Fear in many of the old Women at Dalton, who we may safely affirm had no Ears, lest the vicious Bull at Eliscales had broke out of his pasture and was committing Havoc at the upper End of the Town: even when they were told it was only the Doctor sounding his bugle Horn their Fears were not removed, for as some of them had heard that the Walls of a City called Thebes were raised by the powerful Sounds of the Lyre, they saw no Reason, if that were true, why the antique Tower of Dalton might not be destroy'd by the fare sounding Blasts of the Doctor's Bugle Horn.

When He arrived at Edinburg *[Edinburgh]*, the Deficiancy of his Education, and his want of Skill in the profession he was intended for, were too evident, and he was the But *[Butt]* of many a Joke on acct. of his Whims and pretended Qualifications.

However highly he estimated his own Abilities, his fellow Students were far from forming the same Opinion of them; they saw things as they were & consequently duly appreciated his Talents .... (To be continued)

31st (Tuesday) - Prices: Wheat 45/- per load. - Oats – 10/6 per Bush. - Barley the average or what is commonly called the Candlemas price – 15/- - Potatoes – 3d . Apples 2/8 – Nuts -2/8 per Hoop – Beef – 6d – Mutton – 6d – Veal – 5d – Pork – 4and a half pence per lb.

CHAPTER 6

ASHBURNER WILL
BE A BEGGAR
1806

JANUARY

9th (Thursday) - Thunder & much lightening

10th (Friday) - Rain, Lightening in the night

FEBRUARY 1806

18th (Tuesday) - Continuation of A Biographical Sketch of William Close

When the Days of Probation were ended the Doctor took his Departure from the Metropolis of Scotland, and after experiencing a few Trifling Mishaps in his Journey arrived safe at his Father's Fireside, where, having recd. a Few Shakes by the Hand and a hearty Welcome, he began his Tale of Wonders, which was heard by his Father and Mother with so much Satisfaction, that they both declared that their Money & his Time had been employ'd to very great Advantage during his Stay at Edinburgh: they too concluded that their Son's assiduous Application to his Studies cou'd alone enable him to make such just and various Observations and descant so learnedly on various Branches of Science, but at the same Time they lamented that they had not bound him an Apprentice to some eminent Man in that City, by whose Skill and Abilities he wou'd have been so much improv'd that instead of a Surgeon he might now have departed from the Scotch Capital a compleat [complete] MD. When we cannot have things as we wish them, it certainly is a virtue to sit down contented with them as they are. So the parents of our Doctor now seeing they cou'd not make their Son a physician were happy and satisfied that they had educated him for the noblest and most useful Profession that ever had employ'd the Attention of Man. -

With this consoling thought they retired to Rest and now the first thing to be determined was where the Subject of this Sketch was to commence his professional Career; after much Debating and Consideration, the ancient Town of Dalton was at last fixed upon, for it's excellent Situation and also because the Surgeon there, Mr. Brockbank had entirely given himself up to Liquor which wou'd in all Probability speedily terminate his Existence and the extensive Practice fall entirely into the Hands of their Son Wm. [William].

These undoubtedly were weighty Reasons and when they were communicated to the young man he readily afsented [assented] to the Proposals.

20th (Thursday) - Leonard Coward of Littlemill near Dalton, a youth of very promising Talents who died of a Consumption, was this Day interr'd: he had arrived at his seventeeth Year.

Continuation of A Biographical Sketch of William Close

Proposals made by his parents and a convenient House

and shop were soon after taken and the Family removed to that dirty Town of Dalton, which, according to Mr. West, ' was once the pride but is now become the Shame of Furness', a very true Observation, for a Town of the same Size is no where to be found where the Inhabitants are so ignorant and of such ill Behaviour. - A more favourable Opportunity has seldom offered than that which now presented itself, for they had scarcely got fixed in their new Habitation when Death called away Mr. Thomas Brockbank and left more Room for the Expansion of Mr. Close's increasing Reputation and his medical practice.

The first Year of his Residence at Dalton was not marked with any production of his mechanical Genius, nor any signal Exertion of his professional Skill: he saw, with pain the difolute *[disolute]* and disorderly Behaviour of the Children of the lower Classes and the llamable *[lamentable?]* Conduct of the Parents themselves by the Influence of whose bad Examples the Manners of their Offspring were corrupted. To Remedy this or even to attempt to stop its farther progress was certainly praiseworthy, and to this Object Mr. Close now turned his Attention.

The first Step was to draw a Few of the Children from their idle Habits by some enticing and innocent amusement, for Idleness generates many Vices, and he wished to know what Reception his Plan woud meet with from the Parents. He of Course addrefsed some of the more respectable Inhabitants laying open his plan and explaining his Motives, which met with a more flattering Approbation than he expected and they promis'd that some of their Children shou'd attend him, when he was at Liberty from the Calls of his Profession, to be by him instructed in Playing upon various musical

Instruments. The Example and proficiency of a few
induced more to Attend, and much Good resulted from
the Establishment. A Reformation of Manners was in a
great Measure affected by Mr. C's excellent Example,
and the Time that used to be spent in Idleness and
Mischief was now appropriated to useful and pleasing
amusement: but its Utility extended to a few individuals
only, and little Advantage has been reaped from this
laudable and disinterested Attemp [*Attempt*] to reform
the dissolute Manners and scandalous Behaviour of the
Inhabitants of this idle and beggarly little Town. -

Wherever there are many poor, idle Inhabitants, many
Crimes are committed in the Neighbourhood. And if
the Clergyman and principal Inhabitants be addicted
to Vice and Immorality, the lower Classes follow
their Example and generally exceed them. At Dalton,
I am sorry to say, the Truth of these Observations is
too evident. Public teaching and the Example of our
Superiors constitute the Basis of Morality: and the
Pastor distinguised for his Talents and Virtues has great
influence over his Flock.

But here the Clergyman, whose name I forbear to
mention that Posterity may not know such a Character
ever was admitted to holy orders and so disgraced the
Gown, is most notorious for Drunkeness and Lying,
and frequently ascends even the pulpit in so shameful
a State of Intoxication as renders him unable to do his
Duty; frequently, I say, the solemn funeral Service is
hiccupt over in a Way most distrefsing to the Auditors
and this Minister of the Gospel scarcely able to follow
the Corpse to the Grave without Assistance. What an
Example for his Flock! Moreover his common Discourse
is replete with Obscenity, Lies, Oaths amd Immorality.

If a Story be told in the Neighbourhood which savours strongly of the Marvellous, some one is ready to say,

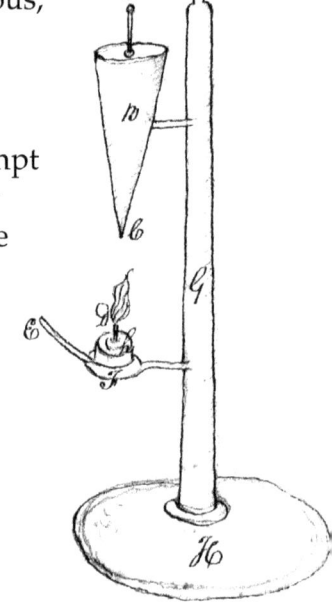

'that's one of the Parson of Dalton's Lies.' When Mr . Close's laudable attempt to ameliorate the Manners of the rising Generation at Dalton had fail'd in some Measure of the intended Succefs *[Success]* , he applied himself in Conjunction with James Charnock, a Blacksmith at Newton, to the Construction of a lamp for Burning Tallow or Kitchen Fat, which was well received and answered the intended purpose, a Figure of which is here added to give some little Idea of this ingenious and useful Invention.

Explanation of the Figure

H – An old pewter plate or Trenches of wood.

G – a piece of Wire fix in the plate – or piece of Wood in the Trenches.

F – a piece of Metal of Tin , pewter & Lead raised , fixed into G firmly.

E – a moveable piece of the same mixed metal containing a Wick ……..

D – when being lighted heats the part E so that the tallow or fat drops down into H and feeds the flame D, which by E the handle of the moveable part may be carried instead of a candle.

C – the point from which the Tallow drops , the Drip of which is regulated by....

A – which is a piece of wire passing thro the Tallow contain'd in the hollow iron part B.

Now as it is necefsary [*necessary*] for a Person going to a Necefsary in the Dark to have so much Light as is necefsary for him to do his necefsary Businefs, it behoves the said person, whom Necefsity compels to make this necefitous Journey, to take especial care that he Stumble not in the way for shou'd it purchance so happen ' tis then thousand to one that he pours the melted fat out of ' H' , and is reduced to the Necefsity of doing his Necefsary Businefs in the Dark – this by Way of Caution – I have frequently heard it said that Riches lead to Luxury and Luxury to Vice this is not the Case of Dalton - ' Tis Idleness leads to poverty and poverty to Vice. -

In the year 1802 Mr. Robt. Fell, an Opulent Banker, Mercer and Cotton Spinner at Ulverston, erected a Weaving House at Dalton for the Employment of the poor Children there, who were taught the Business and at the same time received whatever they cou'd cam [*come*] by their Labour in that way; but few, very few of the parents have sent their Children there, they had rather see their Children play in the Streets than earning sufficient for their Maintenance by honest and commendable Industry; that Scheme of Consequence like Mr. Close's has hitherto fail'd. What a Happinefs [*Happiness*] it must be to well disposed Parents to see their Children industriously earning Wages adequate to their decent Maintenance.

MARCH [1806]

*[One particular piece of
'entertainment' in Georgian
times, though now classified as
a bloodsport, was that of cock
fighting. This was not outlawed*

in Great Britain and her overseas colonies until 1835, though no doubt it continued in some places illegally. Cockfighting is still legal in some countries]

11th (Tuesday) -12th (Wednesday) - On the 11 and 12 a Main of Cocks was fought at Dalton, Jno. Ashburner of Scales against Addison vulgarly called Long Addison or the Holly – cropper, 2 guineas each Battle and 10 guineas the Main which was won by Long Addison. I Prophecy that Ashburner will be a Beggar if he live 10 Years from this Time, or his Intellects will be deranged.

26th (Wednesday) - This Evening I saw two Fishes caught at Roanhead of the Kind Lumpus? Or Sucking Fish *[Probably a Lamprey]* by one Irvin from Scotland who has a large Net there; one of the fishes was replete with Spawn. The same person has caught some Salmon trout and many Flatfish this Spring, also a few Shad

[Of the herring family] not comon *[common]* here.

31st (Monday) - Prices: Barley 15s. - Oats – 11/6 per Bushel Onion Seed – 18d per oz. Early cabbage plants 2d per score.. Red Cabbage – 4d per score. Blue peas – 12d – white do. [ditto] 8d per quart – Beef 7d – Mutton – 7d – Veal – 5d Pork – 5d – Lamb – 1s per lb – Salmon 2s/4d per lb.

Wages: Man servant - £26 per annum and meat and Lodging. Woman servant £8 per annum and ditto.

APRIL [1806]

1st (Tuesday) - John Hartley, the farmer at Crooklands, sowed Oats and Barley this Morning: it is the first sow'd in Furness this Season. The late fine weather has made the Grass spring abundantly; fruit Trees promise much Blossom and are very forward; Plumbs in particular are pushing out into Bloom -

[The following are some non -charitable remarks by Fleming]

2nd (Wednesday) - Thus accustomed to Idleness from Day to Day it becomes at last habitual and its Effects upon the Community lamentable. Swarms of Beggars pour out and disperse themselves over the Country, living on the Charity of the Industrious and getting their Clothing by a much cheaper Method than by purchase. Their Necefsities *[Necessities]* sometimes compel them to make free with the fattening live Stock of their Neighbours, and there the Blame is generally fixed upon Old Anthony; but there are many Anthonys or in other Words many who follow the same unlawful practices.

8th (Tuesday) - The Revd. Mr Powell, Vicar of Pennington died a Fortnight ago: the living is given by the Chancellor of the Duchy of Lancaster (the Earl of Derby) to the Revd. John Sunderland of Ulverston. The Vicar of Pennington, till within a Few Years nominated by the parishioners; but they not agreeing among themselves on the Death of the Revd. Mr Stainton; who shou'd be his Succefsor, *[Successor]* it was proposed by William Nicholson of Rowend, who was always the promoter of Mischief, that they shou'd play at Shake – Cap for a Parson. Upon this the Chancellor nominated Mr. Wm Bifsell *[William Bissell]* - who was succeeded by Mr Powell – who is now succeeded by Mr Sunderland all appointed by the Chancellor: thus by the Folly of our Stubborn illnatured Fellow the Tenants of the Manor of Pennington lost the Valuable privilege of Cheering their own Clergyman. Salary about £150 per annum.

10th (Thursday) - Whilst Mr. Close was buried in the Construction of his Lamp, a light more bright than it cou'd glanced from the refulgent Eyes of Mifs [Miss] Charnock, Daughter of the Blacksmith mentioned above, into his Breast and caused such an Inflamation in his Bosom as cou'd not be cured by medical Skill; the flame burnt with unabating Violence for some months before the timorous Gentleman could resolve to declare his Passion to the divine Object on whom all his Affections were centered.

The unruly Passion is difficult to subdue, so the first Opportunity that presented he humbled himself before her and requested her patience to hear him exert his oratorical abilities on a Subject which nearly concerned his Happiness. he granted him the desired Indulgence, and he proceeded to lay open his Heart in such a lovely Stile of natural and affectionate Eloquence, that he made a Breach in the young Lady's Heart.

The respective parents were now informed of the Attachment, and like prudent parents of prudent Children did not raise any silly nonsensical Objections to the Match on account of Fortune but at once gave their Consent to the matrimonial Junction of the parties were agreeable to each other. This judicious understanding and the nuptial Knot was soon after tied as fast as the parson of Dalton cou'd do it.

Mr C's appearance at this Time did not say to the World that he was in a State to revel much in the carnal Delights of a matrimonial connection; but the Marketplace at Dalton where he lived is situated on a Limestone Rock with an excellent Stream of limpid Water flowing at the Foot of it, and is well supplied with Fish & other light Food, all which are favorable to

procreation; had the contrary been the Case few wou'd
have an Idea that any thing could ifsue from the Loins
of this Disciple of Esculapius *[Latin God of Medicine]*
which cou'd animate lifeless matter, for he seemed as if
the vital Spark was almost extinguished within himself.
But after all he proved himself a Plenipo *[To have
complete or full powers]*:

Matrimony brought new Ideas; and, as the Inhabitants
at the upper part of the Town had their Water to fetch
from some Distance, he now set himself to work to
ease them of that Trouble, and make the Water; by the
Force of its own Current raisd itself to the Height of 27
feet and flow into the Middle of the Marketplace of its
own Accord. But the foolish and ignorant people have
smil'd at Mr. C. and his ingenious apparatus when they
saw him confine the Stream of Water so that it might
flow thro' the Taphole at the Bottom of a Tub, and by
it's thus increased Force rais *[raise]* the Water in a Tube
to the Height of 14 inches; and their Ridicule, against
which he was not proof, caused him to relinquishhis
hydraulic Experiments.

14th (Monday) - The Remains of Thomas Atkinson
of Dalton, were interr'd this Evening at Dalton. He
was for many Years Steward to the Manor of Plain
Furnefs *[Furness]* & Muchland with Torver etc. and
conscientiously discharged his Duty:

William Atkinson his Son succeeded him in his
Stewardship etc. Filius patric difinilis *[! ? - Probably
'Filius patris dificiles']*

*[An excellent description by Fleming on the hierarchy at a
typical funeral in Georgian times]*

It is a singular Custom, still follow'd at Dalton by the more respectable Inhabitants at Funerals, to divide the people who attend the Interment into three Clafses [Classes] ;

The First Clafs [Class] consists of the richest and nearest relations, who have a warm Dinner provided – the Second, consists of the poorest and more distant Relations, together with their richer Acquaintances and Friends, who partake of a cold Dinner; - and the third, of the Farmers & people in the Town, who are not Relations or opulent Acquaintances, these have Bread and Cheese.

[More observations of Wiliam Close]

About this Time a Gold Ring of great antiquity, with an Inscription in Arabic, was found by George Slater, the Farmer at the park, near Dalton, as he was plowing in one of the Fields belonging to that Farm. This valuable Antique was brought by Slater to Mr. C. to decypher, who finding it beyond his Comprehension made a Composition of Brimstone etc. to take off the Characters, in doing which he broke the Ring to pieces, and thus entirely destroy'd the most estimable piece of antiquity which has ever been found in Furnefs both for it's Beauty and preservation.

[To be continued]

28th (Monday) - This day a fair for Cattle and hiring Servants was held at Dalton, also another at Ulverstone, in opposition to the former. The Cattle had dull Sale; Servants were very high; Men from £25 to £30 per ann. Women from £8 to £15 per ann.

MAY [1806]

[Comments by Fleming on Close's updating of West's 'Antiquities of Furness']

Continued Biography of William Close

Without either Genius or Learning fit for the Task, he next undertook, for a trifling Sum, to become the Editor of West's Antiquities of Furness, which required Abilities superior to what he pofsefs'd *[possessed]*, to produce an Edition better than the former.

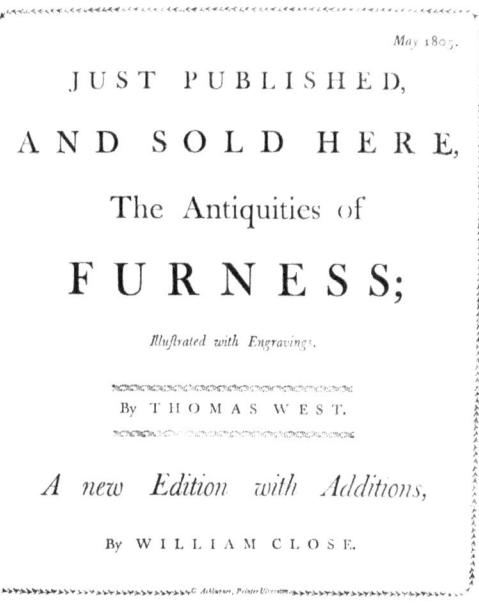

May 1805.

JUST PUBLISHED,

AND SOLD HERE,

The Antiquities of

FURNESS;

Illustrated with Engravings.

By THOMAS WEST.

A new Edition with Additions,

By WILLIAM CLOSE.

William Close's Revision of West's
The Antiquities Of Furness

The Publisher who made the Bargain with Mr C – was sensible of this as soon as The Work began to be put to the press; for tho' the greater part of it was printed from a Copy of the former Edition, the Editor thot *[thought]* it necessary to make some Alterations, which were so full of grammatical Errors, bad Spelling and Nonsense that the publisher was under the Necessity of Applying to another person to alter and correct the proof Sheets.

Tho ' he was not master of all the classic Elegance which is required in an author who wishes his productions to be admired, he used the greatest Diligence in the Work, and the Memories of all the old Women in Dalton and the Neighbourhood were ransack'd to furnish Materials for the Instruction and Amusement of the Gentlemen and Ladies who shou'd become purchasers of this improved Edition.

People who have formed their Judgement from this Specimen of his Abilities as an Author, are of Opinion that he will not readily acquire a Fortune by Literature, his first Attempt being so far from fulfilling the Expectations of his Readers.

6th (Tuesday) - Last Night, Thomas Wilkinson, a Farmer at Stank, was seized with a violent pain in the Head and bleeding at the Nose; A Surgeon, Mr Close, was sent for from Dalton who attempted to stop the Bleeding by filling the patient's Nostrils with Cotton: soon after the Blood burst out at a Tumour in the Gums on Roof of the Mouth: but his nostrils continuing stopped, he went to bed and in the Night was suffocated with the coagulated Blood.

9th (Friday) - The Blossom upon apple pear, plumb and cherry trees is abundant, but it is full of Maggots and Insects, of which the Easterly dry Winds are said to be the Cause, and they will in all probability destroy the Rudiments of the fruit, These Winds are also said to have caused the Complaint, by some called the Influenza, which has been so prevalent & troublesome all this Year, hitherto.

20th (Tuesday) - The Gooseberry Trees are nearly depriv'd of their Leaves by Caterpillars, and the Blossom on Fruit Trees does not expand freely. Nancy Ashburner, Wife of John Ashburner, Malster and Millar at penington Mill, who cut her throat on Tuesday 13 Instant, died this Evening, having lived eight Days without Food.

JUNE ¹⁸⁰⁶

1st Sunday) - Very hot and dry

4th - Went to Ronhidd *[Roanhead]* to see the large net on Duddon Sands and found in it a curious Fish, the name of which the Fishermen confess'd themselves ignorant of.

At our first approach the Tide had not so far ebbed from the Net to allow us to take it, and it was making every Effort to escape; I teased it with a Stick in the Water which caused it to leap with amazing agility & Violence against the Net, and in it's Attempts to escape from me it frequently emitted an Inklike Liquid which hid it for some Time from our Sight by tinging the Water of deep Black. When taken it uttered a Kind of Groan, and often filled its Body with air, which it forced out again at an Aperture under it's Breast with such force as to cause a noise which might be heard at a Hundred Yards Distance.

We took it to John Atkinson's, the Farmer at Ronhed, and put it into a large pot of fresh Water just drawn from the Well: as soon as it was immerged in this Water it again emitted near a Quart of the black Liquid and almost immediately after died.

It's Head was about the Size of one's Fist, the Eyes large and prominent when in its proper Element, but they in some Measure sunk into it's Head and became dull as soon as it was exposed to the air.

It had Eight Appendages to it's Head each about five Inches long with which it cou'd clasp anything which was put to it, and contract or extend them; with these it adhered firmly to the side of the Bason *[Basin]* where it last discharged the Ink from The Body, which was not unlike a Sole but much thicker, was on the Back brown and hard as stiff Leather, but the belly was white; it had no Tail, and was surrounded with a soft Fin. It frequently, when out of the Water, rais'd up the hard Substance upon it's Back and drew in the Air; and when it emitted the Air again from the same Aperture under the Breast from which the Ink ifsued, it stretched out it's Head and about 3 Inches of it's Neck from under it's armour. On it's back was a bony Tubercule not unlike one of the Thorns upon a Ray. The whole Fish was so clear and Transparent that the Motions of the fluids within the Body were clearly to be distinguished. The Fig. Below which I imperfectly sketch from Memory may give some Idea of the Fish.

Having investigated this I find it to be The Cuttle Fish

This is intended to shew the Fish placed on it's Belly and it's Head stretched out, but so humble is the Sketch that that it is scarcely sufficient to indicate the Form of this race, and, I may say curious Fish. I have seen in Buffon *[George-Louis Leclerc, Comte de Buffon, French naturalist, 1707-1788]* the name of Inkfish given from it's emitting a Liquid like Ink to facilitate it's escape from it's Enemies; but do not remember to have seen a Description of the Inkfish. Mem: *[Memo]* to investigate it.

6th -Dalton Fair – Cattle shewn in abundance and a great many sold at good prices -

7th - Fine and hot. Went in company with Mr Wm. Townson of Whinfell to shoot crows at the Rookery at Dendron: Mr Jno. Gardner, senior, attempted to amuse us with a Delineation of the character of Mr Singleton the Clergyman at the Chapel there, in which Mr. G. insisted upon the Revd. Clergyman's being guilty of Vices shocking to be related and the most shameful for a Man to commit: among other Crimes, he accused him of keeping and maintaining in his House, one Jackson who carried on a criminal Connection with Mrs Singleton, her Husband at the same Time knowing and conniving at it:

Also that Mr Singleton with the Knowledge and Connivance of his Wife was guilty of a criminal Connection with a Mrs Atkins, Housekeeper at the Moor Side and that he performed the Duty of husband on her for the sake of obtaining his Belly full of Victuals.

The most shocking Circumstance that need be conceived is, that this Man of the name of Jackson, who performs family Duty for the Wife, is her Nephew, and that the Clergyman allows the unnatural and I may call it, incestuous Connection.

If this be True, O tempora o mores a Clergyman who ought to be our Instructor and Guide in the paths of Virtue, who by his Example should point out to us the Way to eternal Happiness and create in us an abhorance of Vice and Love of Virtue, if he be really guilty of ye Crimes which are laid to his Charge ought not to be allowed to cover his polluted Body with the Garb of

Sanctity but for the Good of Society be stript *[stripped]* of his Cafsock *[Cassock]* and degraded from his Office. If such are imposed upon us for our Instructors what will in a short Time be the State of Society? If we are trained up after their Example, what must be our Situation in a future State? This is one of the Men who tells us that our Actions in this World must determine our Reception in the next, that our Happiness or Misery after Death, Depends upon our virtuous or wicked Actions in this Life. Surely this Man, if the Accusation be true, cannot believe what he preaches, his precepts and Actions are so are so opposite, nor can he expect it to have any weight or Influence on his Auditors.

19th (Thursday) - Hay Grass is very thin this year owing to the dry Season -

30th (Monday) - P. Hartley married.

JULY [1806]

Prices : Beef – 8d Mutton – 7d Veel – 6d Lamb – 7d Salmon – 8d per lb. Ducks – 16d. Hens- 14d. Oatmeal – 22/-Flour – 33s. Per cwt. Old Potatoes 3s. Per Hoop. New Do. 1D per lb. Peas – 8d. Per Hoop. Cabbages -1d each. Cucumber – 4d. ea. Gooseberries – 2 and a half d. per Quart. Cockles – 1d. Do. Old Hay – 14d per stone.

Lime – 16d. Per Bushel.

Port Wine – 16s. Brandy – 24s. Rum – 17s. Holland's Gin – 20s. Ale – 2s. Common British Gin - 10s. Per Gallon. Coals – 24s. Per cwt. Peats – 4s. Per Cart. Deal Timber – 3/6 per solid Foot. Land in general from 35s. To 75s. Per Statute Acre. Licence to kill Game - £3-4s-0d. Per annum. Tax on Game Dogs – 10s. Per ann. - on other Dogs – 6s. Per ann. Shot – 6d. Per lb. Gunpowder 3/6 Do. Plain single Barrel Gun - £5-5s-0d. Plain Double Barrel Do. - £9. Servants – Men from £20 - £30 and meat per annum. Maid servants - £5 - £12 per ann.Day Labourers – 3s. Per day.

3rd (Thursday) - Hay Grass is exremely scarce, particularly where the meadows were pastured late in the Spring and on a gravelly Soil. -

9th (Wednesday) -

A Good Grace After A Scanty Dinner
The Lord be thanked,
For this good Banquet
Although it was but small,
Had there been more Meat,
We cou'd have done wi' it
But God be thank'd for all.

11th (Friday) - This Morning at about 2 o'clock a violent Storm of thunder, Lightning, Rain and Hail came on, and continued incissantly [*incessantly*] till 4 o'clock. Some Damage at Fells' Malt Kiln on Swarthmoor.

12th (Saturday) - Between 3 & 4 o'clock the Lightening struck the House of Mary Fell on Swarthmoor adjoining to a Malt Kiln: it divided the End of the House from the Chimney to the foundation, descended by the Chimney into the Room where M. Fell was in Bed, where it Burst a Set of Drawers to pieces and dispers'd them about the Room without doing the Lady any Injury: it likewise penetrated in another Room, in one of which it was attracted by an Iron Fender placed upon the Chimneypiece and reduced to a shapeless Mass two Brass Candlesticks wh. *[which]* were placed at each End of the Fender: it demolished the windows and plow'd up the Ground adjoining the House to a considerable Depth. A strong sulphureous *[sulphurous]* and very disagreeable Smell remains in the House; thro' the Mercy of the Almighty no Lives were lost.

Cicero says, that all men of Genius are melancholy: and as there is a Seriousness and Melancholy in the Doctor's Manner which is far from pleasant to many, and particularly those who conceive that it arises from an Idea of his possefsing superior Abilities and that his Taciturnity is the Offspring of Vanity rather than of his Modesty or Diffidence, these are only few of his Acquaintance who look upon it a Mark or Indication of Genius but as arising from a different Source.

[Fleming does not relate this second entry to anyone in particular – but it seems likely to be another reference to William Close. No further entries of note are entered for this month. It is surprising, however, that Fleming does not mention the coast road accident and subsequent death of Major John Perryn, on July 21st. He was thrown from his gig and the tragedy was reported in the Lancaster Gazette. Perryn was buried at St. Cuthbert's Church, Aldingham, though it is only very recently that the grave has been discovered inside the church]

AUGUST [1806]

3rd (Sunday) - Harvest begun in Longslacks near Ulverston, Yesterday; Barley.

7th (Thursday) - John Hartley, Farmer at Crooklands near Dalton, began this Morning to reap his Barley, which was sown on the first of April. The Crop was abundant.

9th (Saturday) - There was much Lightening and thunder last, which did great Damage at Low – Wood near Backbarrow.

12th (Tuesday) - Grouse very scarce upon Pennington Moor and the adjoining Commons, but Shooters numerous.

14th (Thursday) - Harvest in general commencing.

17th (Sunday) - It has been the Custom from Time immemorial for Reapers to offer themselves in the Market Place at Dalton in Furness every Sunday morning during Harvest, to be hired by the Farmers not only in the Neighbourhood but by those from Cumberland who constantly repair thither for that purpose. This day being the first this Season, great numbers of Irish came over to reap who caused the prices to be lower than usual.

Reapers – 3s. Per Day with meat, Beer and Lodging; which is = to 5s. Per day. Reapers hired per Stouck [*Stack*] of 12 sheaves – 3d per Stouck.

[Now an outline of the life of Sir William Huddlestone, English Civil War veteran, by William Fleming]

Sir William Huddlestone of Millom Castle, in the County of Cumberland, was one of the Barons, who in the year 1215 compelled King John to sign the Magna

Charta at Runnemede; and one of his Descendants, also named Sir William Huddlestone, in the Rebellion against Charles the First, rais'd a Regiment of Horse at his own Expence for the Service of the King, in which were Seven of his Sons, of whom Five were killed at the Battle of Naseby the 14 June 1645. In this Rebellion Sir William Huddlestone sustain'd a Loss of more than thirty Thousand pound, and moreover was afterwards compell'd by the parliament to pay the Sum of two thousand two hundred and forty eight pounds.

21st (Thursday) - Sultry, Thunder and Rain. Grain, the Farmers say, has never in their Memory been known to ripen so rapidly as it has for the Six Days last past; now the greatest part of the Grain in Low Furness is ready for the Sickle but Reapers cannot br found to cut it.

24th (Sunday) - Reapers 4/6 per Day with Meat, Drink and Lodgings.

Three Dead Bodies of Men wash'd on Shore in Duddon were buried at Dalton, two this Day and one Yesterday

SEPTEMBER [1806]

15th (Monday) - Reaping in general finished & much Grain got from the Fields.

30th (Tuesday) - Prices: Apples – 13d. - Nuts – 2/0 – Potatoes 3d per Hoop. Codfish – 1 and a half pence per lb.

OCTOBER [1806]

5th (Sunday) - The Birthday of Sarah Fleming junior

(one Year old) and the Day her first Tooth made its Appearance.

6th (Monday) - Two men thrown ashore by the Tide on the West Side of Walney, supposed to be two of the passengers in the Dublin packet, which was lost about three weeks ago, when near one hundred persons perished . -

7th (Tuesday) - The new Fair for Cattle at Ulverstone was held this Day but the Shew of Cattle was not great nor the Buyers numerous; many of the Farmers in Low Furness attended; but did not take any of their Cattle.

The new Fair at Broughton which was kept on Friday, 3 Instant was very well attended and a great number of Cows and Sheep offer'd for Sale.

8th (Wednesday) - The forward Crops of Wheat come up freely and appear green.

9th (Thursday) - Fruit at Ulverston market so plentiful that Apples were sold at from 6d to 10d per Hoop at 6 Quarts. Chiefly summer Fruit.

10th (Friday) - Six more of the unfortunate Men lost in the packet, are found on the Lancaster coast thrown up by the Tide, upon each of which some property was found.

14th (Tuesday) - A Company of Players at the Whitehorse Inn, Dalton consisting of 7 or 8 performers, the Theatre a Hay loft over the Stable and the Price of Tickets for attendance. Pit – 1/- , Gallery – 6d.

[A final assessment by Mr Fleming of the Ulverston Volunteers, now the Ulverstone Volunteer Light Infantry]

21st (Tuesday) - When the Corsican Usurper had seated himself on the throne of the Bourbons in France, and envious of the Liberty and happiness of Britons had brought together his Mirmidons *[Myrmidons]* to Bologne, threatening with his formidable Army to subvert our Constitution and deluge the Island with our Blood, he encouraged his Soldiers to this hazardous Invasion by promising them the plunder of our rich Capital and unbounded Liberty of ravaging our conquered Country and enriching themselves with the Spoil.

List of Ulverstone Volunteer Light Infantry, Royal British Legion Club, Barrow in Furness

To oppose the Corsican Tyrant and defend our Wives our Children and our Property, a number of men voluntarily offered themselves and were trained and exercised so as to act with Troops of the Line.

Ulverston and the Neighbourhood produced a Corps consisting of about two hundred and fifty Men who were remarkable for their Steadiness and good Discipline; this Corps was in a great measure & supported from a Subscription made by the Gentlemen in Furness, whilst those people of property who lived in Furness Fells, secure in their native Hills, contributed very little towards their Support.

After having continued near two years their Fund failed, for the Extravagance of the Officers could not be supported; On examining their Accounts it was found they had spent near three thousand pounds and were £600 in Debt.

The people who had subscribed finding the Money not expended in the Way they expected, refused to contribute any thing more towards the Support of the Corps. Of Consequence they were disbanded and the Colours were this Day deposited in the parish Church at Ulverston and their Arms, which were supply'd by the Government, delivered up. This fine Body of Men was greatly approved of by the reviewing Officers who transmitted to Government most flattering accounts of their Discipline and orderly Behaviour.

23rd (Thursday) - Sharp frost, the small Holes of Water frozen over to the thickness of near quarter of an inch thick.

29th (Wednesday) -

Who would have known these Bottledraining Men,
Members of Dalton Club, but from my pen;
Men who for Deeds of drinking now have bore
The Palm of Merit fifty Years and more?
[Part of a lengthy poem by Fleming to the Dalton Club]

31st (Friday) - Ulverston Hunt commenced on Monday 27 & continues the whole of this Week. Richd. *[Richard]* Tower , Mayor. Butler's Company of Comedians came to Ulverston and will perform tomorrow Evening.

NOVEMBER 1806

10th (Monday) - Bridget Hunter of Tytup married to Jno. Parker of the Farm near Bootle in Co. Cumberland.

[A Catalogue of Books at the prime Cost belonging to William Fleming of Pennington]

DECEMBER 1806

31st (Wednesday) -The Winter hitherto has been remarkably mild, so that the Fields have more the Appearance of April than Decem. Yet it is not healthy; a Complaint is prevalent here which may not improperly be called an Epidemical Cattarrh.

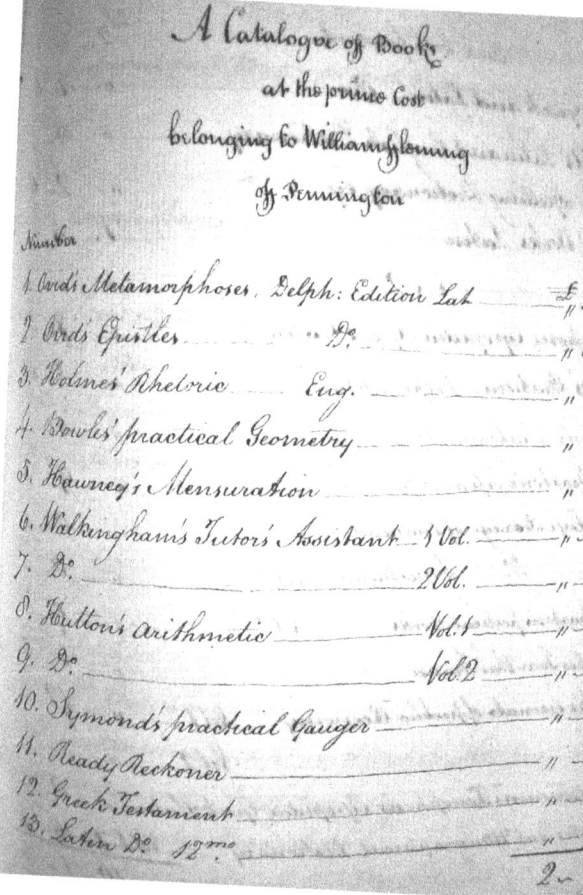

Catalogue Of Books belonging to William Fleming

CHAPTER 7

WAR WITH NEARLY
ALL THE WORLD
1807

JANUARY

20th (Tuesday) -Thomas Atkinson of Manor Abbey died this Morning in a Fit of Apoplexy, caused by immoderate Drinking of Spirits; His Father died of the same but in a more distrefing *[distressing]* Manner:

The Family retired to Bed leaving him in a State of Intoxication sitting by the Fire; in the Morning they found him reduced to a Cinder, tho' still retaining his perfect Figure and most of his clothes not injured by Fire.

22nd (Thursday) - The Atkinson Family has for some Time resided at the Manor Abbey, as Farmers; The Grandfather of the late Thomas Atkinson was in very low and reduced Circumstances, but to the Surprise of all his Neighbours, suddenly emerged from poverty. It was the general Opinion that he had the good Fortune to find some hidden Treasure concealed about the Ruins of the Abbey, which from hard labour and Poverty raised him to Ease and Opulence, for the Transition was quicker than is generally produced by Industry and Parsimony.

His two Sons, the older of which resided at the Abbey and the younger a Surgeon at Dalton, both hastened their Deaths by immoderate Drinking and died in the prime of life.

23rd (Friday) - Thomas Atkinson of Manor Abbey interred at Dalton.

Price of Barley for Malting from 15s. to 16s. Per Carlisle Bushel.

26th (Monday) - Last Week some Oxen belonging to -----*[first name blank]* Powell, the Farmer at Olbeck *[Holbeck]*, took Fright in the Field where they had been accustomed to pasture; Some of them broke thro' the fence and ran to Leece, nearly burst; others laid down in the Brook and wou'd have been drowned had not the Farmer and his Servants dragged them out of the Water with Ropes: the Rest of them ran into a Corner of the Field where the *[they]* remained immoveable, large Drops of sweat following each other down their Sides.

The Cattle having thus taken Fright several Days succefsively the Farmer, alarmed for their Safety, ordered some of his Servants to keep Watch and if possible find out the Cause of their Fright.

The Watch was stationed for some Days & tho' the Cattle were still repeatedly terrified as before, nothing was seen nor any probable Cause cou'd be afsigned. It is something Strange, but the weaker part of the neighbours solve the Mystery by attributing it to a preternatural Apparition.

30th (Friday) - The Farmers in General forward with

plowing [ploughing] from the mildness of the Weather. Coals 27s. For 16 cwt.

FEBRUARY [1807]

16th (Monday) - Barley for Malting something lower than at the Beginning of the Season. Now selling at 14s. Per Carl. Bush.

18th (Wednesday) - Hay now selling at 1s. And 1s / 2d per Stone.

Woodcocks breed numerously in the Woods on the Banks of Caspian Sea (Bell's Travels).

25th (Wednesday) - This Day is appointed for a general Fast.

28th (Saturday) - The Frost and bright Sun in this Season begins to injure the Wheat which was remarkably forward; in Consequence flour and Oatmeal are advanced in price.

The Barometer was never so high since October as it is at present; the Roads are covered with Dust.

MARCH [1807]

Recipe for making Bread of Potatoes *[See ' FOOD AND DRINK RECIPIES ' in the Appendices]*

20th (Friday) - Copy of a Handbill

Whereas it is reported that certain young Gentlemen

in this Town have lately been guilty of issuing many false Notes, and that a person, commonly known by the Name of Squeaking Tommy has for some time past been in the Habit of exchanging such Notes for Cash. Notice is hereby given That if any of the said young Gentlemen shall be found issuing or the aforesaid Squeaking Tommy receiving Cash, for any such bad Notes, they will be considered as Disturbers of the Harmony of the place, and may by a perseverance in such bad practice in time come to a Chord. Ulverston, March 20. 1807.

[In Georgian times forging money or issuing false goods was a capital offence. This crime was known as 'Uttering'. Several people were executed at Lancaster Castle for perpetrating this felony]

Anecdote

When Joe Harrison was in Business at the Town Mill in Ulverston, his wife Mary who, by the Bye, was not very remarkable for the Sweetness of her Temper, went up one morning to the Mill and accosted her Husband with; 'Why Joe, What News this Morning? -------'News? by the Blood, yonder old Jack Jones wedded this Morning' ------'Ah.....hang him for an old Fool ; but ye men are all so: if I was dead, old as thou art, I warrant thou wou'd wed the Devil's Daughter sooner than Mifs *[Miss]* _____*[Name missing!]*
'Nay, nay Mary, I think our Laws wouldn't allow me to wed two Sisters........'.

24th (Tuesday) - A Fair for Cattle and Hiring Servants, held at Ulverston, as advertised for some Weeks past. -

25th (Wednesday) - Ld. Geo. Cavendishes' Farmers met this *[a word is missing – morning?]* at Harvey Mason's at Dalton to hear the Determination of his Lordship's Stewards, regarding their Farms in Low Furness, their Rents were advanced in some Farms to near one half more and in others to near double the old Rents; In Consequence the Farmers, who have been for some Years' conspicuous as dashing Fellows, retired [?] a little Chapfallen.

Cattle Fair, AT ULVERSTONE.

A FAIR FOR CATTLE WILL BE HOLDEN AT
ULVERSTONE,
On Tuesday the 24th of March, 1807;

WHERE a large quantity will be shewn, suitable for GENTLEMEN GRAZIERS, and BUTCHERS; this *Fair* has received the greatest encouragement from the FARMERS who purpose selling some of the Handsomest CATTLE bred in the *North* of *England*, and will be annually holden on *Tuesday* before *Easter*, which will suit *Preston*, *Bentham* and other *Fairs* in that week.

A SHEW of HORSES;
And *MALE* and *FEMALE SERVANTS* to be *HIRED*.

Ulverstone OCTOBER *Cattle Fair:*
The CATTLE FAIR will as usual be held on the 7th day of *October*, next.

J. SOULBY, *Printer,* Ulverstone.

APRIL 1807

2nd (Thursday) - Yesterday the Ballot took place at Ulverston for Men to serve in the Levy en Masse, for which Lancashire furnishes 14,151 as its proportion of 200, 000 to be raised: the No. of men in pennington Eight.

John Hartley of Crooklands sow'd his first Oats.

3rd (Friday) - A little frost – the roads dusty. Seed time begun in some places.

4th (Saturday) - Frost still continues and hinders Seedtime from being generall.

7th (Tuesday) - John Hartley sow'd Barley in Maidenlands first.

11th (Saturday) - The Farmers in general very busy in their Seedtime and the Ground in fine Order for breaking under the Harrow.

Hay – 12d. and 13d. Per Stone, Beans 20s. Per Bushel Barley – 14s. - Oats 11d. Per Bushel - Wheat 47s. Per Load – Eggs 5 for 2d. Beef – 6 and a half pence per lb. - Butter 13d. Per lb of 16 oz. Mutton 7d – Veal – 6d.

Pork – 5d. Per lb. - No Lamb yet in the Market at Ulverston.

14th (Tuesday) - Thunder, lightening, Hail and Rain came on with great Violence, and extended from the East as far as Crooklands near Dalton, where I then was, the Rain falling in Torents to the East of that place, whilst the other part of the sky to the West was calm and serene the Sun shining in all his Splendor and not a Single drop of rain falling to the West ....the Brooks overflowed their Banks and the Evening was stormy.

[William Fleming replies to a letter – from?....... James – Lt. James Hodgson ??]

My Dear James,

Your kind Letter which I received in due Time gave me and the Rest of your Friends great Pleasure, as by it we received the gratifying Information of your

good Health, which is a Blessing not enjoyed by every
Individual who is wafted across the Atlantic, to your
Sunburnt Shores: pray be careful in preserving it, for
you perhaps may not know the Value of it till you
have lost it irecoverably *[irrecoverably]* - At the same
time that I am advising you in Regard to your Health,
I as a Friend, must also give you a little Advice on
another Subject, tho' in some Measure connected with
the former; and that is to beware and avoid the Rock
upon which your brother has split: I know you are not
unacquainted with his present Situation, for Hartley
has taken upon him to make that pretty well known
at St.Vincents. Your Mother too is implicated, for your
Brother has involved her upwards of Three Hundred
pounds still remaining to be paid, besides some Drafts
upon her which she has not accepted. I will say no more,
for the Subject is painful to me, and of Consequence will
be more so to you, but from the above you will easily
conjecture in what State things are on this Side the
Water. - your Letter I have not by me, or I wou'd answer
each of your Interrogations in regular Order; not that I
have been carelefs in preserving your Epistle, but your
Sister wished to see it, of Course I gave it to her and she
has mislaid it, so that I can only give you the News of
the Country as it occurs to my Recollection;

First, of your Friends; they are all in good Health, most
of them beg me to present their Love to you, and the
Rest their best Compliments, which I hope you will
receive join'd to the good Wishes of your correspondent,
who would have been happy in your Company last
August and September in his Shooting Excursions.

I killed many Birds last Season and Some Hares. I keep
an excellent Greyhound that seldom misses the Game if
fairly started. I had it a Whelp and the past Season was
the first of it's …............*[Words unintelligible]*

In the next Place I write inform you of some of your
Acquaintance who are entered into the matrimonial
State: About a Week ago Sarah Fisher with...........*[First
name missing]* Redhead. -

A Fortnight ago Agnes Hartley of the Townend,
and Sister to Hartley of St. Vincents to one Prescot a
Customhouse Officer at Liverpool – Sometime ago, John
Thompson the little spruce Mercer in King's Street to
Mifs Banks of Walney . - then Mr. Jo. Yarker has got a
Share of a Ticket in the State Lottery which has now just
done drawing, which had the good Fortune to come up
a prize of Twenty thousand and Twenty two pounds,
but tho, Fortune has thus smiled upon Mr. Yarker, she
has frowned upon Wm. Dobson of the Braddyll's Arms,
who at Candlemas sign'd over his property for the
Benefit of his Creditors –

Wm. Atkis Fell has commenced Attorney at Ulverston:
his Brother Tom is still with Robt. Fell – Richd. Towers
is dashing away with the money which his Uncle
squeez'd from his Clients: and now as I am making
mention of Richd. Towers I must inform you, as in
all probability you are ignorant of the enormous Bill
he brought against your Mother at the death of Mr
Robinson, it was little short of Sixteen Hundred pounds;
to discharge it, took all the Money she had spared
together with the piece of Mounbarrow *[Mountbarrow?]*
Estate, the Money arising from the sale of the Furniture
at Her Tarnside and all the Cash she had by her within
a Few Pounds. From this you will judge that her Affairs
are not in so flourishing a State as you, without Doubt,
expected them to be; but I wou'd not have kept you in
the Dark in Regards to her Affairs, therefore I mention
this. -------

Your Brother's Affairs in St. Vincents; I find are greatly deranged, so much that perhaps before you receive this his partner may have decamped.

I am sorry for it, and I have the Intelligence from authority which makes it impossible for me to Doubt the Truth of it. Your Letters had generally led us to suppose them different, and I have not yet told your Mother to the contrary, nor do I intend it except some Particular Occassion require it.

In your next Letter pray let us know in what Situation their Affairs are if you know it, for it can answer no good purpose to deceive your Friends here in that Respect, nor do I think it is your Disposition to amuse with a false Statement and lead us into Error. Your Sister received a Letter from you Yesterday you do not mention the french Fleet which is in your Quarter of the World but we have a good Account of them in the Newspapers of Today. I am now approaching the Bounds of my Sheet and will conclude with wishing that you may soon acquire an independent Fortune and be enabled to return with Honour to your Native place, when we may again............the healthy Moors of Kirkby and the fertile Fields of Low Furness in quest of Health and amusement. Adieu! my dear James, when you have a leisure Hour employ it in writing to

Your affectionate etc .

W. Fleming.

[The sad death, at a young age, of Fleming's sister]

20th (Monday) - Mifs *[Miss]* Mary Fleming, of
Pennington, my only Sister, departed this miserable
Life, in the Twenty sixth year of her Age------

21st (Tuesday) - The Farmers are busy in their Seedtime.
Saw the Cuccow *[Cuckow or Cuckoo]* the first Time, this
Spring.

24th (Friday) - Mifs Mary Fleming was interred at
Pennington this morning, Age 26. A Consumption the
Consequence of Fever, terminated her Existence in the
prime of Life.

28th (Tuesday) - Dalton Fair was well attended and a
great Number of Cattle were sold but not at advanced
prices.

29th (Wednesday) - The Fields have now put on their
Summer Livery, the spring is astonishingly rapid.

30th (Thursday) - William Fleming *[Junior]* baptis'd this
Day – born Feb. 3. 1807.

MAY [1807]

5th (Tuesday) - The Sun Inn, Ulverston

Went this morning to Ulverston in Consequence of
Mr John Sunderland, the Vicar of Pennington, having
claimed the Right of nominating and appointing one of
the Churchwardens for the Parish of Pennington, which
is contrary to the Custom there, the Churchwardens
for Time immemorial having been appointed by the
Sidesmen.......these are: William Fleming, Thomas
Nicholson, Thomas Fell and John Ashburner.

Mr. Dowbiggin the Deputy refused to swear in the Churchwardens appointed on Easter Monday last past by the Sidesmen of consequence the old ones continue till the Matter be settled.

7th (Thursday) - Yesterday, Samuel Case of the Tan Yard at Crooklands was married to Agnes Addison Daughter of a Weaver in Dalton of that Name and Neice to Thomas Thompson, Shoemaker who, reports says, purchased her a Husband with £200.

15th (Friday) - This Day and Tomorrow a Main of Cocks will be fought at Dalton.

30th (Saturday) - Many Farmers say their early Potatoes are kill'd by the severe and cold Winds blowing sometime now from the East.

31st (Sunday) - The East Wind continues and is exceeding cold and unseasonable; a good Shower of Rain might perhaps destroy the Caterpillars and other Insects which are destroying the Gooseberries and Fruit tree Blossoms.

[Lists of the Parish of Pennington Collections, Churchwardens, Constables, Poor Law Payouts etc from 1675 onwards – See selected examples in OVERSEERS OF THE POOR in the Appendices]

JUNE 1807

2nd (Tuesday) - The east Wind still prevails and is so very cold that the Hay Grafs *[Grass]* comes very slowly forward.

5th (Friday) - Rain and warmer but the Grass is not yet plentiful & Hay very scarce.

6th (Saturday) - A very great Number of Cattle were shewn today at Dalton fair and many sold but at prices much inferior to what they have been for Seven Years past; which is probably owing to the Scarcity of Grass--

7th (Sunday) - Caterpillars and Insects are devouring all the Blofsom [Blossom] which is extremely abundant; and the Gooseberries which are a failing Crop this Year are left naked on the trees.

8th (Monday) - Grain which was sown early looks well and promises an abundant Crop, yet the Markets keep advancing and fat Cattle sell very high but lean ones low-

17th (Wednesday) - Early Hay Grass in some places ready for the Scythe; John Hartley the Farmer at Crooklands began to sow his Sud [Sod?] Grass on Monday tho' the weather was not then very promising for fine Haytime-

20th (Saturday) - All the Caterpillars have left the Gooseberries.

26th (Friday) - The Rain yesterday not plentiful enough to moisten the dry Ground sown with Turnips which have come up badly hitherto, and those that are up, are now at a stop from the Dryness of the Ground, and as is generally the case when Vegetation is retatrded in the young Turnips, the fly has devoured them totally

29th (Monday) - The Tench at Stainding [Standing] Tarn near Dalton took the Worm very well the three Days past; the Anglers were numerous and all the Fish taken, some of which were very large, were full of Spawn-

30th (Tuesday) - Tried to take some tench at Standing Tarn, but none wou'd touch the Bait.

JULY [1807]

1st (Wednesday) - Matthew Dixon of Walthwaite was kill'd yesterday by falling down one of the Iron Ore pits at Whinfield.

2nd (Thursday) - Samuel Case reared *[an old word for erect or to build]* his Dwelling house at Yarle Well Tanyard yesterday. - Matthew Dixon Interr'd at Dalton this afternoon.

4th (Saturday) - The Crop of Hay this Season is not abundant, but the Weather is very favourable for making it well and much Grass is cut down; the price of Hay Grass is high, for the old Stock is consumed entirely. -

6th (Monday) - Rain is very much Wanted to make the Grain shoot out into Ear freely and also to water the Turnips which are now suffering greatly from the Fly, and if the Weather continue will be entirely devoured.

7th (Tuesday) - John Hartley finished his Haytime this Evening and the Weather has been so favourable that he got the Whole of his Crop of Hay into the House without a Drop of Rain. -

8th (Wednesday) - Salmon and Salmon Trout have been very plentiful for a Fortnight past, the prices at present are, Salmon 10d. Per lb and Salmon trout 7d. -

9th (Thursday) - A Continuance of hot and dry Weather, which burns up the light pastures and hinders the late sown Turnip Seed from vegetating – Fresh Herrings at Ulverston Market the first Time this year, price 3 Halfpence each -

Cure For The Bite Of A Mad Dog *[See MEDICAL Section in the Appendices]*

10th (Friday) - Exceeding hot and dry: the Dust very troublesome anjurious *[injurious]* to the Hay adjoining the public Roads, particularly where much used in carting Iron Ore.

Poem - On A Spirit Dealer going by Sea to Liverpool

Drown him ye Waves, a watr'y Grave he merits, Who has so oft with Water drown'd his Spirits.

11th (Saturday) - Put down a new Sole and Cheeks [?] to the pump at Rowe of the Best English Oak I cou'd procure; the old one was put down about fourteen Years ago and is now entirley rotten ; the Cheeks the same. Also put a new Door and Case between the peathouse & pafsage to the back Kitchen –

Margt. Ashburner Dalton d. *[died]* yesterday ------

12th (Sunday) - Mr. J. Case junr. Dined with me at Ulverston; we afterwards paid a Visit at Conishead Priory that once delightful but now neglected Mansion, which in any Remembrance appeared regally magnificent but now wears the Weatherbeaten Garb of fallen pride. -

[So much for West's 'The Paradise of Furness'! A well known Furness landmark, it was founded as an Augustinian Priory and continued till the dissolution of the monasteries by Henry 8th. For many years it was the family seat of the Braddyll family. The old priory was demolished and a new building built in 1821. Today it is a Buddhist Temple and meditation centre, known as the Manjurishi Kadampa Meditation Centre]

14th (Tuesday) - The gentle Shower on Sunday has made an astonishing improvement in the Grain which was shooting out into Ear, and forwarded the weak Turnips very perceptibly , yet much of the Ground which was sown in the late dry Weather requires sowing over again, the young plants being devoured by the Fly as they sprung up.

15th (Wednesday) - Great plenty of Herrings were taken by the Boats on 13th and sold yesterday at Whitehaven at 4d Dozen. None of them contained any Spawn, but were particularly fat and delicious and not so large as are generally brought by the Manks [Manx] Boats; this is the Commencement of the fishing Season and when farther advanced the fish perhaps may be larger.

19th (Sunday) - Mrs Lumley, Wife of General Lumley and Daughter of Mr Sunderland of Ulverston died last night at her Father's House.

[The lady in question was the former Mary Sunderland, who married Brigadier General Lumley by Special Licence at her father's house, Littlecroft, on October 3rd 1804. General Lumley was the youngest son of the Earl of Scarborough and had served in Ireland, Egypt, South Africa and as the next chapter reveals, on General Whitelocke's disastrous attempt

on Buenos Aires. After Mary's death, he served under Wellington in the Peninsular War. It would seem that in the short time of their marriage, Mary hardly saw much of her husband and given her secretive 'late' marriage and early death, it would seem likely it was an arranged affair as Mary was most likely suffering from some illness.

Postscript - I have noticed that more than one source has the marriage details wrong, stating that Lumley married a Mary Sutherland from Ulverstone. See marriage entry below]

Marriage: 3 Oct 1804 St Mary, Ulverston, Lancs.
Honble. Wm. Lumley - Brigadr. General, Bachelor
Mary Sunderland - Spinster
Witness: Thos. Sunderland; Elenr. Sunderland
Married by Special Licence by: Jn. Sunderland, Minister
Source: LDS Film 1040491 [Parish Records]

20th (Monday) - Mary Hodgson married this Day Week at Liverpool to a person of the name of Siddey *[possibly Fiddey]* a Native of America and according to his own Account of himself a Merchant there------------

[At the foot of the page it says Charles Town, South Carolina]

[Another example of William Close's talents]

Mr.Close proposes the following Species of black varnish, to be used as indelible Ink, in Cases where the permanancy of Writing is of Importance.

Take of Oil of Lavender 200 Grains, Copal in powder, 25 Grns. Lamp black from 2 and a half to 3 Grains. Dissolve the Copal in the Oil , with the Assistance of a gentle Heat, in a glass Vial, then mix the black with the Solution on a Marble Slab. This composition must be kept in a corked bottle and stirred up with a piece of wire before it is used. A paler Colour, but sufficiently black for common writing, is produced by using 2 and a half Grains of lamp black and Half a Grain of Indigo.

When written with, the Oil evaporates from the paper, leaving the black defended from the Action of almost every Species of discharging Liquor by the Copal, which remains behind; for though the Writing will be much acted on by being rubbed with an essential Oil, and the Colour diffused through the paper, the original Characters will retain a greater Degree of Blackness, by which they may be always distinguished.

An Ink may be made in a similar Manner, by dissolving 17 Grains of Copal in 120 Grains of Oil of Lavender, and then mixing in 60 Grains of Vermillion in fine powder.

21st (Tuesday) - To all appearance the Harvest will be much later this year than it has been the last two Years; there is not one field of Grain in the Neighbourhood of Dalton or pennington which begins to look yellow and portents approaching Harvest.

22nd (Wednesday) - Many people have been obliged to sow their Turnips over again, which are now in a promising State, if too much Rain does not follow.

23rd (Thursday) - On Monday 13th the Revd. John Sunderland Vicar of pennington came to the House of Thomas Nicholson of Channelhouse attended by the Revd. Robt. Walker his Curate, to take the Tythe of Wool: but not being satisfied with the ancient Custom of doing it, followed in the parish from Time immemorial, he was at the Trouble of bringing a pair of Scales and wished to take it by Weight, to this T. Nicholson objected, as not according to Custom and contrary to the exprefs *[express]* order of the *[? - word unintelligible]* which says that the Wool shall be tithed according to the Custom of the place:

In consequence Mr Sunderland returned without taking Tythe at any place in the parish---------

24th (Friday) - On Wednesday 22nd. Edmd. *[Edmund]* Winder, a Shoemaker was run over by the Stage Coach at Ulverston and died soon after.

[This is the only entry Fleming makes on this subject, but according to the Lancaster Gazette, Edmund Winder was buried in Ulverston churchyard on this day, aged 86 years. The Gazette also reported the trial of the Stage Coach driver at Lancaster Castle. He was named as John Hardy, 30 years of age. The trial was reported in the Lancaster Gazette of Saturday, August 22nd, as follows:]

THE KING against JOHN HARDY - This was a prosecution against the prisoner, for killing one Edward [sic]

Winder: - Mr. Clark, who conducted the prosecution, observed, that it was one of considerable importance, as it brought before the public a case, as he conceived, of great cruelty and misconduct on the part of the prisoner, in the discharge of his duty as driver of one of the public coaches, from Ulverston to Lancaster.

He feared the public had, of late, strong reasons to complain of the very negligent manner in which the drivers of public coaches discharged their duty; for many of them, by their conduct at least, seemed to be of opinion, that they might, with impunity, drive their carriages at what rate they pleased, or stop or turn them aside, on the public road, just as it suited their own pleasure.

If such an opinion prevailed in the minds of these men, it was high time it should be corrected; for if children were playing in the road, whose innocence and want of foresight betrayed them into danger; or if aged and infirm persons were on the road, who with difficulty could make their escape upon the approach of danger; as it was the unquestionable duty of the drivers of carriages, upon coming near to persons of the above description – a duty not less pointed out by humanity, that by the law of the land – to stop their horses, and to exercise to to utmost degree of caution and tenderness, so that the life of no human creature might be taken away by by any imprudence on their part.

The deceased was a man of 86 years of age, and was walking upon the road from Ulverston to Lancaster, a short time before he was run over.

When the forewheel had passed over the body, the prisoner, not withstanding he was remonstrated with by a byestander, inhumanly persisted in driving on his carriage: and, when the hinderwheel had passed over the old man, the prisoner continued driving on, unconcerned at the melancholy event which had happened.

The old man languished for a few hours and died. The Jury found the prisoner guilty of – Manslaughter.

We hope this case will impress upon the minds of the drivers of public carriages a due regard to the lives of his Majesty's subjects.

[According to 'Lancaster Gazette Records – Or Leaves From Local History' - 1801 – 1851, the prisoner, John Hardy, was fined 1s. and sentenced to be imprisoned for 12 months]

26th (Sunday) - Mrs Lumley was interr'd yesterday with great pomp in a Vault made last Week at the East End of the Church at Ulverston close adjoining to the Walk and about the midway between the Church End and the Ladies Walk.

Sunderland Family Vault in St. Mary's Churchyard, Ulverston.

27th (Monday) - The Farmers are very busy in getting their Hay; the late unsettled Weather makes them watch every Opportunity that offers ---- Turnips advance very slowly, but the Weed among them very rapidly and will if the Weather continue Rainy do a considerable Injury to them......Some of the full Crops of Grain are beaten down by the Rain and to all appearance will rise no more till separated from the nourishing Root by the laborious Hand of the Reaper -

29th (Wednesday) - Fine weather which will rejoice the Farmers who have been retarted [*retarded*] in their Hay time by the wet Weather – An Embargo was laid on all the Vefsels [*Vessels*] on this Coast the 27.

30th (Thursday) - A Charming Day, the Farmers as busy as Bees, amongst their Hay.

Hay, and Turnips which advanced slowly [*word-s.....*
missing?] the late wet weather and are exceeding

full of Weed. Some Fields in the Neighbourhood of Dalton begin to put on a yellow Livery, particularly the forward crops of Barley. The Alteration of the Grain at Pennington is greater than at dalton, owing probably to the Soil being lighter; and the Harvest from Appearances if the Weather be favourable, may commence there in the Course of a Fortnight -

A Grave perukemaker *[a wig maker]* this morning... asked me if I wou'd not choose to have my Hair cut in the present Mode, by which , he meant that all the Hair shou'd be removed except a little Tuft before, like old Time, but differing from him in this, that a small Rat's Tail is suffered to remain behind; to which I answered No, for I intended to keep my Hair, that he might not entirely forget how to drefs *[dress]* .

Ah, God blefs *[bless]* you Sir, replied the Friseur *[Hairdresser]* the Times are hard with us now; but Shou'd Beards go out of Fashion too, Barbers and Lice must both be starved.

31st (Friday) - Old potatoes – 6d. Per Hoop . New ones 10d. To 12d. Per Ditto. Peas – 8d. do. Salmon – 10d. - Salmon trout – 7d. Per lb. Butter – 11d. Beef -7d. Mutton & Lamb – 6d. Veal – 5d. Per lb. Eggs -6d. Per doz. Young Ducks – 15d. Chickens – 1s. Geese – 2/6 each.

AUGUST [1807]

1st (Saturday) – The Fair at Broughton this Day was well attended many fat and lean Cattle shewn *[shown]* but met with a dull Market.

2nd (Sunday) - Fruits of all sorts are plentiful this Year, especially the late Apples, and plumbs which now begin to be ripe and meet with a ready Market at Ulverston at 6d per Doz.

4th (Tuesday) - The Master of a Flat *[Flatboat?]* detained at Roanhead by the general Embargo, was yesterday Morning, found dead in his Bed; the Coroner and a Jury attended there in the Evening and gave in their Verdict 'Died by the Visitation of divine providence.'

Mr. Robinson, Surgeon at Dalton examined the Body and pronounced that he had died in a Fit of Apoplexy, and in Consequence of a continued State of Intoxication with Spirits, for some Days previous to his Difsolution *[Dissolution]*. The Body interr'd this Morning -

Our Ancestors were contented with good wholesome home brewed Ale and did not heat their Blood and destroy their Constitutions with Spiritous Liquors, but lived healthy to a good old Age.

Now, in this Age of Luxury and pride, few will take the Trouble to brew their own but have it from the Common Brewers, who mix it with intoxicating Drugs, prejudicial to Health.

Spirits are more used than Ale, and are still more injurious and many are the Victims who fall a Sacrifice to the inordinate Use of them; for the Liquor Merchants like the Brewers make use of rectified Spirits Ginger and Cayenne pepper with other destructive things, which, with little genuine Spirit and much Water compose the greater part of what is commonly drunk, and if taken to Excess, drives Men to Madness, and many in that shocking State descend to pluto's gloomy Regions.

It is necefsary *[necessary]* to enquire, and certainly
would be satisfactory to ascertain, whether many of the
sudden Deaths, which have been so numerous for the
last 10 Years, have not in a great Measure been owing to
the excessive Use of this pernicious Beverage.

It is lamentable to see so many of our Fellow creatures
without the Warning of Sickness, and often in
the Height of their Mirth, suddenly drop into the
Grave; and if the Cause was found to originate in
the pernicious Compositions of the Spirit Dealers, it
certainly calls for the Interference of Government to
put Stop to their destructive practices, and not allow
so many, by the adulteration of their Spirits, to rise so
suddenly into Opulence, at the Expence of the Lives of
so many valuable Subjects.

5th (Wednesday) - When I saw the Body of this poor
Fellow, who so suddenly and unexpectedly was
snatched from his Family, borne to the Grave, I cou'd
not help saying to myself, as if with some kind of
Doubt; And is this the Man, who only the Day before
Yesterday was enjoying himself in the highest Mirth
and utmost good Humour, whose Sallies of Wit excited
the Mirth and Laughter of his Companions and from
whose Breast every Care was banished; Was it the
Agility of this Man which we all so much admired with
the Stare of Astonishment; and so soon that Laughter –
moving Tongue is silenced for ever, and those nimble
Limbs become so stiff and incapable of Motion. Had
he been conscious that the period of his Existence had
been so near, instead of that festive Joy which then
[The word looks like ...motivate?] his Face and Actions,
we shou'd have seen nothing but melancholy Misery:
But Providence kindly conceals that from us, as the
Knowledge of it would mar all the pleasures of Life.

6th (Thursday) - The tax on property which came in this Year, besides it being so heavy and oppressive, is enforced by one Parker, the Inspector of the County, with so much Insolence & tyrannical Authority, that he has raised a Ferment in this part of the Country which cannot be soon allay'd.

In the present State of Things, when Grain is so much reduced in price and the Value of Cattle so much inferior to the former Years, there is little prospect for the Owners of small Estates and Farmers but Beggary.

Few people can rest satisfied when poverty stares them in the Face and fewer are willing to toil and sweat when they are certain that the produce of their Labour will immediately be wrested from them by the haughty officers of our supreme Magistrate to stop the hungry mouth of uselefs *[useless]* Dependants.

Enough of this is visible in our Neighbourhood, where we daily see Military Officers, who never in the course of their Lives were of twopence Service to the State, supported by Government at Home in uselefs Idleness and Luxury, while many a poor *[brave is written over the word 'poor']* Fellow who has long exposed his Life and lost his Limbs in Defence of his Country, is neglected and ready to perish with Want for Charity has little left to bestow on him. The little that remains from the Tax gatherers is scarcely sufficient to satisfy the Cravings of the Clergy, who lay their insatiable Hands on everything that comes within their Reach and like the Fox in the Fable do all they can to lay their Fingers on the Rest nor cease striving for it, till they are fully satisfied that their Exertions are vain and that it is placed beyond their Reach----

7th (Friday) - ...the Barometer is only at Changeable and rises slowly, though every Appearance indicates the Return of fine Weather, which will be acceptable, for much Grain is beaten down and requires it; the Harvest will be considerably later than it was the two last years, let the Weather be how it may, fine Weather will forward it a little.

8th (Saturday) - The Harvest commenced this Day and a small paddock of Barley at Parkhouse and another at Rampside were reaped which are the first in Furness, this Season.

10th (Monday) - …...the Grain is visibly advanced towards ripe within the last 4 days and much in the Neighbourhood of Ulverston and Pennington will be ready for the Sickle in the Course of next Week if the Weather continue as at present.

Ann Shaw of Rampside interr'd at Dalton this afternoon.

11th (Tuesday) - The fine weather has brought many Visitors from the Lakes to view the magnificent Ruins of Furness Abbey. I have observed that those who have the Shabbiest Equipages are the most provokingly insolent; but these haughty animals like the Ruins before them must soon yield to the all devouring Tooth of Time & vanish into Dust; their Elegance and pride will die away and their Beauties be lefs [less] durable than the Weeds which spring out from these mouldring Walls and may sooner fade than the Flowers they produce......

12th (Wednesday) - I went this morning at 4 upon the Moor to shoot Grouse, the Game were plentiful and the

Gentlemen numerous but not many Birds were killed owing to their Shyness and the Dogs not being able to hunt well on Account of the Heat.

13th (Thursday) - Oats at Ulverstone Market on the Decline but Wheat advances in price owing to the prospect of War with America, and the Difficulty of bringing Grain from the Baltic since Bonaparte has got possession of Danzig and other ports in the Seas.

[An interesting entry in the journal, as it would be another five years before America finally declared war on Great Britain]

14th (Friday) - Very heavy Rain come on this morning and continued all day......Much of the heavy headed Grain is weighed down with Water.

15th (Saturday) - Saw RA [?] from St. Lucia who gave me a bad Account of TH *[Thomas Hodgson?]* also informed me that Mr Donnald [?] was broke and run off, and all the property sold before TH arrived in the Island ..…..

Prospect of war with America

[If the above is correct, then it would appear the affairs of Thomas Hodgson are not going well]

16th (Sunday) - Many Reapers offr'd themselves at Dalton this Morning to hire for the ensuing Week but few of the Farmers were in Want not much of their Grain being ripe.....If the Weather be fine a great Number will be wanted next Week and the Harvest apparantly at the strongest.

[Now - a few poems by William Fleming]

17th (Monday) -

Epigram No.
What's the Reason that Dolly so plump and so fair,
So long for a Husband has panted
That she had no fortune, her Suitors saw clear,
And that was the thing they most wanted.

No
John Briggs Case was very hard
It cannot be denyd;
Tho' by his Trade he money made
He for a Living dyed.

Epigram No.
Says Tom to Peg in roguish Sport
Your legs' too long and mine too short.
But handsome ones they'd make, I know,
If mine were but between the two.

18th (Tuesday) - ....the Harvest approaches and Grain will be generally Ripe in a Fortnight & promises an abundant Crop.

19th (Wednesday) - ....the Farmers near the Sea
Shore find their Grain ripen faster than they expected
and Reapers are much wanted. Some Fields in the
Neighbourhood of Dalton are ready for the Sickle and
much will be cut down in the Course of next Week.
Grain in general will be ripe in a Fortnight and the
Harvset promises to be a very short one.

20th (Thursday) - J. Hartley began to reap his Barley
this Day which is just a Fortnight later than his
commencement of Harvest last Year. There were some
Oats at Market from Concle near Rampside which sold
at 12 /- per Carlisle Bushel.

21st (Friday) - A Cargo of fresh Herrings from the
Manks [*Manx*] Coast came to Ulverston and were sold at
1/3d per Score. They cost the people who brought them
1/6 per Hundred, of Consequence their profits upon
them were something more than what is commonly
called moderate profit.

22nd (Saturday) - Went upon the Moors and killed a
brace of Grouse which are very Scarce this Season upon
pennington and Kirkby Moors.

23rd (Sunday) - Birthday of Sarah Fleming senr. Age 23.

Grain ripen so suddenly as this Season and a great
Number of Reapers were hired for the ensuing Week
at 5/6d and 6/- per Day with Meat Beer and Lodging
which is more than is generally given the first Week of
hiring at Dalton.

24th (Monday) - Probably in the Course of next Week
the Harvest will be nearly finished in Furnefs and

providence & hope will blefs us with fine Weather to get the abundant Crops of Grain into the Barns and Stacks in good order -----

25th (Tuesday) - .…...fewer Irishmen than usual have come over to work at the Harvest this year.

27th (Thursday) - My Aunt Elizabeth was prevailed upon by some of her Acquaintance to attend an Afsembly *[Assembly]* at D------------*[Dalton]* where many of the Sons and Daughters of the most respectable people in Low F------ *[Furness]* were present. The little Knowledge she had of the Capering Science was acquired of an itinerant Master, commonly known from his diminutive Stature, by the Name of Lile Nicholson, whose Terms were so low that the poor Fellow was obliged to teach both by Day and Night to procure a Livelihood: My Aunt was one of his Evening pupils and as Time had since elapsed, she was not perhaps, one of the most perfect in the Room, but by paying Attention to the Figure she did tolerably well in the Contra Dances till an unlucky Circumstance raised a Laugh at her Expense which put her quite out of Countenance and spoiled her Dancing for ever.........She chanced to hear a Lady, to whom Exercise had given the florid Glow of Health and opened the Pores, complain of the Heat of the Room which had thrown her into a violent perspiration;

My Aunt too was not quite as cool as a Cucumber and immediately caught this fashionable Manner of expressing the unpleasant Effect of the Heat; when the Dance was finished she immediately directed his Steps towards two of her Acquaintance with the new phrase ready to drop from her Tongue's End and addrefsing *[addressing]* herself to them in a Tone loud enough to be heard by Half the Company;

'Oh dear, how hot this Room is, I declare I'm all of a Pispiration *[Perspiration]* and completely tired;

I wish you would make me a little Room to sit down and ease myself betwixt you!

A loud peal of Laughter succeeded my Aunt's Eloquence and tho' she was ignorant of the Cause of their Mirth, she soon found, by the side Glances which were thrown upon her and the continued Titter, that herself was the Subject.

She, poor Soul, had never studied the fixed and established Meaning of the Words and unfortunately in her Imagination a different Idea was connected with it: she wished only to be relieved from the uneasy Sensation she felt from Fatigue, and innocently supposing that the Disorder of some part of the Dress caused their merriment, she went into another Room to ascertain it, but on Examination finding that very part was consonant with her own Ideas of Decency, she, without saying a Word to anyone, slipt *[slipped]* out of the House and made the best of her Way Home, not a little mortified that she shou'd be the Laughing Stock of the Company without being able to find out the Reason.

30th (Sunday) - Reapers hired at Dalton for the ensuing Week at 5/- per Day and Board and Lodging.

31st (Monday) - Rain in the Afternoon but none so heavy as to hinder the Reapers from continuing their Labour.

SEPTEMBER [1807]

1st (Tuesday) - Went to shoot at Dalton – 3 Brace. -

3rd (Thursday) - ...two Cargo's of fresh Herrings at the Market at Ulverston which were generally sold at one penny a piece; but some taken into the Country were sold at 15 for a shilling.

4th (Friday) - Went to shoot at Holmbank: dined with Geo. Ashburner and killed 5 Brace partridges.

5th (Saturday) - Rain began to fall extremely heavy in the Morning and continued unabated till 10 o'clock in the Evening when the Brooks were swell'd higher than ever remembered and most of the Bridges in Furnefs were washed down.

6th (Sunday) - Much Grain was carried away by the Floods, caused by the Rain on Saturday, and deposited on the Sands below Ulverston.

7th (Monday) - Reapers hired at Dalton for the ensuing Week at 5/- per diem [*a daily allowance for expenses*] tho' many of the Farmers in Furness have finished Reaping.

8th (Tuesday) - Yesterday and today I killed 8 Brace of pertridges in the Neighbourhood of Scales, where hazel Nuts were in Abundance on the low Bushes.

9th (Wednesday) - Let to farm to James Huddlestone the younger of Roosecot [*Roosecote*] at the yearly Rent of £140, that part of my Estate at Rowe in pennington which is now occupied by William posthethwaite.

10th (Thursday) - Potatoes – 6d. - Apples – 10d. - Nuts – 6d. Per Hoop in the Husks. new Oats 12/- per Bushel – new Wheat 4 / 6 per Load.

11th (Friday) - Went to Newton to shoot and killed five Brace of partridges.

12th (Saturday) - Harvest nearly finished and few Reapers hired at Dalton and those only at 3/6 per Day.

The Estate at Townend sold in public Sale a Few Days ago for the sum of £1124 and was purchased by a Man named hart; the Admeasurement *[process of measuring]* is about 12 Customary Acres; and not one of the five Tenements under the Lord of the Manor of pennington which pay parcel Harriots [?]

[old world term?].

14th (Monday) - Hares have become very Scarce in Furnefs owing to the destructive practice of the poachers taking them in Nets in the Night.

15th (Tuesday) - There is very little Grain reaped in Osmotherley and Lowick.

16th (Wednesday) - Went to Dalton a Shooting in the Afternoon and killed 2 and a half Brace of Partridges.

17th (Thursday) - Went to Newbarns to shoot, killed 3 and a half Brace. Grain dry and the Farmers busy as Bees in getting the Harvest into their Barns and Stacks, as the Weather does not appear to be quite settled or to promise a favorable Harvest Home.

18th (Friday) - Went this Morning with my Greyhound to course at Leece, kill'd 4 Hares.

19th (Saturday) - Returned from Newbarns & killed 1 Hare and 2 Brace of partridges.

20th (Sunday) - Some Farmers carting Grain in the afternoon.

21st (Monday) - Went over Duddon Sands into Cumberland to shoot; the Sands not Good and the Weather Stormy ….....The greatest part of the Grain is housed in Millom and the adjacent parts ….and the Wheat seed time is forward there, tho' the season has not been favorable for preparing the Ground.

22nd (Tuesday) - Went out about Lanthwaite and killed 3 and a half Brace of Partridges. Observed that Beans were a failing Crop here as in Low Furnefs.

23rd (Wednesday) - Went to Whitbeck & 1 killed 4 Brace of Birds. Looked over the Estate at Townend and the Manor of Whitbeck which is intended to be sold on Friday.

24th (Thursday) - Bootle Cattle Fair. Went out to shoot and killed 8 and a half Brace of partridges and a Land Rale *[Land rail or Corncrake]* : find the Beans a very bad crop here too, and am of the Opinion that the Land here is not so good by £50 an Acre as in the Neighbourhood of Dalton, where an Estate was sold in parcels on Tuesday last at the most extravagant price of 150 pounds an Acre.

25th (Friday) - The Manor and Tithes of Whitbeck together with the Estate at Townend sold in public Sale at Ulverston and purchased by Lord Lonsdale for the Sum of £9170 or thereabouts.

26th (Saturday) - Killed 1 Hare and 3 Brace of partridges in the Morning and returned from Cumberland in the afternoon.

27th (Sunday) - Apples – 1s. Per Hoop. - Nuts 10d. Per Do. Potatoes – 4d. Per Do. - Butter – 13d. Per 16 ounces. Oats – 12s. Per Carlisle Bushel. - Wheat 50s. Per Load – Cattle are much lower in price, even fat cattle are lower owing to the price of Tallow and Hides , but Beef remains at 6d. Per pound.

28th (Monday) - Dry with the Wind at West, but not so as to make Grain fit to lead into the House. Killed 1 Hare.

30th (Wednesday) - Some of the Barley that has remained in the Fields during the late Weather is beginning to sprout in the Stack but the greatest part was got into the Barns or Stacks before the Rains set in -

Best Gunpowder 4s. Per lb. - Shot – 10/6 per Bag of 20 lbs. Flints – 8d per Score – Game Certificate - £3 ..4s..0d... Dog Tax – 11s. Per annum.

OCTOBER ¹⁸⁰⁷

1st (Thursday) - Potatoes – 5d. Per Hoop. The Farmers complain that the potatoes planted in low and wet Ground are much injured with the Rains which have prevailed for the last Fortnight.

2nd (Friday) - Fair for Sheep and Cattle at Broughton well attended, but they went off at prices inferior to any Farmers have experienced for some years, and a number were sold.

3rd (Saturday) - Went into Osmotherly to Shoot, kill'd 1 Hare & 1 Partridge – the greatest part of the Grain there remains in the Fields, some not reaped, and much greatly damaged by the late Wet Weather.

This Morning, Mifs [Miss] Hunter of Walney, a Lady aged & infirm was married to a person of the name of Troughton who is Curate of Walney and not Half her Age; and odd as it may appear, she purchased this Husband with the whole of her Fortune (about three thousand pounds) which she made over to him before their Appearance at the Altar of Hymen where she added her own dear person to the Bargain.

The Revd. Gentleman, I suspect, had a much more

earnest Desire to be united to the Fortune of the timbertoed *[having a wooden leg]* Damsel , than for the profession and Enjoyment of her sweet Person, and I am afraid, he is not pofsefed *[possessed]* of much Good Sense, as to treat her in the endearing Manner her Sacrifice Merits ---

4th (Sunday) - Grain spoiling greatly that has remained out in the Fields.

5th (Monday) - Heard a Report yesterday that James Hodgson was dead in the West Indies but know not how the Report originated as I cannot trace it as yet from any authentic Source.

7th (Wednesday) - Fair for Cattle at Ulverston was this Day, and a number were shewn, but Buyers were wanting.

8th (Thursday) - Wheat at Ulverston Market this Day something *[somewhat?]* lower in price.

10th (Saturday) - The House at Townend near Lindal, which formerly was a public House known by the Name of the Anchor, is again licensed for the same purpose.

[The Anchor Inn at Lindal was clearly an 18th century public house, but according to this entry in Fleming's journal - closed down. Here is the re-opening! The pub was finally closed and demolished in 2009-2010]

11th (Sunday) - ….the Grain near the Shore in pretty good Order and some of the Farmers embraced the Opportunity particularly at Roanhead, raised five Stacks

12th (Monday) - Fine in the morning but a heavy shower at 10 o'clock hindered the farmers in getting more of their Grain.

13th (Tuesday) - So many potatoes are spoiled with the wet Weather that they are advanced to 7/6 per Bushel; higher than usual at this Season.

15th (Thursday) - Went to Highfield House to shoot; kill'd 1 Hare.

16th (Friday) - Potatoes from fear of scarcity are got up to five pence per Hoop of 6 Quarts.

17th (Saturday) - .the Hills of Westmorland and Yorkshire appear to be covered with Snow to a considerable Depth. A Few Woodcocks have been killed in the Course of last Week but our Woods have not been afforded them in numerous Flights.

20th (Tuesday) - I went to course with my Greyhound at Leece but found only one Hare which I killed and presented to MC [?] of that place with whom I dined.

21st (Wednesday) - This Morning I was attacked with a very severe Rheumatic pain in the Hip and down to the Ancle [Anckle] Joint so that I could not sit, stand or walk without the most excruciating pain similar to the Cramp when most accute [acute].

22nd (Thursday) - Potatoes at Ulverston Market this Morning at 3d per Hoop which is considerably lower than they were expected to be sold at this Year so many are destroy'd by the Rains.

23rd (Friday) - ...the Rheumatic pain continues most acute and confines me to my Room , and it takes away from me the power of using my right Leg.

24th (Saturday) - Many Cattle were shewn yesterday at Dalton Fair but the Buyers were few and they were bought at low prices from the Fear of a Scarcity of Fodder.

25th (Sunday) - I am still confined by the Rheumatism to my Room : took Salts this Morning which failed to operate.

26th (Monday) - Took more Salts which had the desired Effect in operating but failed in giving me the expected Relief from Pain. Mr B [?] attended me and advised me to looss *[lose]* a little Blood from the Arm by the Lancet; to this I was averse preferring the Application of Leeches to the part affected.

27th (Tuesday) - Applyed Six Leeches, 3 upon the Foot and 3 just above the Ancle *[Anckle]* Joint where the pain was now become most acute, and the Foot bled copiously for five Hours which gave me great Relief.

28th (Wednesday) - Took some of Dr. James' powders with a little of Glauber's [?] powders to promote insensible perspiration.

29th (Thursday) - On Thursday last the Estate at Brackenpark was sold in public Sale for the Sum of 2140£ it measures about 33 Acres customary and was purchased by William Postlethwaite of Lindal.

30th (Friday) - Yesterday Evening the parish Apprentice of Thomas Lowther farmer at the Anchor near Lindal was stopt [stopped] by a Foot pad in [on] his Return from Ulverston at the High bridge and after being knocked down and much abused was robbed of about 16 shillings the Fellow who committed this daring Act was apprehended this Day and proves to be a plaisterer [plasterer] from Lancaster who wrought at the House now finishing by Miles Burton at Stonecrofs [Stone Cross].

On his Examination he at first denied the Charge but being clearly identified he confessed the Crime he stood charged with and was committed: he is now confined in the black Hole at Ulverston till tomorrow, when he will be taken to Jail to stand his Trial at the next Afsizes [Assizes].

NOVEMBER [1807]

1st (Sunday) - The Rheumatic pain by which I have been so long tormented has since the Application of Leeches removed from the Hip and now remains in the Leg and the Ancle Joint. James' powders operate in some Measure as a purgative and prove of great Service.

2nd (Monday) - Woodcocks said to be remarkably plentiful The Ulverston Hunt commenced this Day, Wm. Blundell, Esq. Mayor, and is expected to be well attended. Dalton of Thurnam came to the Town yesterday Evening.

[Probably a reference to the Dalton family of Thurnham Hall in Lancashire, a long term family seat, approximately six miles south of Lancaster]

3rd (Tuesday) - Great plenty of the wild Fowls called here Duckeros [?] are now upon the Coast about Roosebeck and Rampside and are taken in great Numbers by the Fishermen in small Nets of Thread stretched horizontally about a Foot from the Bottom by Means of small Sticks put down in the Sand, where the Birds feed. When the Tide flows the Nets are covered and the Fowls are diving for small Mussels which they eat, Shells and fish together; & get entangled in the Nets where they remain till the Tide ebbs out, when they are taken by the Fishermen and brought to Market, and sold at one shilling the Couple. The Feathers are taken off by dipping the Ducks in boiling Water, and when they are properly drawn and cleaned they are laid in Salt & Water 10 or 12 Hours, then then taken out and again clean wiped and stuffed with Sage and Onions and roasted; Thus cooked they are esteemed a great Delicacy by those who are fond of the strong fishy Flavour. This Bird is of the Duck Tribe; the Male Black with a Few white Feathers in the Wings and a yellow spot on the Bill like the Coot: they seldom frequent our Shores but in stormy Weather.

4th (Wednesday) - Ulverston Hunt well attended.

5th (Thursday) - Potatoes at Ulverston Market advanced from 4d the Hoop to 5d. which probably be about the Average price this year.

7th (Saturday) - Woodcocks plentiful and these price from 2/6 to 3/- an expensive Delicacy, and to my Taste, not superior to the lefs [less] esteemed partridge.

8th (Sunday) - Lean Cattle are now exceeding low, and even at these prices there is little Demand for them:

Barley too does not yet appear to be equal to the last year's price, which will be much against the Farmers ....
[The writing abruptly ends here – could Fleming have left out the word ' wishes '?]

[More on William Close]

9th (Monday) - Mr Close, I am informed intends soon to publish, not as before a new Edition of some Author, but an original Work, in which, I hope, he will succeed better than in his Edition of Mr West's Specimen, & as an Author he cannot expect to rank high except his desriptive powers are much improv'd, his Diction more polished and his Ideas more connected. His warm attachment to the Character of an Author and his earnest Desire to attract Admirers may induce him to an Attempt, which, if it fail of succefs *[success]* will hold him up to Contempt.

11th (Wednesday) - Wheat is advanced to 47s.per Load and Oats to 12s. per Bushel .

12th (Thursday) - Found great Relief from my rheumatic pains since the Frost commenced so that I can this Day walk with the Afsistance *[Assistance]* of a Stick.

13th (Friday) - This day I walked to Dalton in the Morning and returned in the Afternoon.

14th (Saturday) - I found no ill effects from the long Walk I took Yesterday but am fatigued and find my Limbs a little stiff and as if unwilling to perform the same Journey again till they have had two or three Days Rest.

15th (Sunday) - How happy and comfortable a Man finds himself when relieved from acute pain and recovered from any of those dreadful Diseases with which humanity is afflicted: with what a grateful Heart he sighs out his Thanks to God whose merciful Hand has healed his Infirmities and restored him sound to the Smiles of his joyful Family and the pleasures of Society. What sublime and pathetic Emotions arise in his Breast are only known to those who have suffered under some dreadful Calamity.

16th (Monday) - The general price of potatoes this year is 6/6 per Bushel; measured in single Hoops at the Market they are sold at 5d per Hoop of 6 Quarts.

17th (Tuesday) - Walked to Mansrigg and by Newland with J. Case jr. -

18th (Wednesday) - Went out a little with my Gun and kill'd a Brace of partridges.

Mrs. Sarah Fell Widow of the late Thomas Fell of Beckside and mother of the late James Fell of the same place died on Saturday and was this Day interred at the parish Church of Pennington. Her Age 90 years -

19th (Thursday) - Beef at Ulverston this Day was very low, the prime parts – 5d. Per lb. - the Quarter together was sold at 4d. Per lb. - pork – 5d. - Mutton – 6d. - Butter – 13d. Per lb. Eggs – 1d. each – Wheat – 47s. Per Load – Oats – 12/6 per Bushel.

21st (Saturday) - William Townson of Whinfield was this Morning married at Dalton. His Wife was Ann Atkinson eldest Daughter of the late Thomas Atkinson

Farmer at the Furnefs Abbey. His Age about 50; her Age about 40 years.

22nd (Sunday) - 'It is not good for a Man to be alone' ….. Mr. Townson undoubtedly felt the Truth of this Observation and was sensible that he was fitted for domestic and social Duties before he suffered himself to be coupled by the Matrimonial Chain with his present Bride. Close he may clasp and strain her to his Breast, 'while Winter's Sighs sound hollow in the Wind ' …..

26th (Thursday) - Potatoes at Ulverston this Day were 6d. Per Hoop – Oats 12/6 per Bushel – Eggs – 1d each.

27th (Friday) - More Snow and Hail from the Northwest with a brisk and cold Wind so that it is much drifted and doubtlefs [*doubtless*] many Sheep will perish....

29th (Sunday) - A Freestone pediment and Iron Railing put over the new Vault belonging to Mr Sunderland in the Churchyard at Ulverston. The first Corps deposited in this Vault was the Wife of Gen. Lumley Daughter of Mr Sunderland who died this Year.

DECEMBER 1807

1st (Tuesday) - Many unfortunate Accidents have happened to the Ships in the late stormy Weather and many with the Crews have gone to the Bottom, and numbers of our Soldiers have perished in the Transports which were conveying them from Ireland & other places.

What Numbers of our fellow Creatures the present destructive War has in one Way or other sent 'to that

Bourn(e) from whence no Traveller returns', what Treasures it has exhausted and what unspeakable Misery it has caused in the World, for now nearly all the Empires of the Globe are at War with each other. 'Delirant Reges plectuntur Achivi ' [?] but in this Contest Kings themselves have become Sufferers; some have lost their Lives and others their Kingdoms and are become Wanderers without any fixed Resting place and dependant on others for Refuge and Subsistence till Death kindly shall shall close their Eyes forever.

What numbers of his Subjects were sacrificed to gratify the Ambition of that Madman Charles the 12th of Sweden, who nearly ruined his Country, neglected to cultivate the Arts of Peace and delighted in nothing but the Effusion of human Blood. What Numbers have been sacrificed to gratify the Ambition of the present Ruler of France and how many languish at this present Moment in prison, whom the Fortune of war has deprived of their Liberty.

2nd (Wednesday) - Much Rain fell in the night and this Morning the Snow is entirely gone and the Green Surface of the Earth again relieves the Eye. The glaring Whitenefs *[Whiteness]* of Snow is unpleasant to the Sight and when it has been long fixed upon it, the Eye turns with pleasure to some darker Colour, but still prefers green to every other.

4th (Friday) - Potatoes yesterday at Ulverston Market advanced to 7d. Per Hoop: Beef was from 4d to 6d per lb. and Wheat and Oats keep advancing but Barley remains at 15s. Per Bushel.

5th (Saturday) - A Vefsel was yesterday Evening or early this Morning driven by the Fury of the Winds on Shore at Lousea *[Lousy]* point, Duddon Mouth ;

She is loaded with Flax & Coals and has not received much Damage; it is expected she may be got off again the next Spring Tides.

6th (Sunday) - The Vefsel cast on Shore, as mentioned Yesterday, is discharging, and the Goods are found free from Injury. The Newspapers of last Night bring us Accounts that Rufsia *[Russia]* and Sweden have declared War against England so now we are at War with all the powers on the Continent and how the Contest will end God only knows; if France and her Allies can stop our Trade and Manufacturers, Beggary must be the Consequence.

7th (Monday) - Thomas Fisher of Dalton, Matthew Denney of the same place and Malachi Cranke of little Urfwick *[Urswick]* have taken the Royalty of the Manor of Bolton cum Adgerley belonging to the Earl of Derby and this Day began to sink a pit in a Field called Longlaskeds [?] belonging to Harbarrow *[A farm near Stainton with Adgerley]* , in Expectations of finding Coal, a little of that valuable and useful Mineral having been found in a Freehold Enclosure adjoining those called Whinnals, belonging to John Gardner of Dendron. I hope the Undertakers will be so fortunate as find that or if they fail, some other Mineral that may repay them the Money expended in so laudable an Undertaking.

Many Attempts have already been made but none of them have proved succesful, probably the Coals lay deeper than has hitherto been tried, tho' pits were sunk to a considerable Depth at Stank.

8th (Tuesday) - Appearance of Snow , much of which has fallen since Winter commenced and many Lives of valuable Subjects lost in it.

10th (Thursday) - Cattle continue at low prices, particularly Gelt Cattle, and Beef is now from 4 and a half pence to 6 pence per lb. - Butter – 13d. Eggs – 1 and a half pence a piece. Potatoes continue at 6 and 7d. per Hoop and Wheat is at 48 and a halfs. per Load. Oats at 13s. Per Bushel and Barley 15s. per Do. -

11th (Friday) - Substitutes hired this Year to serve for those ballotted for the old Militia, cost from 25 to 30 pounds.

12th (Saturday) - Many of the People emply'd at the Cotton Mills in this Country are dismissed, and almost an entire Stop is put to that Branch of our Trade by the continental War which now rages with destructive Violence: Robberies and Housebreaking are the Consequence of so many people being cast out without the Means of gaining a Livelihood: accustomed to Extravagance whilst the Wages of their Industry were so enormous, they can ill bear with pinching poverty and the Means of Maintenance are procured by Violence since they have become void of Employment and of Consequence destitute of Subsistance. Acts of Violence have been very frequent of late & are many of them committed by these people.

13th (Sunday) - Fisher and Company go on rapidly with their Shaft in Search of Coals.....Tomorrow intend to begin with Boring, Rods being prepared for the purpose. Thus Succefs [*Success*] in this Undertaking may enrich Individuals but probably will not be advantageous to Furnefs in general with those people who consume Few

Coals, the Saving from the Difference in the price, will, no Doubt be sunk in the Increase of the poor rates.

14th (Monday) - The Measles have been very favorable till lately, when the cold wet Weather seems to affect those afflicted with them, and they have been fatal to many. The Smallpox I hope, will never again make their Appearance in Furnefs, tho' many stupid people still resist Vaccination.

16th (Tuesday) - Many of the Farmers in Furness are apprehenfive of a Scarcity of Fodder and offer their Cattle to sale at prices inferior to the low Rates they have sold at for some Time past. Cattle, Barley and Iron Ore are the chief productions of Furness which are exported together with Slate, and bring Money into this isolated Corner of Lancashire; All these have for some Time past been upon the Decline in price; and the Deficiency of Value is much felt here.

17th (Thursday) - We have Accounts that very considerable Lofses *[Losses]* have been suffered by the Farmers who have rented extensive Sheep Walks, from the late heavy Falls of Snow being so much driven by the Violence of the Winds into the more sheltered parts of the pastures, where the Sheep had drawn to.

18th (Friday) - Grain of all kinds advanced at Ulverston Market today.

20th (Saturday) - Many children have died daily in Ulverfton *[Ulverston]* & the Neighbourhood of the Measles, which do not come out freely, owing perhaps to the thick and close cold weather.

21st (Sunday) - Gerard, in his History of plants, makes mention of the Goose – tree, Barnacle tree, or the Tree bearing Geese, to which he gives the Name of Britannica Concha anatiferce [*concha anatifera?*], and thus describes the production.

'There are found in the North part of Scotland and the Islands adjacent called Orchades [*Orkney Islands*], certain Trees, whereon do grow certain Shell Fishes, of a white Colour tending to Rufset [*Russet*] ; wherein are contained little living Creatures; which Shells in Time of Maturity do open, and out of them grow these little living things, which falling into the Water do become Fowls, which we call Barnacles, in the North of England Brant Geese, and in Lancashire Tree Geese; But the others that do fall upon the Land, perish and come to Nothing.

Thus much by the Writings of others, and also from the Mouths of people of those parts, which may well accord with Truth. But what our Eyes have seen, and Hands have touched, we shall declare ......'

There is a small Ifland [*Island*] in Lancashire called the Pile of Foulders [*Fouldrey or Fowdray - Piel Island*] wherein are found the broken pieces of old and bruized [*bruised*] Ships, some whereof have been cast thither by Shipwreck and also the Trunks or Bodies with the Branches of old and rotten Trees, cast up there likewise, whereon is found a certain Spume or Froth that in time breedeth unto certain Shells in Shape like those of the Musfle [*Mussel*] but sharper pointed and of a whitish Colour; wherein is contained a Thing, in Form like a Lace of Silk finely woven as if were together of a whitish Colour; one End whereof is fastened unto the Insid [*Inside?*] of the Shell, even as the Fish of Oisters

[Oysters] and Muscles are; the other End is made fast unto the Belly of a rude Mafse [Mass] or Lump, which in Time cometh to the Shape and Form of a Bird; which is perfectly formed, the Shell gapeth open, and the first thing that appeareth is the foresaid Lace or String, next come the Legs of the Bird hanging out; and as it groweth greater, it openeth the Shell by Degrees, till at length it is all come forth and hangeth only by the Bill; in a Short Space after it cometh to full Maturity and falleth into the Sea, where it gathereth Feathers, and groweth unto a Fowl bigger than a Mallard and lefs than a Goose; having black legs and Bill or Beak and Feathers black and white, spotted in such Manner as is our Magpie, called in some places a pie – annet [?] , which the People of Lancashire call by no other Name than a Tree – Goose; which place aforesaid, and all those parts adjoining do so much abound therewith, that one of the best is bought for three pence: for the Truth hereof, if any doubt, may it please them to repair unto me, and I shall satisfy them by the Testimony of good Witnesses.

[Fleming on Gerard – A History of Plants. In the above Fleming is no doubt quoting one John Gerard – Born 1545, Nantwich, Cheshire. Died 1612, London. He was a noted botanist and herbalist. It was believed that the goose barnacle once produced barnacle geese!]

23rd (Tuesday) - Old Gerard after relating the before mentioned improbable Story, proceeds thus,

'Moreover, it shou'd seem that there is another sort hereof, the History of which is true and of mine own knowledge; for travelling upon the Shores of our English coast between Dover and Rumney *[Romney?]* I found the Trunk of an old rotten Tree, which with some

Help I procured by some Fishermens' Wives that were attending their Husbands Return from Sea we drew out of the Water upon dry Land:

On this rotten Tree I found growing many Thousands of long crimson Bladder, in Shape like unto puddings newly fitted [?] before they be sodden, which were very clear and shining, at the nether End of which did grow a Shelfish, fashioned somewhat like a small Muscel, but much whiter, resembling a Shellfish that groweth upon the Rocks about Guernsey and Jersey, called a Limpet , many of these Shells I brought with me to London, which after I had opened, I found in them living things without Form or Shape: in others which were nearer come to Ripeness, I found living things, that were very naked, in Shape like a Bird: in others, the Birds covered with soft Down, the Shell half open, and the Bird ready to fall out, which no Doubt; were the Fowls called Barnacles.

I dare not absolutely avouch every Circumstance of the first part of this History concerning the Tree that beareth these Buds aforesaid, but will leave it to a further Consideration: howbeit that which I have seen with mine Eyes, and handled with mine Hands. I dare confidently avouch and boldly put down for Verity. Now if any will object, that this tree which I saw might be one of those before mentioned, which either by the Waves of the Sea, or some other violent Wind lad been overturned, as many other Trees are: or that any Trees falling into those Seas about the Orchades will of themselves bear the like Fowls, by Reason of those Seas and waters these being so probable Conjectures, and likely to be true, I may not without prejudice gainsay or endevour to confute the place. The Boards and rotten planks whereon are found these Shells, wherein is bud the Barnacle, Half a Mile from the main Land, called the pile of Foulders. They spawn as it were in March and April: The Geese are formed in May and June, and come to fullness of Feathers in the Month after.

24th (Thursday) - The Rods *[Roads]* are so glazed with the hour Frost and the Fog, that they are almost become impafsable [impassable] and many Accidents have in Cosequence happened, such as broken Arms and the Dislocation of Joints, and few venture out without a Fall. Since the Commencement of the Foggy weather a Complaint has generally prevailed of a pain at the Temples, oppression of the Breast and Difficulty of Breathing.

25th (Friday – Christmas Day) - I have frequently heard if the Sun does not shine out clear on Christmas Day, there will be a Scarcity of Fruit the year following. If the Abundance or Scarcity of next year depend on the Effulgence of the Sun this Day, I am afraid we must not gratify our palates with the Taste of an Apple Dumpling or Gooseberry Tart next year, for the bright Luminary has not once shewn his face Today.

26th (Saturday) - Grain of all kinds except Barley is still on the Advance; and Soap and Candles are now at Eleven pence and one shilling per pound, owing to the War with Russia from whence great Quantities of Tallow used to be imported at a cheap Rate: but that is now put a stop to as also of Timber which upwards of 4d per solid foot, and probably soon cannot be purchased any price.

27th (Sunday) - The Dock Gates at the Ulverston Canal are broken down and must be replaced with new ones. The Owners of the Canal, I fear, will not find it a profitable speculation, for it continued navigable only a short Time, except at the Height of the Spring Tides, and all the Dues have not been sufficient to keep it in due Repair.

[Fleming's report on the commencement of the Peninsular War and smuggling in Ulverston!]

28th (Monday) - Portugal is fallen into the Hands of the French, and port Wine advanced from 35s to 45s per pipe *[A measure of 1008 pints]* in Bond, exclusive of the Duty.

A Few weeks ago we had some at a lower Rate, for the Master of a smuggling Smack had the Audacity to run his Vefsel *[Vessel]* to the Head of the Canal at Ulverston and landed his Casks upon the Quay, pretending they were salted Herrings, as such they were overlooked by the Custom House Officers and soon disposed of.........

31st (Thursday) - Grain of all sorts, except Barley, keeps upon the Advance in our Markets, but Beef and pork are moderate in price. Beef from 4d. to 6d. per lb. and pork from 4d. to 5d. per lb. except the Hams which when cut off sell at 6d.

CHAPTER 8

THREE SICK CLUBS
1808

The Year 1808
Commences with war and all the Horrors attending it:
and England has now to contend with France, Spain,
Holland, Germany, poland, prufsia, Rufsia, Denmark
and all the Turks and probably America will soon be
added to the Number of our Enemies.

JANUARY

1st (Friday) - A Company of Astley's Men came to
perform at Uston *[Ulverston]* and erected a Circus
adjoining to the Theatre behind.

2nd (Saturday) - The Westmorland and Yorkshire Hills
are covered with Snow apparently very Deep.

3rd (Sunday) - Communicants receiving the Sacrament
this Day amounted to no more than Seven, including the
Clergyman, the Clark *[Clerk]* and the Churchwarden.

5th (Tuesday) - This being old Christmas Day, the Bees
in their Hives, at 12 o'clock last night, celebrated the
commencement of the Day with Music, which they
annually repeat; being sensible that this is actually the
Day which ought to be kept holy in Commemoration of
the Birth of Christ. This Story I have heard frequently

affirmed as a Truth by people who said they have watched the Hives repeatedly to ascertain the Truth of it, and are perfectly convinced that it only happens at the Time above mentioned.

6th (Wednesday) - The Measles which have proved fatal to so many Children in Ulverston are something abated of their Virulence since the Weather became more moderate: and the small pox, in the Metropolis, has carried off a great number of those children who were not innoculated with vaccine Matter.

7th (Thursday) - The Receivers of the Property Tax attended this Day at Ulverston: the Assesment upon the parish of pennington has amounted to upwards of 314£ [*Note the pound sign comes after the sum of money*] for the last Year, an enormous Sum for so small a parish: the poor Tax for last year amounted to more than 120£ tho' only a few years ago, there was not a pauper maintained by the parish; but since the lower Rank became so extravagant and arrived at such a pitch of pride in Drefs [Dress] that they far exceed their Mistresses in fashionable Clothes, our Workhouses are crowded with them and their illegitimate Offspring and, if this Evil increase as rapidly as it has done, for a few years past, the total produce of the Lands will not be sufficient to discharge the heavy Taxes imposed upon them and maintain the poor which they are burdened. The Cotton Mills bring Numbers upon the parishes where they are situated.

8th (Friday) - Pork at Ulverston Market yesterday got up to 5d. & 6d. per lb.

[William Fleming gives a description of activities at the Dalton Book Club]

9th (Saturday) - This was the Half Yearly dining Day at Dalton Book Club, which now consists of about 40 Members, who meet on the Second Saturday in each Month, in the Afternoon, at the Great Rooms at the Cavendish Arms, to choose Books for the ensuing Month, when each Member spends three pence, and pays into the Fund for purchasing Books , Seven Shillings and six pence annually, which Books are sold on the second Saturday in June, none but Members being admitted to the Sale; the Money raised by the Sale remains in the Fund and goes in part to buy new Books for the following year.

10th (Sunday) - Yesterday Capt. Gardner, the Master of a coasting Vefsel belonging to Ulverston, fell from the round Top upon the Deck and was killed. This happened at Hammerside Hill.

11th (Monday) - Went to shoot this Morning and kill'd one Brace of partridges, the Birds I found were all in the rough pasture Fields and exceeding shy. Hares are become extremely scarce in pennington, where they used to be particularly plentiful, ' till the destructive and illegal practise of netting them in the Night became known to the villainous part of the Neighbourhood and their Detection difficult if not dangerous, as they are chiefly the lowest and most abandoned Members of Society.

12th (Tuesday) - This Morning I went to see the Coal Works near Dendron. Three of the owners and three hired Men were at Work.

The pit is sunk about Seven Yards, where they began to bore, which they have persevered in for three Weeks &

have got to the Depth of thirty seven yards, when they this morning pricked a Spring from which the Water rose so rapidly on withdrawing the boring Rods, that the Men were forced to ascend the pit and erect a Stage or rather lay a Floor about 7 feet from the Top, which is higher than they expect the Water to ascend;

I waited 'till they commenced the Boring again, which is through some hard Substance , and during the Time I stopped which might be about 2 Hours, they only bored one Inch and could not ascertain what kind of Substance they were working upon; however they advance very slowly and with great Labour , but the Men do not expect the Difficulty to continue long -

13th (Wednesday) - Thomas Fisher who has one Half of the Coal concern before mentioned, is the oldest Son of Joseph Fisher, a Farmer, at Dalton in Furnefs, where he received the little Education which is commonly acquired by the Sons of illiterate Farmers whose Finances compel them to keep their Children at Home to do any little Work about the Farm they are capable of performing. At the Age of 18 he was hired by the Stone Mason at Hawcoat to work in the Freestone Quarry there, and continued some Time, till taking a Dislike either to the Employment or his Master, he returned to his Father and afsisted him for some Time in the Cultivation of the Farm.

Soon after we find him employed as a Maltmaker and a Kiln being offer'd to sale, he purchased it and commenced Malster in which Occupation he laboured diligently and his Efforts were crowned with Succefs. Finding himself deficient in the necefsary Qualifications for Businefs, he went to learn Accounts and took great pains to improve himself, employing his leisure

Hours in reading and revising his Book of Accounts in which he had set down the Questions belonging to the different Rules of Arithmetic he'd gone thro' at School. He soon made Money sufficient to discharge the Debt he had contracted to purchase the Malt Kiln and carry on Businefs. He now got himself elected a Member of the Bookclub at Dalton and indulge his speculative Fancy: he purchased shares in many coasting Vefsels which produced good Reckonings.

Money now flowed in upon him, and every thing appeared to prosper which he took in Hand, except a Love affair or two, in the prosecution of which his Ardor had carried him beyond the Bounds of prudence for when he had got Smock Tail in his Teeth, he was a very Bulldog, and wou'd break through every Impediment to the Indulgence of his vulvic propensity, he was pofsefsed *[possessed]* by a Rabies that hurried him beyond himself, and the Gratification of this Appetite, which was almost insatiable drew from him considerable Sums. He next, in Conjunction with his two Brothers, made a Trial for Iron Ore in some Fields called Deepdales, a little to the North East of Highfield House, near Dalton, and this Undertaking failed of Succefs.

But the Expence when divided among three, was inconsiderable.

He next commenced Slate Merchant in partnership with the Widow of one George Dodson, at Kirkby, and Report says he did not treat the poor Woman in the most honorable Manner and drew her into so many unnecefsary Expences that she was compelled to give up her Share of the best Quarry in Kirkby, as this was reputed to be, for the small Renumeration of 800£ the whole of which Sum it cleared him within the Space of one Year after. His Affairs were now more prosperous than before: he purchased Lindal Cot of Mrs Ireland, the Tithes at Stainton of Charles Gibson, Esq. and built himself a House at Dalton, farmed a Quarry of blue Slate in Langdale, pursued his favorite Diversion with the Mifses and freely moistened his Clay with the intoxicating produce of our West India Islands, in which he was heartily joined by some of his partners in the Coalpit.

His present Speculation is the Trial for Coals, the Succefs or Failure of which Time must shew.

14th (Thursday) - Malachi Cranke, who pofefses [*possesses*] one fourth share of the Coal pit, with Fisher & Co. was the Son of James Cranke a painter of Little Urswick, where he lived in a Stile [*Style*] something higher than his Income wou'd allow and of consequence at his Death left his Children very little but the good Education he had allowed them. He left three Sons & two Daughters but we shall only mention the former, of which John was Fellow of Trinity College, Cambridge and now pofefses a good living, not far from Barnard Castle, in the County of Durham, where he seldom enters the Church not being at all Timis Compos Mentes [*Mentis*].

James chose the Brush and Easel and became a painter of no great Eminence and Malachi, at his Father's Death not knowing what Employment to follow for a Livelihood, as his youth had been spent in Idlenefs [*Idleness*] and Extravagance with little Cash to pay for the purchase he bought an Estate in the parish of Dalton called Hindpool and commenced Farming, built a new House upon the Estate and entered into the Follies &

Amusements of the Age with afsociates *[associates]* of Fortune.

In the Midst of his Career of Debauchery and pleasure, he paid his Addrefses *[Addresses]* to a Middle aged Lady who sometime before had experienced a Disappointment and after a short Courtship he married Mifs Ellen Fell of Beckside in pennington with whom he receives at different Times a portion of about two thousand pounds. This sum redeemed the Hindpool Estate which he left to Farm and returned to little Urswick.

The prudence of his Wife aclamed *[acclaimed]* him in some Measure, but the Fondnefs *[Fondness]* for Liqor *[Liquor]* was not to be altered, and strange of it appears to all her former Acquaintance she is latterly become addicted to the same degrading Vice.

About two years ago he and some others sunk a pit or two near Boltonheads, in Expectation of finding Iron ore, but it did not succeed . He now labours constantly with the other partners in their new Undertaking which if it succeeds will no doubt enrich the Individuals concerned but may not ultimately be of much Advantage to the Country at large.

16th (Saturday) - Matthew Denney (as he is commonly called, and improperly signs his name) the 3rd partner in the Coal pit of Fisher & Co. of which he has one fouth *[fourth]* Share, was the natural child of a Woman of the Name of …................. *[There is a blank space here]* who afterwards was married to William Denny the Farmer at parkhouse, near the Furness Abbey, where he was brought up a Husbandman.

With an Education which qualified him to read a verse
in the New Testament and scrible *[scribble]* an illigible
[illegible] Hand, he was noted among his youthful
Companion, for those little Tricks which somtimes
[sometimes] gain in the pofsefsion *[possession]* of what
belongs to another without the purchase, but when
found out seldom redound to our credit or procure us
the disirable *[desirable]* Character of which honest Men
are generally proposed.

But as 'get it' was his Maxim and 'keep it if you can', we
need not be much surprised at the Methods employ'd
for the Acquirements of what he esteemed the Summum
Bonum *[Latin for the 'highest good']* not being in every
Instance the most honourable: but there are many
people in the World beside Matthew, who suppose, that
to be rich is to be happy; and certainly to be pofsessed
of Independence is convenient enough, but it is the Use
we make of Money which coduces *[conduces]* to our
Happiness or Misery.

He was now arrived at an Age when the thoughts of
a Matrimonial Connection began to enter his Head,
but yet a Wife without a Fortune was an intolerable
thought, and yet what pretensions could he have to any
other, when neither his person nor his Character were
unexceptionable.

After paying his Addrefses to a Widow in Dalton,
named Garth, who was pofsessed of some Money and
an only Child, a Daughter, he succeeded in prevailing
on her to depriving her own Child of it's Patrimony and
casting it upon the World to procure it's Subsistance by
it's Industry.

The next began the Businefs of a Butcher in Dalton and, as soon after there was none of the Trade but himself, he bought and sold at his own Prices, and no wonder at It's succeeding even beyond his Expectations till some little Tricks in Trade being found out his Costomers [*Customers*] one after another left him, so that in a little Time he had no Businefs to follow for he was now become too notorious.

After bringing him one Son and two Daughters, his Wife died; but he was not long in getting another, who was also a Widow with one Son and one Daughter and the Rent of a small Farm near Broughton to bring them up. And this he had fixed his Hawk's Eye and was a weak, sickly Youth, died and the Daughter, being then nearly of Age, deprived him of his prey. His second Wife had now brought him two Children, and the Expences of the Family became more heavy, tho' conducted with the utmost Frugality; so he made another attempt at Butching, which Trade he still follows,tho' since he entered into the Coal Scheme and laboured daily with the other partners in boring.

He has left the Management of the Slaughter House chiefly to his son.

17th (Sunday) - The Fellow who robbed and abused so shamefully the parish Apprentice of Thomas Lowther of Townsend in pennington, as mentioned some Time since, took his Trial for that offence at the general quarter Sessions at Lancaster on Tuesday last, when he was fined one Shilling and to be imprisoned till he had discharged all the Expenses of the Trial etc.

18th (Monday) - If we can put any confidence in
the Accounts we have received by the American
Newspapers, we are not long to be upon peaceable
Terms with that Nation.

*[Another interesting entry. Still more than four years
to go before America declares war. Also, what American
newspapers is Fleming reading?]*

19th (Tuesday) - In the fine warm Days of the last
Summer, a Boy named Smith about 16 years of Age,
procured an old Door, and launching it out upon the
Tarn at great Urswick, to which his Mother's Garden
was adjoining, he placed a Chair upon it, in which he
seated himself and with the Ends of some old Oars
paddled over the Tarn to the great Astonishment of his
Neighbours; the Door being sunk by his Weight about
3 inches below the Surface of the Water, he appeared
to the Spectators to be sailing on the Water seated in
a Chair only. However, though he had repeatedly
entertained the Spectators with this novel Spectacle,
which required much adroitnefs *[adroitness]* in the
Navigator to keep a proper Balance he at last lost the
Equilibrium and fell overboard, but being an expert
Swimmer, he reached the Shore in Safety.

20th (Wednesday) - This Morning, the Widow of the
late, Mr Geo: Lowry of Ulverston appeared at the Altar
with her third Husband, a Widower, from Kendall with
7 children. To her former Husbands, who were both
easy good natured Men, she play'd the Tyrant, and they
quietly submitted to be henpecked, and the later *[latter]*
of them to see his children by a former Wife abused by
her.

21st (Thursday) - Grain of all Kinds except Barl'y keeps upon the Advance at Ulverfton Market, port too is getting up, but Butchers' Meat of other sorts is about the same as last mentioned, and probably may continue so till after Candlemass, potatoes are at 6d and 7d per Hoop and Apples at from 18d to 2 ' per Hoop.

22nd (Friday) - It is remarkable that the Frost the two or three Nights past has done more Damage to my Artichokes that were not covered with Litter, than all the severe Frost we have had this Winter, and tho' I have now covered them carefully – they are so cut that probably few of them will survive.

23rd (Saturday) - about Noon there came on a Sleet and it froze so very intensely at the same Time,that in two or three Hours the Ground was perfectly glazed over, the Branches of the Trees, from the Ice adhering to them, became five Times thicker than before, and the Icicles descending from the Hedges gave them a novel and not unpleasing Appearance, but such I hope, they won't long retain.

24th (Sunday) - Betty Harrison of Barrow married to one Barrow, the Master of a Vefsel trading between Liverpool & Ulverston.

25th (Monday) - Early this Morning Thomas Fell of Holebigrow *[Holebiggerah]* in Pennington, died in the 46th year of his Age; the Complaint which put a period to his Existence appeared to the Surgeon to be brought on by hard Labour; tho' he had a Sufficiency he was remarkably saving and laboured with unremitted Afiduity *[Assiduity]* on his Farm, which he greatly improved; and frequently after the Toils of the Day were ended, he wou'd go up to the Common to inspect his Sheep, of which he had a good Flock: in following there he frequently over heated himself and returned Home in the chill damp Air of the Evening almost stiffened with cold, and thought his Constitution was naturally strong, this had such ill Effect upon it that it most probably brought on the Disease of which he has lingered for some Months, and till near his Decease experienced but little pains. He has left a Wife and three young Children.

When we see our Neighbours thus leaving us one after another, and even the most healthy and robust dropping into the Grave, it reminds us that we are not immortal, but may be unexpectedly snatched off in the Midst of our Schemes for future Happiness and Enjoyment of Ease and pleasure.

How many Labour to acquire what they suppose will contribute much to their comfort in old Age, and in the Acquirement and eager pursuit of their Object, contract some Disease which terminates their Days long before the Time their Imaginations had fired upon for the End of their Labours and the Commencement of enjoying the Fruits of their Industry and Frugallity, which few wou'd be stimulated to practise, was the Boundary our Existence never exactly known for as Pindar well expresses it ......

'But wrapt Errors is the human Mind,
And human Bliss is ever insecure;
Know we what fortune yet remains behind?
Know we how long the Present shall endure? '

[John Wolcot, a satirist writing under the pseudonym of 'Peter Pindar']

(Fleming Note : See pindar's 7th Olympic Ode trans'd by West)

'Xenuara Xpnuar avrie' - Money makes the Man is the opinion of many, and we daily see the greatest Blockheads and frequently the greatest Vilains *[Villains]* treated with that Respect which is only due to the wise and virtuous part of Mankind and this for no other Reason but because they have had the good Fortune of having more than a common portion of the Riches fallen to their Share.

A Coat of better Materials than are commonly manufactured and cut in a fashionable Manner even when it decorates the Back of a Rascal, will attract more Regard than a sober plain Drefs *[Dress]* which covers a learned & virtuous Man: by this it seems as if outward appearance was more esteemed than inward Worth; and Men are willing to be deceived by parade [?] for let a person be what he may, if he only dress well and make a Shew of Riches, tho' both his pofsefsons *[possessions]* and his Character are not both worth a Groat, he will meet with enough to shew him the outward Marks of Respect and flatter his Foibles.

26th (Tuesday) - This day my Mother enters into her Sixty ninth Year, and is exceeding agile for a Woman of her Years; but pure Country Air, a dry and healthy Habitation, with moderate Exercise and abstemiousness living often prolongs life with Health and Happinefs to an extreme old Age.

With such Time passes pleasantly away, the few Wants of Life are easily supply'd and their Temperance keeps them healthy and cheerful, for Nature is contented and satisfy'd with a little; on the contrarey *[contrary]* Luxury and intemperance debilitate the Body and cause many to drag an infirm and diseased Body to an untimely Grave and rendered the latter part of their Existence miserable not unfrequently curtails an Estate and forces them to labour for their Living, who, but for the Impudence of their parents, might have been happy with Independance, and avoided the Commission of many little unpleasant Actions which poverty that vile Instigator compelled them to do.

27th (Wednesday) - This Winter has been exceeding severe, and the Severity commencing so soon makes me hope that the Spring will be early and mild, otherwise many of the Farmers will experience the Want of Fodder, which must be particularly distressing, for few can unfeelingly see their Cattle scarecely *[scarecly]* able to sustain life by the Scanty produce of the Ground, without being able to purchase them any thing for Relief – Thomas Fell of Hoibigrow interred this Afternoon at pennington.

28th (Thursday) - Yesterday Evening I lost a Greyhound in the Distemper to which Whelps are particularly liable, and seldom survive. It was four years old and this is one of the few Instances I have known of Dogs being attacked with it when arrived at that Age, but whatever Means have been used I never knew one recover when more than a Year old. My loss in this case is irreparable, it was the only one I had, and by Sportsman esteemed the best in Lancashire. Its Father was purchased at a very extravagant price, in Italy by John Baldwin of Aldingham Esq. and this was the only Whelp which was suffered to be kept, so that this excellent and valuable Breed is now extinct.

29th (Friday) - It is not a little surprising that, when the Country is so burthened with Taxes as they are at present, and all our Manufactories and Commerce at a Stand, the people here shou'd croud [crowd] into the Circus and pay so extravagantly for the repeated Amusement and yet grumble to contribute their proportion of the Taxes for their own Security and the Defence of the Nation. But we are always more ready to open our purse strings for our own pleasures which are voluntary for any thing that has the last Appearance of Compulsion, even our proft [profit] and Advantage is often neglected for the Enjoyment of pleasure which frequently leaves a Sting behind which gives us more pain than all our Enjoyments pleasure. These are too dearly bought which are purchased at the Expense of our Health and purse, but that is disregarded till pain makes us sensible of the value of one and Want of the other; then we are sensible of our Folly and lament our past Conduct as a Misfortune.

31st (Sunday) - Grain continues at high prices, except Barley which now fetches only about 14/- per Bushel; the best Flour is at 28/- per cwt of 120 lbs. The prospect of Scarcity of Fodder and the crop of potatoes not being abundant last year has caused them to sell even now at the extravagant price of 7d per Hoop of 6 Quarts; yet they are far below what they were a few years back when they sold at 15d per Hoop, and at that enormous price many of the Farmers here would not bring them to Market, expecting them still to advance and great quantities were kept thus till they were spoiled, and many poor people were in the utmost Distress for Want of the common Necessaries of Life tho' every precaution was taken to alliviate their Sufferings and provide for their Necessities.

FEBRUARY [1808]

1st (Monday) - Tom a' Lin and his Wife and Wife's Mother they went all three to bed together

The Weather was cold and the Blankets were thin lay close to my Arse and Tom a' Lin

Tom a' Lin and his Wife and his Wife's Mother, they all three went to th' Midden together

One Shit thick and the others shit thin, we'll sew them together said Tom a' Lin

Tom a' Lin and his Wife and his Wife's Mother went all three over a Bridge together

The Bridge broke down and the Women fell in the De' d go with them quoth Tom a' Lin

[The above entry in Fleming's journal appears to be based on a childrens' nursery rhyme dated from around 1560. It goes thus:]

'Tom a' Lin and his wife and his wife's mother
They all went over the bridge together
The bridge was broken and they fell in,
The devil go with all 'quoth Tom a' Lin '

2nd (Tuesday) - The severe Winter has caused the Wheat sown last Autumn to be not so forward as usual, much of it has only just put forth its' Blades and appears very thin , but a favourable will I hope in a great Measure repair the Ravages of the unusually Sharp and blustering Winter.

3rd (Wednesday) - Extremely cold, but the high Wind from Northwest has in the Course of last night dried up much of the superabundant Moisture and made the

Roads cleaner and the Ground more in a Working State for the plow: Some Farmers complain that many of their Turnips are much injured by the severe Frosts and wet Weather. They sold in public Sale this Day at penny – bridge for Eleven pence per Stone of 16 lb which is an exceeding high price to begin with, and probably will be higher except the Spring be early.

4th (Thursday) - Attended the Sales of Pearson a Bankrupt at pennybridge Yesterday and today, who had only just got a Wife and a House neatly furnished with every comfortable Necessary, when he failed in Business and the Decorations of his Mansion were greedily purchased by his Neighbours to adorn their several Habitations which he had carefully selected and brought together for the Convenience of his Family. It is a melancholy Sight to see the property of a Man just settled in the World totally taken away and his Dwelling stript of every Moveable, his every Delight dispersed about the Neighbourhood and become the property of Perhaps his greatest Enemies, even of those who helped to bring the Misfortune upon him. If he be a man of Integrity and sensibility his Situation must be far from a pleasant one.

5th (Friday) - *[Fleming visits Uverston churchyard - See Inscriptions in the Appendices]*

6th (Saturday) - *[Fleming visits Ulverston churchyard - See Inscriptions in the Appendices - the following is of note]*

Mary Lumley Memorial

Sacred to the deposited Remains of Mary the Wife of Brigadier General, the honourable William Lumley and the second Daughter of Thomas Sunderland Esq. who died at Ulverstone the 19 Day of July 1807 aged 34.

There is another and a better World:
A lonely pilgrim I am left in this;
God's Will be done! But if my prayers be heard,
We shall meet again: till then sleep on
Sweet Innocence, thou stranger to Offence;
Thy God hath call'd thee; and that very Voice
That thunders Terror through the guilty Soul
With Tongue of Seraphs whisper peace to thee.
…..................W. L.(William Lumley)

7th (Sunday) - The monument bearing the last inscription was erected in January 1808 by Gen: Lumley, over the Vault in which his Wife was deposited during his absence in the unfortunate and ill conducted Expedition fitted out against Monte Video and the other Spanish Settlements on the River plate under the Command of General Whitelocke, thro' whose unskilled Conduct they failed of Success and for which he is now taking his Trial; the Result of which whatever it may be, his fellow Subjects in general are so exasperated that if he be condemned to die, they will scarecely be satisfied with: for they look upon it as an offence for which he cannot in any Way attone, to order the men under his Command to march into the Middle of an Enemy's Town prepared for Defence, with their Muskets unloaded and the Flints taken away when all the flat Roofs and Windows of the Houses were lined with the Musketry of the Enemy, and thus wantonly to throw away and sport with the lives of many valuable Subjects and the vast Sums of Money which the Expedition must cost the nearly Bankrupt Nation.

People who are thus deprived of Friends and Relations whose power of Resistance was taken away and Death inevitable, cannot manifestly see such Actions perpetrated without calling for that punishment which the Offender duely merited; let his Station and Connections be what they will, his Actions demand a Scrutiny, and as the public are in possession of most of the particulars relating to his unjustifiable Conduct, they suppose themselves capable of appreciating the merits or demerits of the Case before them.

A Few Days wil now give publicity to the Trial and inform us of his Acquittal or Condemnation and be a precedent for others to whom the Succefs of such Expedition are entrusted.

[The above entry in Fleming's journal refers to the trial of Lieutenant General John Whitelocke. He was born in 1757 and died in 1833. Whitelocke was the Commander In Chief of the expedition against the Spanish in Buenos Ayres, South America in 1807. The Court martial was held on the 28th January, 1808 at Chelsea College and for several days following. He was found guilty on all charges, except one. Consequently, he was dismissed from the service. The newspapers of the time, including the Lancaster Gazette, widely reported this]

General John Whitelocke

A satirical picture ridiculing John Whitelocke

8th (Monday) - Tobacco is risen from 4.5d to 7.5d. per oz the raw Article, in Consequence of the expected Rupture with America.

9th (Tuesday) - Walked to Dalton this Morning and dined with Rd. *[Richard]* Cleater.

I am informed that the Coal Company have met with a Seam, the Thickness of which they were not able to ascurtain *[ascertain]* but are of Opinion; it is sufficient to repay them the Expences of working if it prove no more than eighteen or twenty Inches thick as they lay no more than about Fifty yards below the Surface: but the Quantity of Water, which probably is greater than can be drawn by Horses, will be a great Impediment and if they be compelled to erect a Fire Engine will be a great Expense perhaps not less than 4 or 5 Hund. £*[£400 - £500]*.

10th (Wednesday) - *[Fleming visits Ulverston churchyard – See Inscriptions in the Appendices]*

12th (Friday) - …...went to shoot & killed One Hare; one Rabbit and two and Half Brace Woodcock.

13th (Saturday) - *[Fleming visits Ulverston churchyard – See Inscriptions in the Appendices]*

15th (Monday) - here was very little Candlemas Business done at Ulverston this Day. It has been a Custom in Furness from Time immemorial to settle all Money Concerns at Candlemas, such as the Signing of Deeds of Conveyayance and paying the purchase Money of Estates; borrowing Money and executing Mortgages Bonds and promissory Notes, settling Tradesmen's Bills etc. Tho' many Tradesmen now make a Custom of collecting their Bills in the Country every three Months.

A Few Years back, we had nothing but Gold here and strong Canvas Bags were necefsary [necessary] to convey the purchase Money of an Estate, but now the Case is altered and here is scarcely a Guinea to be seen; nothing in Circulation but provincial Bank Notes and a Few of the Bank of England, so that now a considerable Sum may be transported in a Walnut Shell and a Farthingworth of paper by the magical Touch of the Banker becomes an equivalent to an Hundred Acres of Terafirma *[Terrafirma]*; and an Estate by a Mistake of the Owner, may be consumed in lighting his pipe or his Candle , or making himself comfortably clean behind.

18th (Thursday) - Grain of all kinds took a considerable Rise at the Market at Ulverston today; potatoes were at 7d per Hoop and Apples at from 18d to 24d per Hoop – Butter 14d per 16 ounces

19th (Friday) - The Farmers now complain heavily of the Loss they have experienced in their Turnips from the very severe Frosts and heavy Rains which have constantly succeeded. This severe and changeable Weather has caused them to rot, and from the scarcity of Hay, the Destruction of this nututive [*nutritious?*] and useful Root will be more sensibly felt.

It was customary with our ancestors, and continued till within the last twenty years, to buy a quantity of Beef and Mutton at martinmas, sufficient for their family, till the ensuing summer; this they cured with salt and saltpetre and either hung it up in their Open Kitchens to dry, or laid it in casks made for the purpose; this latter they called pickled beef and this and mutton was their chief food all the winter; at Shrovetide they began to cut their Hung Meat and this served them in the spring, so that the markets contain'd little Buthcher's Meat for that Time, but since the Introduction of Turnip Cultivation, and Cabbages with other winter Feed-became plentiful, the Markets have been well supplied with Fresh Meat all the year and little is preserved with salt as formerly.

[Fleming comments on the poor state of the Ulverston Canal]

20th (Saturday) - The Canal at Ulverston is now become nearly useless, from the bad repair it is in, and the Vefsels coming to that port lay chiefly at Bardsea and Waddet Hill *[Wadhead Scar]* which is inconvenient for the Town.

23rd (Tuesday) - Great Numbers of Dogs are lately gone mad and much mischief done by them.

This Day the Chief Constable by Order of the Magistrates issued precepts to the petty Constables to order that all Dogs in Ulverston and the Neighbourhood shou'd be kept up in Confinement or they would be destroy'd as some Dogs affected with the Hydrophobia had been seen about Ulverston.

24th (Wednesday) - James Huddleston entered upon my Farm at Rowe on the 13th. Feby. Inst. and this Day opened the Water – Courses in the Stubbs and floated the Meadows.

25th (Thursday) - The Market at Ulverston was ill supply 'd with Grain this Day and both Wheat and Oats advanced in price, Wheat at 50 s per Load. Potatoes, Butter and Butcher's Meat continued about the same except pork which fell to 4 & three quarters d per lb taking the whole pig but if cut up sold at about 5 & a quarter d per lb.

26th (Friday) - Geo. Coward, a Grocer and Tallow Chandler at Ulverston and Schoolfellow of mine, died about 3 o'clock this Afternoon.

He was a Lieutenant in the Ulverston Volunteers, and among them acquired the Habit of drinking which has been the Ruin of many of them, and to which he has fallen a Martyr, ruined in Constitution and Estate, and has left a Wife and five Children dependant on their Relations for Support, the oldest of them about 7 Years of Age, the Youngest one & a Half:

The Coal Company have found a small seam of Coals about Six Inches deep, or thereabouts, at 53 yards below the Surface.

28th (Sunday) - People are very busy in turning over their Gardens.

29th (Monday) - The cruel and blackguard Diversion of Cockfighting which is so much practised at this Season of the Year and degrades the human Species, who delight to see the Cocks pierce and fear each other to Death, to below the Level of the brute Creation, does not so much prevail as it did about Twenty Years ago, and though many who call themselves, and desire that other people shou'd think them, Gentlemen, frequent the places where these Diversions are going forwards, it is to be hoped that the Legislation will shortly put a Stop to the infamous practice, for those who frequent Cockfights are now generally known by the Denomination of Blackguards.

MARCH [1808]

1st (Tuesday) - Commonly called here Pancake Tuesday. Cockfights Yesterday at pennington; this Day they were at Ulverston, where, I am astonished the Magistrates do not interfere and put a Stop to the cruel practice ---

2nd (Wednesday) - It has been the Custom on this Day, and is still retained in this Corner of Britain, to eat nothing on this Day of animal Food, except Fish; Many Families abstain from butchers' Meat on the Wednesdays and Fridays through Lent, and some lefs *[less]* scrupulous eat anything they can procure.

[Fleming tells an amusing tale of his Grandfather and a rat]

4th (Friday) - My Grandfather, by the Mother's Side,

had much of the Gentleman about him, wore a comely Wig well dusted with powder and greased with pomatum was possessed of much Goodsense, and once in his Life exhausted his whole Stock of Cunning in catching a Rat. After the Death of his first Wife, he let his Estate to farm and boarded with his Neighbour Simpson, at Dendron, but slept in his own House.

One Morning when he went out he negligently left the Door of his Chamber open and admitted a Rat, which made great Disturbance the following Night deprived him of part of his Nights Rest.

The next Morning he rose a little out of Temper with the Intruder, and prepared a Trap which he baited with a nice Morsel, hoping that hunger wou'd compel the animal to devour it to its own Destruction.

But before he set the Trap he hunted it round and round the Room with the Hearth Brush, but the nimble quadruped ran him out of Breath and patience too; so stepping out of the Chamber and carefully closing the Door again, Confound thee, said he but I'll take a more effectual Method of getting rid of thee.

The Room was closed, so that the Rat cou'd not pofsibly [possibly] escape, and my Grandfather took the cruel Resolution of confining it there till it was hungered to Death.

Yet he was not an unfeeling, cruel Man, for his Neighbours frequently observed with what Gentleness and Humanity he always treated the animals subjected to the Service and Amusements of Man.

The prisoner had now remained two Nights in Durance, and its Gaoler persevered in the famishing System till the third, which was the Sunday Evening, where his Rest was no longer disturbed and he concluded the Animal had expired for Want of Food; and now he felt little Compunction for the Cruelty he had exercised against an Animal which had so slightly offended him, but what were his Feelings when he rose in the Morning, and the first Object that met his Sight was the mangled Remains of his Sunday Wig, great part of which the Rat had devoured. He calmly put on his Cloths, and, without a Word to the demolisher of his capital Ornament, walked out and left the Door open for the Rat to escape if it pleased.

6th (Sunday) - Fields, plowed yesterday at pennington by James Huddleston, my Farmer, High Croft, Gillbrow, little and great Swarbricks, out of Lay – Little Close, Stubble the 4th Year, for Barley and to be laid down in Grass – little Carlow and two Dales in Templands for Barley – parrock Meadow and Kettlebarn for Barley to be laid down in Grass. *[Fleming is most likely naming his fields]*

7th (Monday) - Grain of all Kinds are again advanced in price. Wheat to 52s/6d per load. Oats to 14/6 per Bushel – and potatoes continue at 7d per Hoop. Barley and Malt are little advanced, as there Remains much in Low Furness yet unsold – pork is at 5d per lb and the choice parts of Beef sells at 6d per lb. Steaks 7d – Veal is at 5d – no Lamb yet in the Market.

9th (Wednesday) - The Roads have been very dusty for some Days Past, and according to the old saying,

A peck of March Dust is worth a King's Ransom; alluding I suppose to the fruitful year which commonly succeeds a dry March, and hither to this Month has been remarkably so, that the Farmers are got very forward with their plowing.

The Wheats are more backward than usual and in general appear to be thin upon the Ground, particularly in the lighter Soil, and where they lay sloping are affected more by the warmth of the meridian Sun, and their Roots are frozen out, the Crops in these Situations must consequently prove thin.

10th (Thursday) - Provisions of all Kinds at Ulverston Market this Day were on the Advance, and much Grain is laid up in the Warehouses in Expectation of the prices being yet higher.

11th (Friday) - There remains no Snow on the Mountains visible from our Hills.

12th (Saturday) - This morning John Yarker began to sow Oats on the new enclosed Ground [Common] at Rosset Nook, which is the first I have seen this Season, and though the seed is committed to the Ground so early, I doubt not but much; later sown, will be sooner ripe for the Sickle.

(NB - This Grain upon the Fields September the 1st)

13th (Sunday) - This Day, the Revd. John Sunderland Vicar of pennington officiated there for the third Time since he entered upon the Living. His Curate is rather negligent in his Duty, not attending sometimes even on Sundays, nor was he there or any Clergyman for him on Ash wednesday last, when I waited for him at Church from Eleven to 12 o'clock. The Second Time Mr Sunderland did duty at Pennington was on the 6th. Sept.1807

14th (Monday) - Very fine and dry, but the Wind from the North East was exceeding strong and extremely cold, with frost, neverthelefs [*nevertheless*] J.Yarker continues to sow his Grain at Rosset, and says he is determined to keep his Men at the same Employment , if the Weather will permit, till he has finished his Seed Time.

15th (Tuesday) - This Morning Mr Will. Atkis Fell, Attorney at Law in Ulverston and Owner of the Estate called Fellside in the parish of pennington, received the following Note from the Revd. John Sunderland Vicar of Pennington, the Content of which he this Evening communicated to me and of which the following is a copy verbatim et literatim . [*'word for word and letter for letter'*]

Mr J. Sunderland has had an Opinion, respecting his Right as Vicar of pennington, of appointing one of the Churchwardens, which is decidely in his Favour on this Ground, that the Canon Law upon this Subject, strengthened by the written Testimony of a former Bishop of the Diocese, as to the Exercise of this Right in his Time, will set aside any subsequent Custom to the contrary, originating, most likely from the non – residence & consequent neglect of former Vicars –

In case therefore Mr. J. Sunderlands nomination is disallowed, by the parish, the ensuing Easter, he is determined to bring it to Trial & Mr. J.S. Will thank Mr

A Fell to acquaint Mr. Fleming & the rest of the parish that such is his Determination – Tuesday Morning.

16th (Wednesday) - This Morning I laid the above Note of Mr Sunderland before some of the Sidesmen of the parish of pennington, but as all who were interested in the Affair cou'd not be convened on so short a Notice, we thought proper to defer our Determination till Tomorrow -

17th (Thursday) - None of the Sidesmen except W. Atkis Fell, Thos. Nicholson and myself attended to consult concerning the Affair mentioned above between the Revd. John Sunderland and the parish of pennington.

However not thinking that we ought tamely to have a just Statement of our Case drawn up, and consequently examined the Records of the parish and some Witnesses, and wish Will. Atkis Fell to draw up the same impartially and submit the same to Mr. Holroyd or some other eminent Council at the Assizes now holding at Lancaster, that we may know his Opinion of the Case and be informed in what Manner we may lawfully Act in this Affair, and not draw the parish into unccefsary [unneccessary] Expenses of a Lawsuit; without probability of Sucefs [Success].

18th (Friday) - Wheat advanced Yesterday to 55/- per load. Oats were as last week about 14/6 per Bushel – potatoes 7 and a half pence per Hoop, and Butter 14 and a half pence per lb of 16 oz – Eggs 6d per doz – Beef 7d per lb.

19th (Saturday) - This Morning I examined the Case and thinking it drawn fairly & impartially desired Mr W A Fell to send it over to Lancaster by tomorrow Morning's post, that we may become possessed of the Opinion as soon as possible and take our Measures accordingly.

21st (Monday) - The Frost still continues very Sharp & severly cold with some brisk Showers of Snow & Hail and the Wind from the East, which having continued there so long has probably been the Cause of Sickness which generally prevails and is attended with violent Rheumatic pains in the Head and other parts ----

22nd (Tuesday) - About a Fortnight ago, the Revd. Rbt. Walker Curate at pennington, who by the Bye, is a queer Stick, took it into his Head that his Wife, cou'd not possibly live many Days, and therefore made all preparations for the Funeral before she was called hence, that these Cares might not intrude when the Weight of Sorrow fell upon him for the Lofs [Loss] of his Helpmate; and as his Brother liv'd in Grasmere, which is at some Distance, he and one Singleton from Broughton were requested to come over to Pennington to attend the Interment, and of Consequence came last Sunday Week, but were astonished to find the Lady still alive, however as Meat was provided and cooked and a Barrel of Ale brought up from Ulverston, the Gentlemen thought that they shou'd be wanting in Respect to Mr Walker if they did not accept his kind Invition [Invitation] to stop with him a Few Days.

The following Week was spent in soothing the Sorrows of their Revd. Friend & consoling themselves with the Contents of the parsons Ale Cask & which was considerably lightened , but the old Woman continued to breathe. Yet from her silence was supposed to be

speechless and the Moment of her Dissolution near;
On the Sunday following the parson and his Friends
attended Church, and guess what was their Amazement
when at their Return they found Mrs Walker sitting
by the Fire dressed in Silk and the Use of her Tongue
recovered, and when she addressed them as follows -
'Gentlemen, if ye come to shake Hands with Mr Walker
we are glad to see ye, but if ye want a Maintenance
why don't ye apply to your parishes.' This Woman has
been for some Years deranged , but is now recovered of
Sickness , and may probably live for many Years.

23rd (Wednesday) - The Furniture and Chattels of Geo.
Ashburner of Coran [*Probably Cowran – a farming estate
in Pennington*] were yesterday sold in public; he signed
over his property some Years ago, but no Dividend has
hitherto been made.

No Duty, nor Attendance of the Clergyman, at the
Church at pennington this Day or on Friday last -----

24th (Thursday) - Much of the plumb Blossom which
was ready for bursting out, has been devoured by
the Birds in the late severe Weather. The high prices
heve been the Cause of more Grain being brought
to Ulverston Market this Day, has been there since
Candlemas alltogether, but there was no Reduction of
the prices.

There is yet a great Quantity of Grain in Hands of the
Farmers in Furness but they are slow in bringing it out
expecting an Advance.

25th (Friday) - No duty at pennington Church nor priest
attending.

26th (Saturday) - The unusual hard Frost deters the Farmers in general from beginning their Seedtime so soon as they were accustomed to do in former Years , but a Few have sown as usual and Autumn will shew whether of them produce the more abundant Crops.

Early sowing is certainly commendable where the Land is in a high State of Cultivation and the Weather Seasonable, otherwise the Grain wou'd be too luxuriant and the produce small. Barley and Oats are now sown by many Farmers at the same Time, which was not practised a few years back.

27th (Sunday) - Yesterday a Woodcock was killed in plumpton by Mr Woodburn.

28th (Monday) - The Seeds sown in the Gardens this Spring do not make their Appearance, nor can the Blofsom *[Blossom]* of different kinds, which is now ready to burst out an *[and]* promises to be abundant, push forth for Want of Rain and warmer Weather.

Much of the early plumb Blossom has been destroy'd by the Birds, and the Spink *[A finch]* is the busiest of them and well seconded by the Tom Tit; the best Way of preventing their Depredations is to stuff the Skin of a Hawk and place it on a perch in the Garden or near the Trees infested by them.

29th (Tuesday) - Peas for Seed are so scarce that they are sold at the very extravagant price of 18d per Quart, Beans at 9d per Quart and other Garden Seeds proportionably high: but red and white Clover sells at 10d and 11d per pound.

30th (Wednesday) - The Eastern Sky was a little red this Morning at Sunrise which led me to hope for a Change to milder in a short Time. Some Farmers presuming from the Appearance commenced their Seed Time today, but this Evening the prospect of Change for the present was not so promising, tho' we may probably experience it in a few Days. Got my Irish pointer ……. *[Word unintelligible - Sancho?]* …...this Morning.

31st (Thursday) - Oats as high as 15s per Bushel at Market this Day, which was well supplied. Fisher the chapman signed over his Effects, Wm Redhead & Wm. Marr Afignees *[Assignees]*. Revd. Holroyd's Opinion upon the Case stated a few Days ago and find it in our own Favour; produced the same for the Inspection of some of the Landholders who had agreed to pay a proportionable Share of the Expenses already incurred and hereafter to be incurred in any Suit that may be instituted by the Clergyman against any Individual in the parish , and to Oppose any Attorney he may [make?] to introduce new Customs into the parish.

APRIL [1808]

1st (Friday) - Mr. N . & Self visited Mr. F- at Furness Abbey to obtain his Signature to our Agreement for the joint Expenses of opposing the Inovations of our Vicar. His Wife opposed his Signing voluntarily and shewed more Acid in her Composition than is generally found in a Lady whose Honeymoon is not much past the full: however we prevailed: but not so J. Ashburner the Miller, who was the only Man of any propriety in the Parish, who refused to sign --------

2nd (Saturday) - ….…....the Wind shifted from the East to South West and brought on a Shower of Snow: but a thickness in the West predicts approaching Rain which will be very acceptable to the Farmers.

3rd (Sunday) - Returned the Agreement with the Signatures annexed to Wm. Atkis Fell, our Attorney, that a Copy thereof might be sent to the Revd. J. Sunderland in Return for his kind Note copied which was conveyed to us in the same Manner.

4th (Monday) - *[Fleming visits Ulverston churchyard – See Inscriptions in the Appendices]*

5th (Tuesday) - *[Fleming visits Ulverston churchyard – See Inscriptions in the Appendices]*

6th (Wednesday) - *[Fleming visits Ulverston churchyard – See Inscriptions in the Appendices]*

7th (Thursday) - Extremely fine and moderate with a warm Breeze from the Southwest and the Farmers exceeding busy sowing Oats and planting potatoes for a full Autumn Crop.

The high price of produce and the inferior price of lean Cattle has caused much Land to be plowed up this Spring; moreover the uncertainty of our importing any Grain from the Baltic and America leads the Farmers to conjecture that the prices will yet advance, and of Course are desirous of obtaining as extensive Crops as their several Farms will allow: their Exertions, if the future Crop proves as abundant as their Industry merits, will be the Means of keeping our Markets well supplyd, and, if none shou'd be imported, the prices lower.

Furness has always been able to raise Grain sufficient for the inhabitants and to send off much coastwise to other Markets, though the population is nearly doubled within the last thirty Years: in Ulverston and the Neighbourhood the Number of Inhabitants is nearly double what it was fifteen Years ago, and three times the Number there was thirty Years since.......

8th (Friday) - Vegetation which was impeded by the late severe Frosts, now begins to advance, but the Wheats in general are thin and look badly. Many Farmers in Furness, who laboured for an early Seedtime, finished sewing their Barley today and some inform me they will have completed it tomorrow Evening. Peas are so extravagantly dear that few will be sown this Year: the Market price is 16d & 18d per Quart owing to the Wetness of last Autumn, the Crops of Seed peas were chiefly destroy'd and Winter potatoes much damaged, which has made both of them sell very high; potatoes are now seven pence per Hoop of 6 Quarts.

9th (Saturday) - Gooseberries begin to make their Appearance in Abundance where the Buds in the late severe Weather were not destroyed by the Birds.

11th (Monday) - In Consequence of the Threats of the Inhabitants of Kirkby, of inditing [?] the Road from Ulverston over the Moor to that place, we are under the Necefsity of building a Bridge over the Beck which crofses the Road below Rathmos, though there is no great Need for it; for there is a sufficient foot Bridge and the Water is never deep there; however I caused the following Note to be made public at our parish Church Yesterday, and intend to be done at the Market Crofs [Cross] at Ulverston on Thursday next.

To be let – on Saturday next the 15th Inst. At 6 o'Clock in the Evening, the building and compleating *[completing]* of a Bridge over the Brook at Rathmoss on the Highway leading from Ulverston to Kirkby; any person, wishing to contract for the same, is requested to attend there at the Time above mentioned.

12th (Tuesday) - The Cattle Fair at Ulverston this Day was well attended and many Cattle sold at tolerable Prices though none of the Yorkshire Dealeres attended . Some very good fat Oxen were shewn but Calvers were chiefly in the greatest Request.

13th (Wednesday) - *[Fleming visits Ulverston churchyard – See Inscriptions in the Appendices]*

14th (Thursday) - *[Fleming visits Ulverston churchyard – See Inscriptions in the Appendices]*

15th (Friday) - Good Friday, fine and moderate with a drizzling Fog and warm Wind from the Southwest.

16th (Saturday) - Went to Rathmoss this Evening and let the Building of a Bridge on the Highway there, by Ticket to the lowest proposers, who were Richard Rowcliff Farmer at Whinfield and William Woodburn of Kirby they agreed to find all the Matterials and erect the Bridge before the 1st. of June for the Sum of Nine pounds and to give Bond before the Receipt of the said Sum to support the Bridge for Seven Years from the Time of its Erection.

17th (Easter Sunday) - Attended the Sacrament at pennington where only 24 Communicants were and their Oblations amounted to four Shillings and Ten pence, two shillings of which were given to the poor Clerk, one Shilling to Sarah Barnes, and the remaining one Shilling and Ten pence to Sarah Hartley, two paupers belonging to the parish. John walton the Clark *[Clerk]* , having half a Bottle of Wine that remained, drank the same in the Church when we had retired and was tipsy when the Afternoon Service for the Evening was performed.

18th (Easter Monday) - Attended the Vestry Meeting in the Church at pennington with the following Sidesmen, Thomas Nicholson of the Channon House, John Ashburner of the Mill, William Townson of Whinfield, James Nicholson of Low Greaves, when we elected the churchwardens for the ensuing without the Interference of Mr. Sunderland the Vicar or Mr Walker his curate who was present, though the former had given us Notice that he was determined to oppose our Election and nominate one of them; however, finding the Landholders were resolved to contest it with him, he declined it, and left us at Liberty to nominate both the churchwardens according to our established Custom and Right by Common Law.

19th (Tuesday) - Much snow fell driving last Night and in the course of this Day; with very cold Wind from the Northwest. Went to inspect the Ground about Rossed *[Rosside?]* , being informed that Iron Ore appeared there to the Day; but found it was only the Rubish *[Rubbish]* which had been thrown out some years ago, perhaps 60 [word missing - years?] or more, when a Trial was made there for Iron Ore, but did not succeed; two or three Shafts were sunk but little ore found, though it was of excellent Quality.

There is a Bed of Freestone and much black Shale appears in the outbreak of the Banks, not unlike what is found in the Neighbourhood of Coalpits, the Rock appears dip from North West to South East ------

[Next is a fascinating letter from his relative, Thomas Hodgson, who is desperately trying to make money during the latter days of the Slave Trade and is clearly none too keen to be in the army. Berbice is a region of the Berbice River in present day Guyana]

This Evening I received the following Letter from Thomas Hodgson.................

William Fleming, Esq.

Berbice Nov.12th 1807

Dear Sir,

By the present Opportunity I have wrote my Mother requesting the loan of Five hundred pounds, this Sum she will not have at Hand when this is presented her, the present therefore is to intreat your Afsistance in enabling her to procure it, and advising her to advancing it, in which Case I have a very good Prospect of gaining a Competency in a very Few Years. By purchasing jointly with my Friend William Dodgson Esq. Negroes to the Amount of one Thousand pounds say fifteen which are to be hired upon his Estate for 12 months at 2s/6d per Day each as seasoning and learning their future Work, they then will be formed into a Taskgan [?] with some other Negroes to be to be purchased with Money earned during their 12 mos. *[months]* say 213£. 7s..6d a Taskgan of 20 will upon a moderate Calculation bring us in 1000£ Sterling, that Money laid out in the same Way will very soon place me among the independent.

In fact if you comply with my most ardent Wish there is no Obstacle in the Way that can possibly prevent it, my personal Attendance upon them in the Field will be necessary and am now learning my Business as a planter and Cultivator of Cotton under the Idea that my wish will be complied with which may be easily done if you wou'd have the Goodness to lend me your Interest I should imagine that my Mother wou'd have at least 150£ by her in 6 mos.

You might advance 150£ and afsist my Mother in borrowing the remainding 200£ for which I would give you any security on my future property you think necessary, I beg most ardently your Afsistance in this last Effort of mine, and depend upon it your Confidence shall not be abused, its melancholy to even think upon a man spending his Youth in this Country without the least prospect of putting any up for old Age. without a Little Money here there is none to be made here and with a little an immense Fortune is soon accumlated.

I shall of course allow you the regular Interest of borrowed Money in this Country say 6 per Cent which shall be regularly sent yearly – there is only one Guineaman expected here before the Abolition takes place here consequently have only that Opportunity of purchasing New Negroes -----

She's expected here in about a Month when Mr D........ will purchase 15 and when I must give Bills for the Amount of my Half which I suppose will come due in about June next, I shall draw on you for the Amount, but I would rather that you paid it into some respectable House in Liverpool and request them to write me to Value on them for it in which Case I might get 6 Mo. Credit for 4 or 5 Negroes.

Mr Dodgson writes my Mother to which Letter I refer you to Mr. John Todd might perhaps be prevailed upon to advance the 200£, however it must be procured, I would willingly sacrifice all my Expectancy from Lanthwaite & Co. [?] than mifs this Opportunity of trying what Fortune had in Store for me.

Mr.Thos. Dodgson will likely call on you upon this Business – for God Sake don't let your Letter plead poverty but let it give me the pleasing Tidings of the Money being forthcoming - & believe me it shall ever be remembered with Gratitude on the Contrary, I immediately go into the Army---write me by the packet, 2 Duplicates send to Mr. Edward Myers Liverpool to be forwarded to the Fleet & a running Vessel –

I expect a Commission out for an Ensign in a Few Weeks, it went to England in the Chiswick 21st. Augt for Sanction, Consequently is of the greatest Consequence that shou'd know the Issue whether I am to be planter or Soldier ----I hope your Mo. S. - *[Mother, Sister]* Wife and children are all well give my Respects to them and believe me,

Your Friend and well wisher,

Thos. Hodgson

[The Abolition of Slavery Act, passed in the British parliament, became law on 25th March 1807, though it would

be nearly another thirty years before slavery was finally abolished throughout the British Empire. Sadly it would seem, slavery, illegally continues to this day]

20th (Wednesday) - the Hills in Cumberland & Westmorland of which we have a distant prospect appear cover deep with Snow if one may judge from their apparent Smoothness.

21st (Thursday) - Potatoes at Ufton *[Uverston]* Market this Day advanced to 8d per Hoop and Butter to 15d per lb of 16oz - Consulted Mrs Hodgson & Jno. *[John]* Todd with Regard to the Letter received a Day or two ago, by the Diana, from her Son Thomas Hodgson at Berbice but they both declined having any thing to do in the Business; of Consequence, when I find the Mother and Trustee unwilling to lend the least Assistance, I judge it would be highly imprudent in me, who am ignorant of his Affairs and Situation, to advance him the Money unless I had ample Security for the principal and Interest . Besides a Report has reached us from Liverpool that more than twelve Months ago, he married a Daughter of the Edward Myers, a Cabinet maker at Brownlow Hill, Liverpool mentioned in our Letters, but of this matrimonial connection he did not yet think proper, though his conscience must frequently have reminded him that it was his Duty, to inform his Mother.

This and the Representation of her being a gay Lady and living in an expensive Stile, such as the present of her Husband is by no Means adequate to the Support of, may have some Shew of a Cause why his nearest Relatives are backwards in supplying him with the Money he requests from them. They may fear too that his promises and Schemes may like many of his before, be broken and fall to the Ground.

22nd (Friday) - Some Blossom bursting out upon the Orleans plumbs particularly Wall Trees.

23rd (Saturday) - Unhealthy Weather -

25th (Monday) - Some oats early sown are appearing.

26th (Tuesday) - Saw a Swallow this Morning, for the first Time this Season, and it is remarkable that the Fieldfares have not yet taken their Departure.

27th (Wednesday) - The fair at Broughton this Day was well attended but the Cattle fell in price full 20s. Owing probably to the Scarcity of Grass and prospect of a late Spring. The Fields in general are as bare as they were two months ago, and Hay is not plentiful and now sells at 12d and 14d per Stone. Lamb at Ulverston last thursday, which was the first this Season, sold at one shilling per lb – Butter at 15d per lb.

28th (Thursday) - The Fair at Dalton this Day was much the same as at Broughton Yesterday, and few Cattle were sold.

29th (Friday) - Mr. Harrison began to cut his Rape for Green Fodder – Caught some Trouts.

30th (Saturday) - Went to Kirkby pool to angle: caught some sea Fish and Trouts, but was driven off by the Rain about 10am which continued about 3 hours.

MAY [1808]

3rd (Tuesday) - Attended the comissary *[commissary]* at Ulverston and took the Oath of churchwarden for pennington together with John winder, the Farmer at Lowfield House, without any opposition from the Revd. John Sunderland the Vicar, who was present - Received from Mr Dowbiggin, the Register, Eleven Briefs, four for Conflagrations [?] and Seven for Churches and Chapels, all which I delivered to Mr Walker the curate of pennington. -

It is a custom, continued from Time immemorial, for the old and new Churchwardens and the Minister to dine at this Time at Ulverston at the Expence of the parish – the Few fine Days we have experienced lately; have made a considerable Change in the Fields; the Grain has made it's Appearance and the Hedges are clothed in Green; the Cuckow too lends his repeated Note to enliven the pleasant but too dry Weather. -

4th (Wednesday) - Intolerably hot & sultry with very little Wind from the South West.

5th (Thursday) - Grain advanced in price at our Market this Day.

6th (Friday) - 10th (Tuesday) - *[Fleming visits Ulverston churchyard – To be continued]*

11th (Wednesday) - Grass now springs up quick and Ground in good Condition, has got well covered already, tho' lately so bare.

12th (Thursday) - Grain advanced greatly at Ulverston Market this Morning; potatoes too were at an Average 8d per Hoop: - Early Cabbage – 1 and a half pence each – Hens – 18d each – Beef and Mutton – 7d per lb – Veal – 6d – Lamb – 12d. Butter – 14d – Eggs 14 for 6d.

13th (Friday) - Rape or Cole, which was sown last Autumn for Spring Feed, is now in full Bloom and looks beautiful. This Crop is of great Value to those who cultivate, as it may be sown after the Grain is reaped, and if the Ground be in good condition will produce an abundant Crop which comes for Spring Fodder after the Turnips are eaten off. I have only seen two Fields, about Half an Acre each, of it in Furness, but it certainly deserves to be more noticed – the price of the Seed is about 4d or 5d per lb.

14th (Saturday) - 16th (Monday) - *[Fleming visits Ulverston churchyard – To be continued]*

17th (Tuesday) - The Sale of Furniture of the late Geo. Lowry at Ulverston, commenced Yesterday and ended this Day. I purchased one green Wire lodging Room Fender with a Brass Top, price nine shillings – and 6 stained Chairs of Ash, with rounded Backs, price 5/3 each – both the Chairs & Fender are at Mrs 'H' Ulverstone.

[The bloodsport of cockfighting continues - at Ulverston]

18th (Wednesday) - The first Day's fight of a Main of Cocks in the Assembly Room at Ulverston. William Benn of Middleton Place in Cumberland against Mefs *[Messrs]* Tolming, King, Shaw, and Harrison of Ulverstone, for one Guinea a Battle, and five Guineas the Main.

Benn one Battle a Head in the Main at the Close of the Day's Light – Barbarous Amusement.

19th (Thursday) - This is the Second Day's Fight of the Main Benn got all the battles except two. The Admittance to the pit is five shillings a day for each person and Yesterday amounted to about 18 £ -

This Day near to 40 £. Grain advanced greatly at our Market this Day, but potatoes were something lower, and I never saw the Market so abundantly suppl'd. -

20th (Friday) - Went to Dendron to shoot Rooks - The last Day's Fight of the Main which terminated greatly in favour of Benn. The receipt of pit Money this Day added to the two Former amounted to upwards of seventy pounds.

22nd (Sunday) - Hay Grass promises to be abundant.

23rd (Monday) - James Huddleston removed from his Father's House at roosecot *[Roosecote]* to my Farm at Rowe. -

26th (Thursday) - The Blossom which is abundant on most kinds of Fruit Trees appears to set well and promises to afford plenty of Fruit, if the Weather be favorable.

27th (Friday) - Exceeding heavy Rain in the Night and all this Day, so that the Brooks which were almost dry now overflow their Banks and flood much of the Hay Grass contiguous; the Wind blowing strong and cold from the South East -

28th (Saturday) - John Hodgson's Birthday -

31st (Tuesday) - Prices: - Oats 16s. Barley – 15s. per Bush. - Wheat £3 per load – Beef 7d. - Mutton – 7d. - Veal – 6d. - Lamb – 8d. Per lb. - potatoes 7d. per Hoop – Cabbages 1d. Each – Oatmeal – 26s. per cwt –

Flour -37s per cwt . The Rent of a Cotage *[Cottage]* from £3 to £5. Cattle continue to sell low – good Horses are high. Land from £2 to £6 per Acre according to the Quality and Condition. Fowls – 10d. Each – young Ducks – 14d ea. - Eggs 5d per Dozen – Butter 1s. Per lb of 16 oz.

JUNE ¹⁸⁰⁸

2nd (Thursday) - Fine Weather for the Crops of Grain and Hay which promise Abundance: the prospect is consoling to the poorer Class, who now are in some Measure distressed by the high prices of every kind of provisions.

[Fleming mentions Barrow in this next entry. In his day it was a village on the area now known as The Strand, Barrow-in-Furness, before the coming of the railways and the town's expansion into shipbuilding. A good time, by all accounts, in celebrating the king's birthday!]

4th (Saturday) - This being the King's Birthday, a Number of Gentleman met at Barrow, according to Custom to celebrate this day and got most loyally drunk, repeating their wishes for his Majesty's Health till their legs forgot their Duty and their Tongues could only utter Lisps of Loyalty.

In the Ulverston Library I this Day purchased the share belonging to the late George Coward, and applied to the Librarian that my Name might be stuck up in the Library for the Approbation of the Comitte *[Committee]* that I might have the Liberty of taking and Reading what Books I thought proper, after the 8th. of June Inst.

The Anniversary being always held on the second Wednesday in June, when the Numbers dine together and elect a committee to transact the Business of the ensuing Year – Soulby, Librarian -

Yesterday the Revd. Richard Postlethwaite, Rector of Roche, in Cornwall, dined with me, and requested my signature as a subscriber to his Fundamentum Latinitalis or Grammar of the Latin Tongue, to be published by Subscription, price 5s bound – in this, Mr. Postlethwaite, informs me, he intends to correct the Errors and avoid the Improprieties of other Latin Grammarians; to make the Rules as simple and concise as possible: clearly to explain the Rhetorical Figures, and to give a full Account of the metrical Art to facilitate Versification -

How far he may succeed, I know not, being a perfect Stranger to him, but from what I saw of him, and from his conversation, I am led to pronounce that he is very deeply linctured with Methodism, and not competent to the Task he has undertaken, though he is extremely guarded in speaking, he uttered many grammatical Inaccuracies , and made some improper Applications of Terms ; though he was particularly careful in his choice of Words and spoke exceeding delibirately. -

5th (Sunday) - For some Time past great Numbers of Herrings have been caught near Whitehaven, some of which were brought to our Market and sold at 1 and a half d each.

6th (Monday) - Some heavy Showers of Rain in the Morning which hindered the Country People from Attending the Sick Clubs at Ulverstone in such Numbers as usual; (but the Day was more after Dinner and continued fine with the Wind from the West:)

There are three Sick Clubs at Ulverstone, viz, the Friendly Society – the Amicable Society – and the Union Club. -

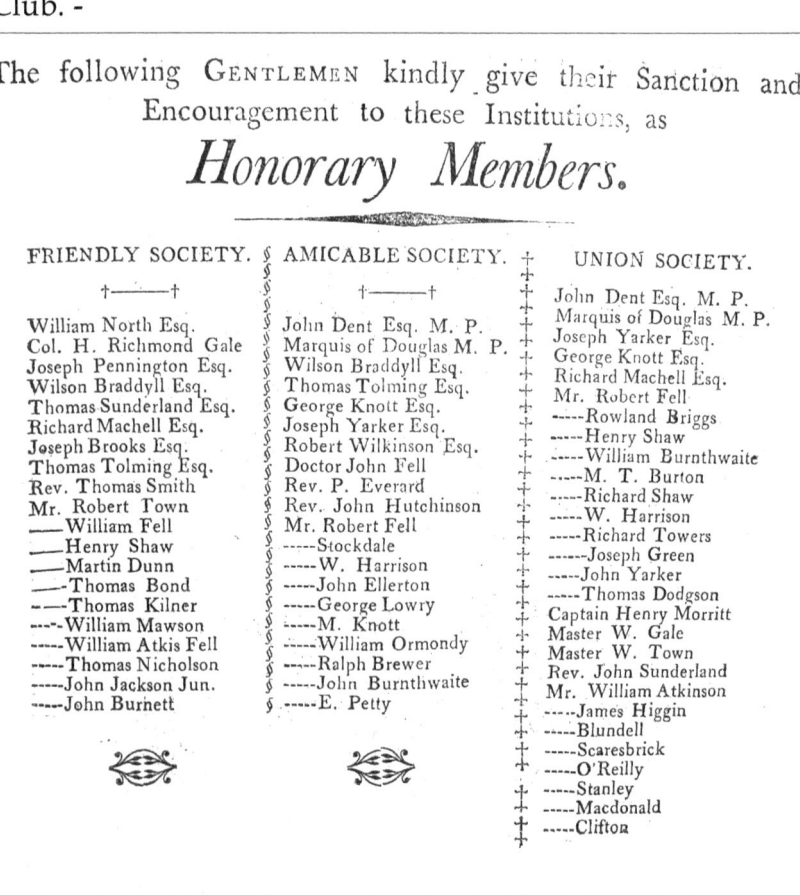

The following GENTLEMEN kindly give their Sanction and Encouragement to these Institutions, as

Honorary Members.

FRIENDLY SOCIETY.	AMICABLE SOCIETY.	UNION SOCIETY.
†———†	†———†	John Dent Esq. M. P.
William North Esq.	John Dent Esq. M. P.	Marquis of Douglas M. P.
Col. H. Richmond Gale	Marquis of Douglas M. P.	Joseph Yarker Esq.
Joseph Pennington Esq.	Wilson Braddyll Esq.	George Knott Esq.
Wilson Braddyll Esq.	Thomas Tolming Esq.	Richard Machell Esq.
Thomas Sunderland Esq.	George Knott Esq.	Mr. Robert Fell
Richard Machell Esq.	Joseph Yarker Esq.	-----Rowland Briggs
Joseph Brooks Esq.	Robert Wilkinson Esq.	-----Henry Shaw
Thomas Tolming Esq.	Doctor John Fell	-----William Burnthwaite
Rev. Thomas Smith	Rev. P. Everard	-----M. T. Burton
Mr. Robert Town	Rev. John Hutchinson	-----Richard Shaw
----William Fell	Mr. Robert Fell	-----W. Harrison
----Henry Shaw	-----Stockdale	-----Richard Towers
----Martin Dunn	-----W. Harrison	-----Joseph Green
----Thomas Bond	-----John Ellerton	-----John Yarker
----Thomas Kilner	-----George Lowry	-----Thomas Dodgson
----William Mawson	-----M. Knott	Captain Henry Morritt
-----William Atkis Fell	-----William Ormondy	Master W. Gale
-----Thomas Nicholson	-----Ralph Brewer	Master W. Town
-----John Jackson Jun.	-----John Burnthwaite	Rev. John Sunderland
-----John Burnett	-----E. Petty	Mr. William Atkinson
		----James Higgin
		-----Blundell
		-----Scaresbrick
		-----O'Reilly
		-----Stanley
		-----Macdonald
		-----Clifton

Honorary Members of the Sick Clubs – Soulby Collection

7th (Tuesday) - One Sick Club at Dalton hold their anniversary this Day; the Members are not very numerous. -

8th (Wednesday) - Dined with Members of the Ulverston Library, of one hundred and four Members only twenty six dined: the Dinner was provided by Worthington at the Sun Inn, the expence was 3/6 each.

9th (Thursday) - Extremely fine & warm. The fair this day attended by amazing numbers of young people, but the young men were not so quarrelsome as frequently happened.

11th (Saturday) - the anniversary and sale of the Books at the Dalton Book Club, of which I am a Member, was held this Day, Mr. Shaw of Lindal in the Chair – Expence of the Dinner and Liquor was 5/- each. -

Mrs. Hodgson's Birthday, 49

12th (Sunday) - Dined with Mr John Case. Yesterday John Woodburn of Croglane, the younger, married Margaret Lowry, one of the Daughters of the late George Lowry of Ulverstone, sailmaker; they were married at Cartmel and dined at Lowick Hall where they intend to reside.

13th (Monday) - This Day dined with Rd. Cleator at Dalton.

14th (Tuesday) - The Coal Company at the South of Adgarley are got to the Depth of 106 Yards, but have not yet been so fortunate as meet with a Band sufficiently deep to work -

A New Iron Ore Company consisting of William Townson of Whinfield, John Thompson of Lindal and Mathew Harrison of Newland have begun to sink a shaft in the Gillrow near the Turnpike Gate in Pennington, they are now at the Depth of about nine yards but have not met with any Ore, though I am of Opinion they will be successful if Water does *[Fleming must mean 'doesn't']* hinder them from sinking to a proper Depth.

15th (Wednesday) - Mr. Jo. Yarker drilling Turnips upon the new inclosed Land on Flan Hill. -

16th (Thursday) – Dr. Harrison began to mow his Hay Grass, which is the first in the Neighbourhood of Ulverston; near Hoad Stile; it consisted of Clover and Oat Grass.

[Note the following letter. Many people in Ulverston are aware of Ulverstone, Tasmania, but here is another Ulverston! Further correspondence from Thomas Hodgson]

17th (Friday) - Received the following letter from Thomas Hodgson.

Pl: Ulverston, Corrantien Coast, Berbice.

Dear Sir,

I wrote you from the Neptune on the 8th Feb last to which beg your reference, since which I have some arrangements in Land & Negroes and nothing is wanting but your own letter to me that the sum of £500 will be forthcoming or Leave to draw on you for that sum at 6 months after sight, which will extend the Time to at least next Feby when I have no Doubt but it will be every way convenient for you to procure the above Sum for which I will send you any Security on my future property you deem needful.

I have every Reason to believe you and my Mother will use all your Interest in putting me in a Way of making a little money which with your joint Assistance and my own Exertions will put the Question beyond a Doubt – We have had one of the wettest Seasons ever known here, a complete Deluge ever since November last.

Of course the Cotton crops is much injured, however the Weather seems to have cleaned up in which case we shall make a good second crop.

You will have the Goodness to forward my Cloase [*Clothes*] if not already done as soon as possible to Mr. Edward Myers St. Ann Street, Islington, Liverpool you may also send 12 Boxes of Candles a box or two of Hams, 2 casks of Old Brewery Ale, a few pieces of chicks [?] and some good Shoes and Sportsman's Boots that lace up to the ankle, a Trunk of Stockings and Negro Hats all of which I can command an immediate sale for and payment by Return of the Vefel [*Vessel*] if you would send me a keg of good Nuts I will return it with Coffee this 11d per lb here - I have not had the pleasure of receiving a line from Ulverston since I left Liverpool, however I flatter myself to hear from you by the Jane which is expected next. Pray give my Duty to my Mother and Respects to all Friends whom I trust are all in good Health and remain.

Dear Sir
Yrs. Very truly
T. H.

[Thomas Hodgson's letter is sent from Ulverston, in what is present day East Berbice – Corentyne, Guyana. There are also villages or towns called Lancaster, Liverpool and Manchester in this region. There follows a post script to this letter]

Send me 2 Coats & 1 Coatee without Linen in Sleeves. 6 white Jeanes Jack made to answer the purpose of Waistcoats if you send *[good?]* two or three doz. of Jeanes Linen an Calico Trowsers I can dispose of them at least at advance of 100 per 6£ and also request the Favour from my Mother or your Wife of a 1 case of preserves put up in white Sugar & 1 Case of pickles for Mrs Dodgson who is one of the most amiable Women in the Country.

Mr. Dodgson has wrote to my Mother will you have the Goodness to answer it, and according to his Wish as you may inform my Mother I can admit of no Excuse as I am confident the Money can be procured with Ease

T. H.

20th (Monday) - Herrings plentiful in our Market at Ulverston brought from Whitehaven and the Coast of Cumberland, where they are caught in abundance, the price of them is 18d per Dozen.

21st (Tuesday) - the Farmers are beginning to be busy making Hay which is an abundant Crop. -

22nd (Wednesday) - Weather extremely hot

23rd (Thursday) - Fine and hot Weather continues but is too dry for the Farmers who have not sown their Turnips; the Wind moderate and going round with the Sun.

25th (Saturday) - Fruit will not be plentiful this year and in particular prove a failing Crop; but Grain of every kind looks Well and promises an abundant supply: at present it sells at extravagant prices. -

27th (Monday) - Oats 17/6d per Bushel – Wheat 3...3...0 per load Barley, of which little remains, 17/- per Bushel – Old potatoes – 8d per Hoop – New Do. 3d per pound – Butter 13d per lb – Beef and Lamb 8d – Veal – 6d – Salmon 14d per lb. Eggs 12d per Dozen. - peas 18d per Hoop in the Shells -

28th (Tuesday) - Herrings continue, plentiful, and great Numbers are taken at the Entrance of the River Duddon. The price is reduced to 1d a piece.

30th (Thursday) - There is an encampment upon the Height of Blackcomb *[Black Combe]* consisting of Eleven persons who are making a new Survey of England.

[Fleming is referring to engineers carrying out the great triangulation survey of Britain, in other words, the Ordnance Survey. This was the first accurate survey of the north of England, led by Lieutenant Colonel William Mudge, 1762 – 1820, Surveyor and military engineer. He was alluded to by William Wordsworth in his poem 'Written with a Slate Pencil, on a Stone, on the Side of the Mountain of Black Comb' first published in 1815]

[Lt. Col. Mudge had a half-brother, Zachary Mudge, who served in the Royal Navy and whose many exploits

William Mudge

were reported by the London Gazette, including, capturing a Spanish lugger and a cutter off the coast of Vigo, Spain in June 1801]

Prices: Old potatoes 7d. Per Hoop – New ones 1d. Per lb. - peas 10d. Per Hoop. Salmon 12d. Per lb. Salmon Trout 6d to 7d per lb. Butter 10d to 12d per lb. - Beef 8d – Mutton & Lamb 7d – Veal – 5 and a half Eggs 8d per Dozen – Ducks – 16d ea. Lead Shot 10s per Bag of 28lb – Powder 3 to 4s per pound.

JULY 1808

2nd (Saturday) - Hay grass sold in public Sale in the course of last Week brought on an average 18/6 per cart which with the Making and Carting Home, it [is] estimated at 4 ' per Cart, will cost the purchasers £1...2s...6d per Cart.

3rd (Sunday) - plenty of Salmon Trout at Ulverston this Morning, brought from Ravenglass and Duddon, the price 7d. per pound.

4th (Monday) - The Smallpox brought into Ulverston by some Beggars.

6th (Wednesday) - The Farmers are now near the Height of their Haymaking and busy as Ants, expecting Harvest at no great Distance; and if the Weather continue as at present, we shall, in all probability, see much Grain cut early in August if not before, for the greatest part of it has been completley headed for some Time, and after a little Rain will soon be ripe.

7th (Thursday) - The assessed Taxes paid at Ulverston to a Mr Richardson from Lowther, Steward to Lord Lonsdale.

8th (Friday) - The property tax in Furness paid this Day to the above mentioned Richardson. - Lord Muncaster held a Court at the House of his Bailiff for the Manor, at the Mill – I had a Deputation as Gamekeeper for the s.d. *[second?]* Manor granted me this Day by Lord Muncaster.

9th (Saturday) - Book Club at Dalton -

The Coal Company near Dendron have bored there to the Depth of one Hundred and fifteen Yards, but have not yet found a Seam worth sinking for: they have begun also near Gleaston Mill. -

11th (Monday) - Early potatoes sold at 10d per Hoop of Six Pounds.

12th (Tuesday) - Went to Jobb for Eels in the pool below the Cottonworks at Lund Becks; caught 6 lbs.

The best Time is at the first flowing up of the Tide, then these Fish are ravenous of their prey and are best taken. As we stood on the Bank, exposed to the burning Rays of the Mid Day Sun, I recollected the Definition of a Bait Fisher, I think by Swift ....

[Jonathan Swift – Born 1667 – Died 1745. Author of 'Gulliver's Travels' that it is ' a Stick and a Line with a worm at one End and a Fool at the other ']

I double felt the Force of the Observation for the Fish
not being in Season, are not worth the Trouble of taking.

14th (Thursday) - Still hotter than Yesterday and
relaxing the Body so much as to make it almost
incapable of any Exertion ..'

15th (Friday) - At about one o'clock this Morning there
was much Lightening and soon after very loud thunder
with heavy Rain. It continued at Intervals the greatest
part of the Day but it was the loudest and the flashes
most vivid in the Evening.

17th (Sunday) - Mr. Knott is begun to sink a pit in the
Cowpark, near Roosbeck in Expectation of finding Coals
there.

19th (Tuesday) - Fisher & Co. have left Gleaston and
begun to bore in a fresh place near Stainton. I am afraid
they will not succeed in finding Coals, they Change
plans so often and try so feebly in all but the first where
they have bored to a cosiderable Depth.

20th (Wednesday) - Went to Rampside to try a Mullet
Net of a new Construction but did not succeed in taking
fish the afternoon was so stormy.

21st (Thursday) - Fowls – 16d. ea. Ducks – 18d. ea.
Salmon - 9d. Per lb. Beef – 7d. - Mutton – 6d. - Lamb –
6d. - Butter – 11d. per lb.

22nd (Friday) - Haytime begins to be tedious from
the sudden and heavy Showers which have taken the
Farmers unawares, for a Few Days past, and hindered
them from finishing their Hay. -

23rd (Saturday) - Employ'd Workmen to remove
the Rubbish from the North Side of the Church at
pennington to make the Wall dry, by means of a Trench
to take off the Water which falls from the Roof, and
hitherto has been suffered to sink into the Wall from the
Earth on the outside being two yards above the Floor of
the Church within. -

24th (Sunday) - Henry Noble the Farmer at Churchstile
was interred at Dalton on Thursday the 21st. Age – 90 –
His Father died Age – 94 – his Grandfather – Age – 104
and his Great Grandfather 115 -

25th (Monday) - Compleated the Drain at Pennington
Church in cutting through the Rubbish, which consisted
of Lime and old Mortar mixed with Stones, and appears
to be the Remains of the ancient Church which was
suffered to fall to Ruin and of which the North Wall of
the present Structure is the only Remaining part, except
the Great Door Case, we found a Wall two yards thick
running North & South adjoining, to, but not connected
with the North wall of the Church : We removed this
old Wall and near it found the Head of an Image of red
freestone in a handsomely curled freestone Wig, and a
piece of Copper much corroded with the impression of
a rude Anchor stamped upon it, on the Reverse nothing
appeared.

26th (Tuesday) - Began to make a Gravel Walk from the
Gate of the Churchyard at pennington to the porch.

27th (Wednesday) - Yesterday Evening William
Postlethwaite, my late Farmer at Rowe sold his Offgoing
Crop of Barley in little Carley and the larger Dale in
Templands, at the Rate of twelve Guineas an Acre:

It was supposed to have about 17 Bushels on the Acre, and the next Year's price probably may be about 15/6d or 16s. The Straw Chaff will pay the Wages of reaping and thrashing except Labourers are very high.

The Harvest will commence about the End of the first Week in August. -

28th (Thursday) - Farmers who did not finish their Hay in the first fine Season are now very busy carting the remaining part in Expectation that Harvest will commence before their Turnips are all hoed, for which dry Days are the most suitable. -

29th (Friday) - The Fields of Grain in this Neighbourhood , but Barley in particular, has now begun to acquire the golden tinge, and will soon require every Exertion of the Farmers: Wheat, I am afraid, will not answer their Expectations, as I have observed some Fields much mildewed, and if the Weather prove wet in the Beginning of August, probably much of it will be unsound. -

30th (Saturday) - Went to inspect a Tree near Bardsea which was struck by Lightening a Few Days ago and retained evident Marks of its dreadful Effects. It had struck the Body of the Tree about 18 Feet from the Ground and pierced it through, then had taken a spiral Direction to the Root and entered the Ground, which it had plowed up in a Tangent to the Circular Body of the Tree at the Surface of the Earth. In its Circuit down the Tree it had made a kind of Groove, which with the discolouring of the Bark perfectly shewed the Direction it had taken. -

This Morning a person by the Name of Sanders, the pupil of Ben: Taylor the noted Bonesetter and his successor in that profession, came from Penrith to Ufton *[Uston or Ulverston]* and put right some Bones in My Son's Foot, which had been dislocated by a negligent Servant. -

31st (Sunday) - The following remarkably fine Day, I hope, indicates a speedy Return of dry Weather, which is now greatly desirable that the Crops may be well fed and got Home in due Season.

Prices: Wheat -£3 per load – Oats 14/6d per Bushel – potatoes 8d 18d ? per Hoop – peas – 8d – Beans 4 and a half pence per Hoop in the pods – Gooseberries 1s. Currants 14d per Hoop – Mushrooms to pickle 4d per Quart – Cucumbers to pickle 3s per 100 – Beef – 8d – Mutton – 7d – Lamb – 7d – Salmon – 9d –

Salmon Trout – 6d per lb . Coccles *[Cockles]* 9d per Hoop – Chickens – 14d ea. Ducks – 15d ea. - Oatmeal 26s. Per Cwt. Fresh Herrings 1s. Per Doz. Shot – 7/6d per Bag of 28lb . - Gunpowder 3/6 per lb. - Game Licence £3...4...0d – Dogs for Game 11/6d Tax per Dog – Sheep Dogs 7s per Dog. -

AUGUST [1808]

1st (Monday) - The Fair this Day at Broughton was well attended and the Few Cattle that were sold fetched something higher prices than lately – New Barley Bread there. - This Day Joseph Yarker began to wrap his Oats upon Flan Hill near Ulverston, which are the first cut in this Neighbourhood; yet if the Weather prove fine much will be ready for the Sickle in the Course of next Week

2nd (Tuesday) - Went to Dalton but saw no Grain near ripe – the Turnips there look very full, but some are rather late. -

3rd (Wednesday) - Mr Yarker carted his Oats and trashed [threshed] some for the Market at Ulverston Tomorrow -

4th (Thursday) - Mr. Yarker sold his new Oats in the Market today at 12/6d per Bushel -

[Recipe for making Yeast – See 'FOOD AND DRINK RECIPIES' in the Appendices]

5th (Friday) - Went to inspect the new Bridge at Rathmoss which is not yet finished.

6th (Saturday) - The Grain ripens remarkably fast and promises a ready Harvest; no Doubt some of the Farmers on the Sea Coast will want a number of Reapers the latter end of next Week.

7th (Sunday) - Early this afternoon a Boy of the Name of Watson Apprentice to William Gibson shoemaker in Ulverston was drowned on Leven Sands when bathing with his Companions who were not able to save his life.

[A tragedy reported by Fleming at the newly erected mill on Walney]

10th (Wednesday) - On Saturday last the Millar *[Miller]* at the Wind Mill lately erected at North End in the Isle of Walney, had his Hand crushed in the Mill and probably will lose all his Fingers. -

The Windmill at North Scale, Walney Island

11th (Thursday) - There has seldom been more Grain at Ulverstone Market than appeared this Day; it's being rather on the Decline makes the Farmers bring out their old Store before the markets are well supply'd with this Year's produce, which no Doubt will bring down the prices considerably.

12th (Friday) - This being the first Day of Grouse Shooting this Season, I went upon pennington, Kirkby and Gosthwaite Moors to shoot; there were as many Shooters as Birds and a good Number were killed by some of the Gentlemen but most of them returned without a single Bird: I killed 3 and a half Brace and one Snipe which were as many as any single Gentleman killed: from the Excessive Heat both Dogs and Men were completley done up before the Close of Day; I returned Home about 3 in the afternoon. -

13th (Saturday) - The Farmers were fortunate who Yesterday Housed their Wheat, and much of the early cut was got in, tho' there was no prospect of change, no opportunity of this Sort should be neglected.

14th (Sunday) - Appearance of Change, which made many Farmers, though it was the Sabbath Day, begin to cart their Wheat as soon as the Service for the Morning was performed. The Rain came on about 5 o'Clock in the Evening. -

Reapers at Dalton this Day were hired at 6s. Per Day & Meat, Drink and Lodging: last Week, not so many were wanted, and the Wages were only about 4s. Per Day –Never were Currants and Gooseberries more plentiful than they have been this year; Cherries were in abundance, but Apples, Pears, and Plumbs are not in general so great a Crop, yet they are not to be complained of; though the Sun did not favour us with a peep at his ruddy Face last Christmas Day, the Crops of Fruit have not failed us, thanks to the Director [?] of that great Luminary, for causing the old women to prophecy falsely. - Revd. J.S. at pennington .

15th (Monday) - The Harvest now at the busiest period. Went upon the Moors to shoot and killed 4 Brace of Grouse, which make in all 7 and a half Brace of which I gave 1 to MG [?] - Do.*[Ditto]* to Mr. Redhead.

16th (Tuesday) - William Kellet of Hawcoat married Nancy Hunter Daughter of James Hunter Farmer at Tytup on Monday 8th Inst. -

17th (Wednesday) - Went on the Moors this Morning and killed one Grouse & 1 Dotterel *[A small wader - a member of the plover family]* upon pennington Moor. -

18th (Thursday) - The promising fine Weather and abundant Crops have been the Cause of Grain becoming much lower today than it has been, and Oatmeal is fallen from 26s. Per Cwt to 23s. In Consequence; Flour too has suffered a propotianate Depression.

19th (Friday) - A Cargo of Herrings came this Morning from the Ifle of Mann [Isle of Man] and were sold at one penny a piece; what an amazing Sum of Money they wou'd make, for people were very eager to buy them at the price.

20th (Saturday) - Yesterday Hannah Walton, Widow of Edward Walton late of Loppergarth, was buried at Pennington. I have frequently heard it observed that there is seldom a Funeral in this parish, but is soon followed by another, which now has proved so. - S. Grouse this Day. 8 and a half Brace.

21st (Sunday) - The Reapers at Dalton this Day were generally hired at 5/3d per Day with Meat, Drink and Lodging for the ensuing Week; but it has been, and still continues the Custom here, when the Rain won't allow the Reapers to labour in the Fields, the Farmer finds them Meat and Lodging, but pays them no Wages, except they be hired for wet and dry Weather, in which Case the Wages are generally lower.

22nd (Monday) - Fine and dry and favourable for the Reapers.

23rd (Tuesday) - Went to Conishead Bank to catch Eels and took five pound Weigh.

24th (Wednesday) - Favourable Weather for the Wheat Crop, which is generally got off the Fields:

Went this Afternoon to shoot Grouse upon Gothwaite

[Gawthwaite] Moor and found the Game exceeding Shy; killed one and Half Brace, which make the whole of Grouse killed by me this Season no more than 10 Brace, but this Species of Game is become extremely scarce upon the Moors, and probably in a Few Years will be entirely destroyed.

25th (Thursday) - Grain of every sort at Ulverston Market this Day was rather on the Advance. New Oats fetched 13/- and old Oats 13/9d per Bushel. -

A Cargo of Herrings from the Isle of Mann came here this Afternoon & were sold at 13 for one shilling.

[Fleming now describes a fascinating walk with a friend from Pennington to the shores of Lake Windermere]

26th (Friday) - Mr. Case, merchant in Liverpool, under the Firm of Case & Murray, came here last Night, and this Morning at 5 o' clock, we set out, pedestrians, to the Regatta on Windermere Lake, by the Way of Ulverston; we pafsed *[passed]* Newland, where there is a Furnace for smelting Iron Ore: the Ground around this place was lately a common of little Value but is now

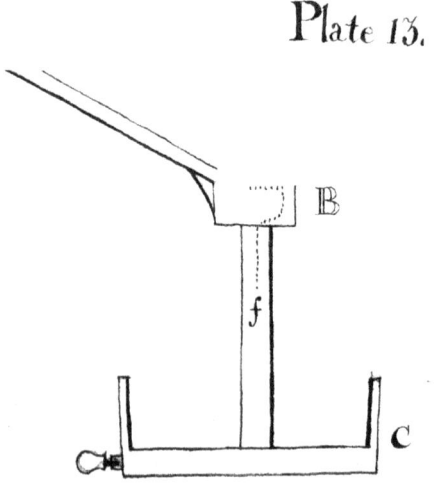

Plate 13.

Close's Lamp - (Letters, description and diagrams of 'Close's Lamp' sent to Mr. Nicholson of 'The Philosophical Journal' by William Close, Surgeon at Dalton-in-Furness).

enclosed & cultivated bearing abundant Crops of Grain.

Along a good Road, we pass'd by Arrad Foot and along the Bank of a deep and broad Ditch or Drain, cut last year for the purpose of carrying off the Water from the new Enclosures between this place and Newland, till we came to Greenodd, where we crofsed the River in a Ferry Boat at the Confluence of the Crake and Leven, the Fare was 2d. Each. After crossing the Water our Road lay along the Banks of the River which flows down from the Lake of Windermere till we

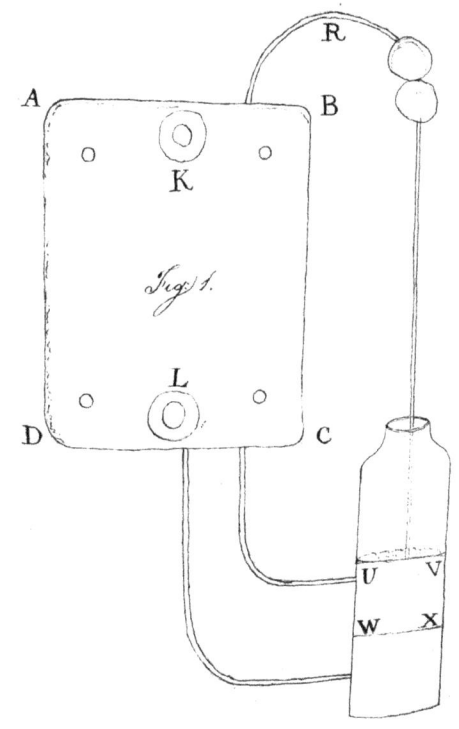

Mr John Fell for many years Surgeon in Ulverston made the following communication to Mr. Nicholson , to be inserted in ' The Philosophical Journal ' for April 1799 . A diagram of a pocket Ribbon Machine for charging a small coated phial with Electricity.

arrived at Low Wood, whither this River is Navigable; a Vefsel loaden with Coals was laying at the Wharf ready to discharge her Cargo.

At Low Wood, besides the Iron Works, there are Mills for making Gunpowder, lately erected by a person of the Name of Barker, who was a partner in the Cotton Works at Backbarrow:

At the Mills we cross the River to the North Side, over a handsome Bridge, lately erected, a little to the West of the wooden old Bridge, which is still standing but not used: we then follow the Course of the River along the North Bank till we come to Backbarrow, where besides the Furnace for smelting Iron ore and the Forge for making it malleable there is an extensive Cotton Mill and much Business was lately done there by the Firm of Birch & Robinson, who about a Month ago were made Bankrupts: the Business is now carried on by the Creditors.

At Backbarrow we again crossed the River to the South Bank and soon arrived at Newby Bridge, where there is a good Inn, the Sign, a Swan; *[The Swan, a 17th century coaching inn has grown dramatically into the large hotel seen today]* we kept along the East Side of the Lake and passed a charming Seat at Fellfoot, belonging to Jeremiah Dixon, Esq. one of the Justices of the peace for Lancashire, whence an excellent Road led us at a little Distance from the Lake, of which we had diversified and beautiful prospects, of the grand Scenery with which the Banks of the Lake are Furnished, we also had perfect Views in pleasing Variety, but there I find, who are accustomed to these beautiful Scenes, are incapable of admiring their Grandeur and their Eyes are more delighted with a View of the plain Grounds of Low Furness waving with abundant Crops of Yellow Grain.

In our Walk along the Banks of the Lake, I observed many plants which are not produced in Low Furness and of which I shou'd have been glad to make some Remarks, had this been the Season for Bottanizing but I had not with me, either Withering, or any means of conveying those which were in a proper State for Investigation, Home, so that I was compelled to defer the Examination of *[these]* till some future Excursion, when I shall be provided with Authors and Instruments proper for the purpose. -

We next passed Storrs Hall, the Seat of St. John Legar, but lately purchased by Mr. Bolton, a Merchant from Liverpool of immense Fortune, who , when this County was threatened with Invasion by Buonaparte, the usurper of the Throne of France, at his sole Expense raised and Supported a Regiment of Soldiers for the Defence of the Kingdom . About two years ago, when Colonel of his Regiment, he was compelled to accept a challenge and killed his Antagonist in a Duel.

Although acquitted by all who were acquainted with the Circumstance of this fatal Act, he took a Dislike to Liverpool and removed to Storrs Hall where he is building a princely Mansion in a sequestered Situation on the Border of the Lake.

[John Bolton, born in Ulverston in 1756, made his fortune from the West India Trade.

Bolton's Place in Ulverston is named after him. He raised a regiment of militia in 1803 when the threat of invasion by Napoleon Bonaparte was at its height. This regiment became known as 'Bolton's Invincibles'.

The duel occurred late one afternoon in 1805 at a place called Low Hill.

Colonel John Bolton By Joseph Allen - *The Walker Art Gallery, Liverpool*

For the second time in a year Major Edward Brooks, an Ulverston man like Bolton, who had asked for an increase in his salary and was refused, challenged Bolton. Brooks missed, but the shot from John Bolton's pistol pierced Brook's eye causing instant death.

Bolton was found guilty of murder but as Brooks had challenged him and public opinion was in Bolton's favour, he was never charged. The duel was the last ever to be fought in Liverpool. The last fatal duel to be fought in England was at Priest Hill in the Royal Borough of Windsor, on the 19th October 1852 between two French political exiles; Frederic Cournet and Emmanuel Barthelemy. Cournet was killed]

Pursuing our Walk we arrived at Bowness at 11 o'clock and after taking some Refreshment returned to the Ferry and crossed the Lake to the Boat House, where the Breadth may be about 500 yards.

Here we found some Hundreds of people assembled, the place crowded with Carriages, the Lake covered with Boats of from 50 Tons Burthen to be scarcely capable of containing two people, all decked out as neat as their Owners cou'd make them; the people too had not been sparing or negligent in adorning their persons, - The Island or Holm, now the property of Mr. Curwen, is a Beautiful place and kept in the neatest Order; it is in the County of Westmorland and may contain between thirty and 40 acres.

The barren Mountains on the West Side of the Lake which about Ten Years ago presented nothing but bare Rock to the Eye of the Owner of this Island is now covered with Trees, chiefly Larches, to the Summit, and the Walks formed on the side of the Mountain are charming. - Numbers of Carriages and Horses crossed the Lake from the Bowness Side to the Boat House, and during our Stay many ludicrous Accidents happened in the passage, unattended by any more disagreeable Consequences than a wet Skin.

There was an Ordiner [?] at the Boat House the Tickets were 10/6d each -

After we had remaind a considerable Time in Expectation of a Boat Race, which, by the Bye, was never intended to happen, we set off on our Return Home, and for the sake of Variety took the West Side of Lake where the Road lays chiefly through thick Woods which hide the Lake from the Eye of the Traveller and has none of those bewitching prospects which the East Side affords.

At some Distance below the Ferry we crossed Cunsey Beck, which is the River that flows from the Esthwaite Water into Windermere, and pafsing Graythwaite the Seat of Myles Sandys Esq, a pleasant Road led us to Stotpark [Stott Park] the Habitation of George Braithwaite Esq. one of the Justices of the peace for Lancashire. Here is a Tower built on an Eminence and commands a good View of part of the Lake; another Tower to the right of our Road, was built by Mr King of Finsthwaite a few Years ago upon the Summit of a high Mountain and affords an extensive prospect.

At 6 o'clock in the Evening we arrived at Newby Bridge, where we dined, and then measuring back our Steps over the plain of Roudsey, crofsed [crossed] the Ferry below Pennybridge and arrived at Home about Half an Hour after Nine o'clock after a walk of Forty Miles.

The Trees which we observed to be generally planted or grow spontaneously in the Course of our Walk were, the Oak, Ash, planetree, Birch, Alder, Willow, Hasel *[Hazel]* Elder, black and white Thorn, Bird Cherry, called in Furness Fells, Hecberry *[Hackberry]*, with some Few of the Spindle Tree, this last and the privet we seldom saw except where they had been planted. The plantations consist chiefly of the Scotch pine, Larch, Silver and Spruce Firs, the Elm, Service and Beech, Spanish Chestnut, many of which appeared loaded with Fruit, some of which I plucked and broke to examine, but suppose from the State in which I found them, that these Trees will not bring their Fruit to perfection in these Mountains -

The Horse Chestnut is common here, so is the Holly, Yew, Savin, Aspen, Hornbeam & the black & Lombardy Popular *[Poplar]*, Taccamahac *[Tacamahac]* in the pleasure Grounds bordering on the Lake.

28th (Sunday) - The Harvest is nearly finished here and there was little Hiring of Reapers at Dalton this Day, their Wages were considerably lower than last Week few obtaining more than 4s per Day.

29th (Monday) - Yesterday Morning, Ellen Townson, Wife of Thomas Townson, who was many Years Farmer of my Estate at Greenmoor House, died suddenly at Ulverston. She was a patient good Woman, and bore every Change of Fortune with a calm and steady Temper. Her Age is about ….......'

[The words end abruptly here – the woman's age is not revealed]

SEPTEMBER ¹⁸⁰⁸

1st (Thursday) - Partridge Shooting commenced this
Day; I went out in Pennington and killed 11 Brace and
one Hare, which with the Grouse I killed upon the
Moors in August make a total this Evening of 21 Brace. -

The Harvest is very forward; there is very little Grain
to cut, and much is carted off the Fields; if the Weather
should prove fine and favourable for a few Days the
Fields will be chiefly got clear of Grain.

2nd (Friday) - The Farmers are very busy this Evening
carting Home their Grain. Went to shoot this Day about
Greenlane and Horseclose killed 8 Brace, gave 2 Brace to
James Nicholson of Low Greaves; these make 29 Brace
killed this Season.

3rd (Saturday) - The Farmers were carting home their
Grain in the Evening. Shot about my own Fields at
Pennington this Morning and killed 4 Brace, making in
all 33 Brace. Gave one Brace to Dr. Redhead and five
Do. to Mrs Hodgson at Ulverston – partridges are very
plentiful this Season.

5th (Monday) - I killed 2 Brace of partridges this
morning which make 35 Brace this Season. Gave one
Brace to James Huddleston. -

6th (Tuesday) - Went to shoot at Newton and killed 10
and a half Brace which make 45 and a half Brace. Gave
two Brace to John Case of Dalton in *[on]* my Return. -
Mem. *[Memo]* Have only seen two Hares this Season

they are become very scarce.

7th (Wednesday) - Killed 2 and a half Brace of partridges this Morning which make in all 48 Brace. Gave one Brace to Geo: Briggs – one Do. to Mr. Kilner, and 4 and a half Do. to Mrs Hodgson – one Brace to Jane Brough

8th (Thursday) - Heavy Rain last night hindered the Farmers from carting Home their Grain;

The Market this Day at Ulverston was abundantly suppl'd with Oats and Wheat, both consequently were lower than before.

Potatoes too came down, the best were sold at three pence Halfpenny per Hoop; Beef at 6 and a half d –

Mutton 6d per lb. -

9th (Friday) - A Very fine Morning and the Farmers particularly busy carting Home their Grain, which was put a stop to by the Rain coming on at Eleven o'clock. Went to shoot For Mr Redhead and killed one Brace, which added to the former make a total of 49 Brace this Season.

10th (Saturday) - Went to Lindal and the Neighbourhood of Dalton to shoot and killed 3 and a half Br. Which makes 52 and a half Brace – Gave 1 and a half Brace to John Hartley and one Br. To Mrs Hodgson.

11th (Sunday) - The Harvest is finished in Furness and great part of the Grain got into the Barns and Stacks: Reapers the last week hired for 3/6 per Day : but few were wanted. -

12th (Monday) - Killed 4 and a half Brace of partridges this Morning which makes 57 Brace.

13th (Tuesday) - J. Gardner and Wife at pennington. Killed in this morning 6 Brace and one Hare, which makes 63 Brace and 2 Hares for the Total.

14th (Wednesday) - Went to shoot and killed 4 Brace, in all 67 Brace. Gave 6 Brace to Mrs. Hodgson.

Great plenty of Herrings and Salmon have been caught at Haverig [*Haverigg*] for two or three Days last past.

15th (Thursday) - Much Grain at the Market this Day and the prices something lower.

16th (Friday) - Nearly all the Grain is taken from the Fields and scarcely a Stouck to be seen. [*Stook - the old term for a stack of corn where the sheaves are piled on end*].

Dr. R. called upon me to shoot him a Brace of partridges; we went upon the new Inclosures at Swarthmoor.

I killed 5 and a half Brace, gave him one Brace; Do. to John Wilson: Do. to Robt. Postlethwaite: Do. to Mifs Fell. - Total killed this Season 72 and a half Brace.

17th (Saturday) - Went to Dendron this Morning to shoot and killed 6 Brace and one Landrail, which this Year for the first [*time*] was by Act of parliament made Game; the Total killed are 70 and a half Brace; 2 Hares and one Landrail.

19th (Monday) - The Farmers very busy sowing Wheat.

20th (Tuesday) - Killed 3 Brace of partridges this Morning wnich made 81 and a half Brace. Gave 1 and a half to Geo. Ashburner and 3 to Mrs H. - *[Hodgson]* This Evening the Estate at Rowe belonging to William Mashiter and containing twenty *[Figure 19 written over this]* Customary Acres, was sold in public Sale, and purchased by a person called John Darley, for the Sum of £1960.

Mashiter purchased this Estate about 16 or 18 Years ago for 740, of course it has increased in Value since that Time 1220: a pretty advance.

22nd (Thursday) - Still fine and dry and extremely favourable for the Farmers to sow their Wheat, some of which is already come up, though there is much yet to sow: Grain rose in our Market this Day, and some new wheat was sold at 56s. per Load, Flour in consequence advanced to 33s. per Cwt.

23rd (Friday) - Killed 1 Brace which make 82 and a half. Wool, which has been low for some Time, is now upon the Advance: the Growth of Pennington Common, which lately sold as low as 7s per Stone, is now at 9' and probably will in a little Time be cosiderably higher.

24th (Saturday) - Cattle at Bootle Fair this day were sold something higher than the late prices, but the Shew was not great. -Killed 1 Br. Which make 83 and a half.

Thomas Tolming of Ulverston built a Vault in the churchyard at Ulverston close behind the Vestry to contain the Corpse of his Daughter who died lately.

26th (Monday) - Killed 1 and a half Brace of partridges, which added to the former make a total of 85 Brace.

27th (Tuesday) - Went this Morning with James Nicholson to Walney to shoot and found the Birds remarkably wild and killed only 3 Brace which I left with Miles Gibson of Northscale, with whom we dined and returned Home in the Evening which was extremely Frosty. 88 Brace.

28th (Wednesday) - The Frost last Night has destroyed all the Tops of the potatoes and Clover Fog, and there was this Morning, Ice to the thicknefs of Half a Crown.

Killed 4 Brace and one Hare, which make a total of 92 Brace and 3 Hares. Gave 1 Brace to James Nicholson and 2 Ds. and the Hare to Mrs. H. - Repaired the Road opposite the Garden at Rowe.

[Fleming now takes us on a remarkable journey on the Stage Coach and other horse powered vehicles to Liverpool via Lancaster. His journal continues with the return journey and his stopover in Lancaster]

30th (Friday) - At Half past 12 I set out on a Journey to Liverpool in Company with G.A *[Most likely George Ashburner]* in the Stage Coach; the Fare from Ulverston to Lancaster is 6/6d.

There were four of us on the inside and six upon the Roof of the Coach: we crofsed *[crossed]* Leven Sands in a straight Direction, and when we arrived at Flookburgh, two more were added to our Number, the coach generally stops here about 15 Minutes, that the pafsengers may take some Refreshment, if they find it necefsary *[necessary]*.

One of the people who took the Coach here was a pleasant facetious Gentleman from Brighton, who enlivened the Journey with entertaining Conversation and removed or rather prevented that Tedium which a samenefs *[sameness]* of prospect, such as the dreary Sands afford, seldom fails to causes.

In about three Hours we had crofsed the Sands and arrived at Hestbank, a poor miserable Inn where the Coach stopped a little while, but the House could afford nothing worth drinking. I *[In]* about an Hour we arrived at Lancaster, a place once dear to John of Ghent *[Also John O' Gaunt]* , and famous for its strong built and pleasantly situated Castle. Lancaster had a few Years back much trade with the West Indies, but now it is removed to Liverpool, its Quays are deserted, its Warehouses empty, and the Town, which a few Years ago, was all Businefs *[Business]* and Bustle, is dull and its Inhabitants inactive.

On our arrival Here I attempted to finish the Businefs which particularly was the Cause of my Journey, but not succeeding according to my Wishes, Mr. A. the Gentleman from Brighton and myself, not being in Time to get places in the Mail Coach, took a post chaise to Garstang, at the Rate of 1/3d per Mile; in this Stage we crofsed the Canal four or more Times, but the Evening was come on, for it was 7 o'Clock when we set out from John of Ghent's Town, and we experienced but little pleasure from the Views of the Country we were travelling through, and could only amuse ourselves with Conversation instructive and entertaining.

From Garstang, which is a small Market Town of little or no Trade, we hired a Chaise to Preston, and proceeded with all pofsible *[possible]* Expedition. In two

Hours we arrived at proud Preston, where much Cotton was manufactured before this destructive War spoiled our Trade with most foreign Nations and increased our Taxes to their present Extent.

Here we supped and took another Chaise to Ormskirk, a Distance of nineteen Miles; when we got there the people at the Inn were all in Bed , and we were compelled to sit in the Chaise for Half an Hour before we could get into the Inn ;

At last the Door was opened and we entered the House, our Eyelids heavy, our Spirits exhausted and Sleep prefsing [*pressing*] heavy upon us, in Expectation of Refreshing ourselves with a warm & comfortable potion, but to our great Disappointment and Vexation, we could procure nothing but a cooling Draught of unpalatable Water, for the Landlord had locked up the Bar, taken the Key to Bed with him, which he would not entrust to his Servants, nor could he be prevailed on to quit the warm Bum of his snoring Wife, under the sweet Banks of whose brawny Bottom he was so snugly laid, and where we left him to enjoy the sighing Breezes which at intervals whisper down that Vale, while we as quickly as pofsible prepared to sniff a purer Air and meet the rising Sun.

About the third Mile Stone, in our Way from Ormskirk to Liverpool, our Driver was overpowered with Sleep, nodded on his Seat and had nearly overturned us into the Ditch, but better Fortune attended us and prevented our being plunged in the Mud. Soon after rosyfaced Aurora; phoebus's bright forerunner, began to shew her welcome face and soon after, the bright Luminary himself, in a skulking Manner and as if he did not intend to favour us, peeped out from behind a watry

Cloud and almost immediately withdrew his Face, just as if he meant only to take a peep at our Driver and with a Face so red, that he seemed to be enraged at finding him in such a Situation and ready to punish him by a Fate like Phaton's *[Also 'Phaeton' - a hypothetical planet between Mars and Jupiter whose destruction led to the production of the asteroid belt]* , but taking pity probably on us weary and dejected, he took another Method of punishing the Sleeping Charioteer, by pouring down a Deluge upon him and unpleasantly disturbing his agreeable Slumbers; the Rain continued till we arrived in Liverpool, a bustling, rich and overgrown Town, perhaps the first in England for Trade, where we alighted, and took up our Lodgings at the Sign of the Saddle at the Foot of Vernon Street adjoining to Dale Street, kept by a person of the Name of Duckworth, fatigued in Body, dispirited and weary, desirous of taking a comfortable and refreshing Nap, but not able to close my Eyes to sleep: Therefore to make the best of a bad Matter, I washed my Temples well with cold spring Water, and after changing my Linen and taking a Moderate Breakfast I began the Day which was …......

OCTOBER [1808]

1st (Saturday) - …......Saturday, the 1st Day of October 1808, unpleasant on Account of the drizling cold Rain and the Wind blowing pretty Strong from the South west.

The Object of my Journey was my first pursuit, but with no better Success than before, I traversed the dirty Streets till Dinner Time, Half past one, when I returned to the Inn where fourteen of us sat down to an excellent Dinner: the Rain continuing the greatest part of the Day made it very disagreeable looking out, the Streets were so remarkably dirty.

In the Evening we retired to Bed at 8 O' Clock, and slept comfortably till the next Morning which was …...........

2nd (Sunday) - …........Sunday October the 2d. as wet and unpleasant as the Day before, with the Wind from the South West. Two of our Fellow Lodgers who sailed in one of the packets for Ireland early Yesterday Morning were wrecked, and returned to the Inn today in miserable plight, and completely done up, sick of the Sea, and out of Humour with the Weather; however a few Glasses of Brandy and Water calmed paddy's unruly pafsions *[passions]* and restored them to Harmony and good Humour.

We had not much Company this Day, only 8 sat down to Dinner, and a stupid Meal it was: the greatest part of this Day was spent unpleasantly and unprofitably in the House; I observed at Dinner today, that every fine dapper Gentleman is not able to cut up a Goose or even a Chicken, and yet would be greatly mortified if not placed at the upper End of the table.

3rd (Monday) - Monday the 3d. of October brought us finer and more favourable Weather and we set out early into the Town to finish our Businefs, but without Succefs we visited the panorama; and the Docks, full of Ships, went upon Change, lounged to the old Book Repository and returned to Dinner at Half after one.

In the Afternoon we went to the Afsylum *[Asylum]* for the Blind, an excellent Institution, to which we contributed our Mite, then visited Brownlow Hill, and made enquiry there of certain Persons concerning a mysterious Affair which I wished to unravel, and got Intelligence that convinced me Report was not always a Lyar *[Liar]* .

In the Evening we went to the Theatre, but a more miserable company of Performers I have seldom seen, not one of them was worth a Straw, except a Mrs Glover:

[Fleming is probably referring to one Mrs Julia Betterton or Butterton Glover, 1779 or 1781 – 1850, an Irish actress well known for her comic roles and Shakespearean readings in the late 18th and early 19th centuries]

Saw there the famed Bruiser [?] , commonly known among the Amateurs of Boxing by the Name of the Game Chicken,a mean, shabby and blackguard looking Fellow, fit enough to amuse those of the same Clafs *[Class]* who delight in such brutal and and inhuman pastime, as seeing a fellow Creature, endowed with Reason, and placed at the Head of the Creation, put himself upon a level with the lowest Brutes. Returned much difsatisfied *[dissatisfied]* with our Evening's Amusement, and in our Way saw Numbers of miserable female Wretches practising every Species of wanton Lasciviousness to allure the unwary to their prostituted Haunts and rob him of his Cash and what is still more valuable, his Health and peace of mind:

They must be the most abandoned of Men and lost to every Sense of Rectitude, who can account it amongst their pleasures to revel wantonly with the shamelefs prostitute, however bedizened with Ornaments, and attractive with paint and other Arts: where Reason rules the Man, he cannot fail to detest the presence of such corrupted Animals and avoid them with as much Care as he would a House or a person infected with the Plague: but, enough of bad Subjects: we supped and retired to Bed about Midnight, and early on the Morning of Tuesday set out in one of the long Coaches on our Return Home, and after a weary and unpleasant Journey, for the Day was remarkably wet, we arrived at Lancaster, hungry and fatigued, for till six in the Evening we had no Dinners.

The pleasure of being jolted in a heavy Coach from 7 in the Morning till six in the Evening without a Morsel to eat, or any Refreshment except a Glafs [*Glass*] of bad Wine, is not, in my Opinion deserving of that Appellation, for I must confess I cannot find out what constitutes the pleasure of travelling: is it, to be hungry without the Opportunity of getting anything to eat? to be thirsty and tired without being able to obtain anything wholesome and refreshing? to be imposed on at every Inn, and if unwilling to throw away your Money carelefsly [*carelessly*] and unnecefsarily [*unnecessarily*] about you to every worthlefs [*worthless*] Servant, to be insulted and neglected? In short to have your pockets picked by every publican, almost, with whom you have anything to do? The persons who esteem the pleasures of travelling differ much in Opinion with me, and I envy them not such Enjoyments.

At the Kings Arms in Lancaster, some poet has given the public a speciman of his abilities in the two following lines which arc painted on a Board and stuck up in the Yard near a pump;

'Whoever washes their Hands here
Must pay two pence towards Bere.'

This Evening I met with J.S. From Dalton, by whom I wrote to Ulverston, and went early to Rest, having got a severe Cold.

5th (Wednesday) - I rose early and having breakfasted went into the Town to buy if possible to accomplish the Businefs I wished to do. About 10 AM met with Mr Henry Walker, cabinetmaker in the New Road, with whom I came to an Agreement to his taking John Hodgson an Apprentice for 5 Years, Mr W. to find him Meat and Lodging during the Term, in his own House, and proper Attendance & necefsaries if at any Time sick, Mrs Hodgson to pay the Doctor's Bills and find him Clothes, with a consideration of Forty pounds. We then waited on Mr Lewthwaite the Town Clerk & attorney at Law to explain the Conditions for the immediate preparation of the necefsary *[necessary]* Writings.

Wrote to Ulverston by the post, but the Bags were making up before I arrived at the Office and I was compelled to pay 6d to the postmaster before he would admit the Letter: this is a heavy Imposition upon the public and ought to be remedied, for the Mail did not leave the Town till the Expiration of Half an Hour after the time I put the Letter into the Office. Mr Wilson, a partner in the Firm of Mason, Wilson and Jenkinson, Attorneys at Law, is Mayor of Lancaster this Year; the Office, may not, probably, be a very lucrative one, and the Honour it confers on the person who holds it is not great.

The Gentlemen of Lancaster and the Neighbourhood have made a new Race Course upon the Moor and expect good Races the next Year: the old course was upon the Marsh to the West of the Town, and was done away by the Division and Enclosure which took place there a few Years ago, from which Time till now the Races ceased, but are expected to be renewed with redoubled Splendor.

Here is very little Trade and not more than five Vefsels [*Vessels*] in the Harbour and two new ones upon the Stocks, and two in the Dock at Glasson.

This Evening I waited till Mr. A. returned from the Theatre; he gave no flattering Account of the Performers which would induce others to repair to the same place for Amusement: supped and retired to Bed at 12, but Sleep, which refreshes the weary Labourer and renews his exhausted Strength, fled from my pillow, and a very uneasy Night I experienced.

Wrote to Ulverston by Mr. A. as I thought it probable that my Letter of Yesterday might remain in the post office too long and detain me at Lancaster longer than I could desire.

6th (Thursday) - Mr. A. set off at 5 in the Morning and probably would arrive at Ulverston about 9.

At Halfpast Nine John H. arrived and after taking a little Refreshment we proceeded to settle his Businefs which was soon completed, his Indenture being ready for signing: we then sauntered about the Town and the Quays, took a look at the Canal over the River Lune; it is a noble building & comletely answers the purpose it was intended for, built something in the Stile of the new Bridge.

The old Bridge is in Ruins and appears as if two of the arches at the East End had been purposely destroyed, perhaps to allow Vefsels to pafs [*pass*] without striking their Masts: but even that seems almost unnecefsary, so few come up the River higher than Glasson.

Dined with Mrs. Fletcher and drank Tea with Mr. Batty.

About twenty years ago Lancaster was in a flourishing State, the streets filled with Merchants its Quays crouded with carts & people, and nobody could be noticed who would not boast of his Ten Thousands: but how different now, these fine Gentlemen who then in the pride of their Hearts boasted of what they never pofsefsed [*possessed*], after ruining most of the Tradesmen who would trust them, are not, if their Debts were honestly paid worth, 100 pounds. How hard for many honest Families to be reduced to Beggary by supporting their Extravagance and foolish pride for a Few Years; but the same may not readily happen again, for from that Time the place has lost its Credit and scarce a Tradesman will trust anyone in it.

The Fishery in the River Lune belonging to Mr Bradshaw of Halton has for some Years been upon the Decline, and the Reason given is, that the Fish high up the River are destroyed at their Spawning Time.

There may, perhaps be another Reason given, and in my Opinion, Mr Bradshaw himself is in some Measure the Cause of the Scarcity of Salmon of which he complains. He has raised the Weare [*Weir*] so that the Fish can seldom get over, and never allows the Gratings of the Locks to be removed that the Fish may run: if Few Fish get up the River to spawn, many cannot be expected to be taken the ensuing Seasons, and in a few Years if the same practise be continued, scarce a Fish will come up the River, and the Fishery, which, I am informed, some Years was worth a Thousand Pounds, will not be worth the Trouble of attending and the Expence of Nets.

If the Salmon were allowed a free Run only Half of one Year, the River would again abound, and become of equal Value, if not superior to what it was before, from the Increase of price, as it has never been lower than 18d per lb. and a great part of the year sold as high as 2/6 & 3s which is an enormous price, and consequently if the Salmon were plentiful, the Fishery would fetch a considerable Rent.

Two Smacks were fitted out here a few Years ago to Fish in the Bay between the Isle of Mann [Man] and Blackcomb, [Black Combe] and succeeded wonderfully; the Town was well and regularly supplied, but the Inhabitants would not pay a price for them worth the Trouble and Expence of Catching: Soals [Soles] were sold at 2d per lb. and other kinds in proportion.

This Day Jno. Hodgson was bound, at his own Desire, an apprentice to Mr Henry Walker, cabinetmaker in the New Road for 5 Years.

7th (Friday) - Breakfasted with Mr Atkinson of Dalton at the King's Arms, and we set off on our Return over the Sands to Ulverston, in the Stage Coach: the Wind blowing from the South West, the Afternoon was extremely wet and the Wind blew a Hurricane.

8th (Saturday) - Went with J. [?] Jackson to dine at Dalton Bookclub, and on our Way I killed one Hare and 2 Brace of Birds which make a Total of 94 Brace and 4 Hares this Season.

10th (Monday) - Went a shooting and killed 1 and a half Brace, the Birds are remarkably shy; these make 95 and a half.

11th (Tuesday) - One Half Year's payment of the afsefsed [assessed] Taxes for this Year upon Horses,

Carriages, Houses, Windows, Dogs, Servants, and the Duty upon Game Certificates, was collected within our parish of pennington.

12th (Wednesday) - James Nicholson of Low Greaves exhibited his Accounts, as a Surveyor of the Highways, and being prepared to quit the Office: John Wilson the Farmer at Midrow is to succeed him.

The Turnpike Road belonging to the parish of pennington, has been put into good Repair by the Commifsoners [*Commissioners*], and from this Day the parish take it into their own Hands, and repair it, when necessary at their own Cost.

15th (Saturday) - Mrs H went to Greenhead Yesterday and returned Home this Evening to Tarnside.

17th (Monday) - Barley for malting is now selling at 15/6 and 16s. per Bushel. Potatoes at 4s. & 4/6 per Do. -Oats at 10s. Do. - Wheat 58s. & 60s. per Load. Beef 7d. - Mutton – 6d – Veal – 5d – Pork -5d & Butter 13d per lb - Apples 18d to 24d – Nuts out of the Husks 3/6 per Hoop. Geese 5d per lb. - Fowls 12d to 18d each – Coffee reduced from 4/6 to 2/6 per lb.

18th (Tuesday) - Killed one Brace of p. which make a Total of 96 and a half Braces this Season.

20th (Thursday) - Cheese from the Fair at Lancaster is sold 7d per lb. Wheat at the Market this Day was upon the Advance. Payday for the Afsefsed Taxes.

21st (Friday) - Went down to Mr James Robinson's at Newbarnes.

22nd (Saturday) - Went to Cocken to shoot and killed 5 Brace and two Hares. Gave one Hare and 3 partridges to J. Robinson – and returned Home in the Evening.

Total 101 and a half Brace of Birds and 6 Hares this Season.

24th (Monday) - Exceeding stormy and very heavy Rain, so that the Brooks have overflowed their Banks and done considerable Damage.

25th (Tuesday) - Few Cattle were shewn at Dalton Fair Yesterday, but they sold at advanced prices; spring Calvers fetched the best prices and were most in Request: few cattle were shewn and these not well fed No Horses of any value to merit Notice.

26th (Wednesday) - Within the parish of pennington there is a Raise or Circle of Stones, yet commonly known and called by no other Name but, White Raise, probably from the quantity of white moor Stones laying on a Heap within the Circle. This may have been at some remote place where Justice was administered, as at the Stone Raise and Dunmailraise in Cumberland, or the Mote-hill in Low Furness. There is another Raise or Tumulus of Stones at about a mile Distance from the former, but without any surrounding Circle of Stones, and may have been the burial place of some Man of note.

27th (Thursday) - Townterm Rent, Tenagium or Tow-terr [?] rent, is a land Rent paid to the Lord of a

Manor, in lieu of boon Services, in some places every second Year, but in pennington every seventh year.

28th (Friday) - Circulated the papers for the new or local Militia, and killed 2 Brace of Birds and 3 yellow Plovers. Total 103½ Brace and 6 Hares .

29th (Saturday) - A Battle at Rowend between two Women.

31st (Monday) - This morning the Battles of Saturday was renewed with greater Fury than before and the Caps and Hair of the Combatants suffered greatly, but no Blood was drawn, except a little from the Cheek of one of them by a Dog which interfered and with its Claws made a slight Scratch no doubt thinking that B-; Sport [*Bloodsport*] would be Dogs' Fun.

Two 19th century women fighting

This Afternoon, Robt. Gorrill sold the greatest part of his Stock of Sheep which averaged about 17s. each taken from Pennington Common, a very high price, his Farm at Highgreaves consisting of about 27 Acres was let by Ticket and taken by a person called Simpson at the yearly Rent of 88£ and all Taxes.

Went to shoot this Day and killed 3 Brace, one Snipe and one Wild Duck making in all 106 ½ Brace this season.

The Markets have for some Time been on the Advance. Barley at 16s.- Oats at 13s. and Potatoes at 4/6 per Bushel. Wheat at 60s. Per load – Beef -7d - Mutton 7d - Pork 5.5d – Veal 6d.per lb. - Cattle too are something higher than they have been the two last Years – Tar is advanced a 100£ per cwt or in other Words has doubled the price it was last Year.

NOVEMBER 1808

1st (Tuesday) - Woodcocks are scarce yet: killed half *[brace?]* which makes the Total 107 Brace, 6 Hares.

2nd (Wednesday) - Killed ½ . 107 ½ Brace. This Afternoon one of the female Bruisers before mentioned came to me with a Warrant to apprehend her Opponent and take her before a Justice of the peace.

3rd (Thursday) - Early this morning I apprehended the fighter and had her before the Magistrate, when she was obliged to find Surety for her Appearance at the next quarter Sefsions *[Sessions]* and for keeping the peace in the Mean Time herself in 10£ and Thos. Fell of Tarnclose in the like Sum.

4th (Friday) - 1 Brace. Off. to Mr. Rd. Cleator of Dalton. The Mayor Hunt at Dalton was this Day and Mr James Jackson of Ulverston was elected to succeed Richd. Shaw, Atty. At Law – killed 6 Hares.

7th (Monday) - Set out at 7 AM in Company with James Park, Atty. At Law, on a Shooting Excursion to Walney, in [on] our Way I killed 3 ½ Brace of Birds, one Hare and one Stockdove or Wild Pigeon. There make the total of Game killed by me 111 Brace, 7 Hares Etc.

Thos. Fell of Biggar met us at North Scale. He had killed a Hen pheasant & 2 Brace.

8th (Tuesday) - We slept last Night at T. Fell's, Bigger [*Biggar*], and early this Morning pursued our Diversion, the Birds were shy and I killed only 2 ½ Brace, which were all we got.

These make the Total 113 ½ Brace this Season; left them with Thomas Fell .

9th (Wednesday) - Slept again at T. Fell's, and took our Departure this Morning from his hospitable Mansion on our Way Home again: dined with the Revd. John Troughton Curate of Walney, at North Scale, crofsed the Water in a Boat and arrived at Pennington about Half past 6 in the Evening, after a pleasant Excursion, but our Succefs in shooting was greatly short of our Expectations : Game, particularly partridges, were vey plentiful but remarkably wild.

10th (Thursday) - Grain of all kinds advanced rapidly this week.

11th (Friday) - I killed one Hare this Afternoon. Total 113 ½ B. 8 Hares.

12th (Saturday) - The Theatre at Ulverston was opened for this Season on Thursday the 27th October but hitherto the House has not been so crowded as Mr Samuel Butler, the Manager, had expected.

13th (Sunday) - Some sacriligious Rascal has stolen one of the Surplices from the Church at pennington; there were only two, a new one and an old one of little Value, and it is something singular that the Fool should steal the worse.

The former theatre on Theatre St, Ulverston

14th (Monday) - Much Snow laid upon the Mountains
to the East. Woodcocks, which by the new Game Laws
are made Game, have hither to *[have]* been unusually
Scarce in this Neighbourhood; the price is in proportion,
2s/6d to 3/- ea. -

15th (Tuesday) - The best Wheat Flour is now at 40s the
Hundred weight, Oatmeal at 2s 6d per Cwt. and Barley
for malting at 16/6d per Bushel – potatoes 4d per Hoop
of 6 Quarts – Candles are advanced from 10d to 14d per
lb. - Soap to 15d per lb. and Tallow in our Market is now
12s. per Stone –

Sugar rose in the course of last Week 2d per lb. - and
Tar is advanced 10 per Cent or double the price it was –
Rum is now at 20s per Gallon – Beef & Mutton 7d per lb.

16th (Wednesday) - A Child in Ulverstone was burnt
to Death, in playing near the Fire the Flames caught its
Clothes.

17th (Thursday) - This Day there used to be about
150 fat Cattle killed at Ulverston, and few Families
purchased less than one Quarter of a Beast to salt for

their Winter provision; but now Beef is plentiful every Market Day in the Year and of Consequence there is no Necessity for salting, and this Day not more than 30 were killed in the Town which were sold at 4 to 5d per lb the Quarter taken together.

The Choice prices were from 6 to 7d per lb. -

19th (Saturday) - Killed one Hare this Afternoon which makes the Total 9 Hares this Season. -

21st (Monday) - This Day the Ulverston Hunt commenced and about thirty Riders appeared *[on]* the Field;

the Hounds threw off at Loperts and killed three Hares which made admirable Chaces *[Chases]* and afforded excellent Sport, after which about 27 sat down to Dinner at the King's Arms in Ulverston, Edward Moysten *[Mostyn]* Esq. the Mayor, was sick and did not attend.

On Saturday last the Coroner's Inquest was held on the Body of an Infant found in the Box of one Mary Jackson, a Servant with James Wright of Rampside; the Jury brought in a Verdict of wilful Murder against the said Servant and she must take her Trial at the next Afsizes *[Assizes]* at Lancaster.

22nd (Tuesday) - This morning the Hounds cast off near Lindale.

In the Evening, the Hunt Ball was at the Assembly Rooms, over the Theatre at Ulverston.

I Removed the Fence between the Bank and Briglat *[Brigflats]*.

23rd (Wednesday) - This Morning the Hounds threw off at Plumpton for the Drag of a Fox, but none could be found, of Consequence the Sportsmen returned much disappointed.

24th (Thursday) - The Hounds this Morning cast off at Low Greaves: in the Evening there was a concert at the Afsembly *[Assembly]* Rooms and a Ball after, which were well attended.

Grain was abundant this Day and the prices something lower than last Week.

25th (Friday) - The Hounds cast off this Morning at Highfield House and killed four Hares. In the Evening, after the Wine had circulated freely, came on the Election of a Mayor for the ensuing Year, when Mr. Strickland

UNDER THE PATRONAGE OF

EDWARD MOSTYN, ESQ.

(MAYOR OF THE HUNT),

ASSEMBLY ROOM,

Ulverston.

On THURSDAY Evening the 24th of November, 1808,
WILL BE PERFORMED

A CONCERT,

or

VOCAL and INSTRUMENTAL MUSIC.

ACT FIRST.	ACT SECOND.
OVERTURE—*ABEL.*	CONCERTO OBOE·· *Mr. SCRUTON.*
GLEE—*STEVENS.*	GLEE.—*PAXTON.*
SOLO FLUTE··Mr.Scruton—*W. J. Park.*	OVERTURE.—*ABEL.*
SONG··*Miss SCRUTON.*	SONG··*Miss SCRUTON.*
OVERTURE.—*W. SMETHERGELL.*	OVERTURE—PLEYEL.

GLEE.—*Stevens.*

SIGH no more ladies, ladies sigh no more,
Men were deceivers ever,
One foot on sea and one on shore,
To one thing constant never;
Then sigh not so, but let them go,
And be you blithe and bonny,
Converting all your sounds of woe to, hey,
nonny, nonny.

Sing no more ditties, ladies sing no more
Of dumps so dull and heavy,
The frauds of men were ever so
Since summer first was leafy ;
Then sigh not so, but let them go,
And be you blithe and bonny,
Converting all your sounds of woe to, hey,
nonny, nonny.

SONG...*Miss Scruton.*

'TWAS at the hour of day's decline,
When to the neighb'ring hills I went,
To tie up many a drooping vine,
By weight of purple clusters bent;
That done beneath a willow shade,
Which o'er beauteous river play'd,
I sat and sung to the waving willow.
Willow, willow, waving willow.

While there I mused and watch'd the stream,
A boat approach'd with lazy oar.
Oh here ah! little did I dream,
Till roguish Casper sprung . . e;
A thousand vows he made me hear,
And I believ'd them all sincere,
While resting near the waving willow.
Willow, willow, waving willow.

GLEE.—*Paxton.*

CUPID come without delay,
Lovely Venus haste away,
With the nymphs and graces fair,
Antidotes to mortal care,
Thus encircled let us be,
Ever happy, ever free.

Not let Bacchus be forgot,
Drunken laugher, loving sot,
Social god of potent wine,
Making mortal man devine,
Thus encircled let us be,
Ever happy, ever free.

SONG...*Miss Scruton.*

WHEN pensive I thought on my Love,
The moon on the mountains was bright,
And philomel down in the grove,
Broke sweetly the silence of night;
O I wish that the tear drop would flow,
But felt too much anguish to weep,
'Till worn with the weight of my woe,
I sunk on my pillow to sleep.

Me thought that my love as I in'r,
His ringlets all clotted with gore,
In the paleness of death seem'd to say,
Alas! we must never meet more;
Yes, yes, my belov'd we must part,
The steel of my rival was true,
The assassin has struck out that heart,
Which beat with such fervour for you.

TO BEGIN PRECISELY AT EIGHT O'CLOCK.
After the Concert a Ball.

Tickets 3· each, to be had of Mr. Soulby, Bookseller, King-street, and of Mr. Scruton, Fountain-street.

ULVERSTON PRINTED BY J. SOULBY.

The Hunt Ball Concert at the Assembly Rooms,
Ulverston – Soulby Collection

of Sizergh, Jnr. was chosen to succeed Edwd. Mostyn, Esq. who made a very eloquent Speech, and the whole Company pushed the Wine about, till they all got, what they denominate, nobly drunk.

26th (Saturday) - Heavy Rain all Day with the Wind from the South West and not favorable for the Conclusion of Ulverston Hunt, as the Hounds cast off at Holebeck, too great a Distance from Ulverston for many to attend in the Rain.

27th (Sunday) - This Morning, Mr. Askeugh *[Askew?]* of Greystock *[Most likely the Reverend Henry Askew, married to Anne Sunderland, Thomas Sunderland's eldest daughter]* preached at Pennington but there was no Service in the Afternoon: Mr Walker our Curate was at Ulverston.

28th (Monday) - Went to shoot but killed but one Partridge only, they were so very shy:

The Total this Season 114 brace & 9 Hares. -

This Evening there was an Account of the Embago *[Embargo]* in the United States of America being taken off, & if it prove true, I hope Trade will flourish again and many who are now distrefsed *[distressed]* find Employment.

[The Peninsular War continues. Spain is now Great Britain's ally]

30th (Wednesday) - Better News this Evening from Spain where a great part of our Army are employed in Aid of the Spainiards *[Spaniards]* to repel the Incursions of the French.

DECEMBER [1808]

1st (Thursday) - The Custom of prefixing the Addition of Sir to the Christian Name of a Clergyman was formerly usual in England. Fuller *[Thomas Fuller – 1608 – 1661]* in his Church History, Book 6. p. *[blank space]* inumerates Seven Chantries, part of a much larger Number, in the old Cathedral of St. Paul, in the Time of Ewd. 6th *[Edward 6th]* with the Names of the then Incumbents, most of whom have the Addition of Sir; upon which he remarks, and gives this Reason why there were formerly more Sirs than Knights: Such priests as have the Addition of Sir before their Christian Names were men not gradualed *[graduated?]* in the University, being in Orders, but not in Degrees, whilst those entitled Masters, had commenced in the Arts. This is the Reason why one of the Vicars of pennington is found Sir prefixed to his Christian Name.

3rd (Saturday) - Club Day at Brad. A. *[Ulverston Book Club at the Braddyll's Arms]*.

4th (Sunday) - No duty at pennington in the morning but the Revd Mr Ponsonby, Vicar of Urswick, did Duty there in the Afternoon. - The late Vicars of Urswick succeeded each other in the following Order.

Revd. Mr Holmes – Revd. John Addison – Revd. William Ashburner – Revd. Mr. Bayles – Revd. Mr Ponsonby, the present Vicar & Master of the Grammar School at little Urswick, which is free to all Furness. -

5th (Monday) - Cut the parrock Fence next to the Highway and laid down the Wood.

6th (Tuesday) - Put up a new Grate in the little parlour at pennington.

7th (Wednesday) - Oatmeal fallen from 26' *[shillings]* to 23' per Cwt.

8th (Thursday) - Thomas Lowther sold his Estate at peaseholmes consisting of about 22 Acres Customary Measure for 1,300 Guineas. -

12th (Monday) - This Evening I killed one Brace of Partridges which make the Total killed this Season 115 Brace and nine Hares.

14th (Wednesday) - Soap and Candles were never known to be as at so high a price here as at present, dip Candles are at 15d. and Moulds at 17d per lb. Soap is at 14d per pound but potatoes are at 3d per Hoop, which is something in favour of the poor.

15th (Thursday) - Oatmeal 23s per Cwt.

19th (Monday) - The pumps and many Spring, are frozen up, and the Sky unspotted with a Single Cloud; people are skating upon the ponds and Tarns, and to all Appearance we shall experience a Sharp Frost. The Wind blows strong from the North East. -

20th (Tuesday) - This Evening John Carter of Loppergarth sold his Estate there consisting of about 19 Customary Acres for the enormous and extravagant Sum of upwards of two thousand nine Hundred pounds. It was sold in parcels. I purchased his Loppergarth Meadow estimated at one Customary Acre for two Hundred and two pounds, a most extravagant price. The other purchasers were James Wilson, a farmer at Lindal, and Thomas Lowther, a farmer at Rowe.

21st (Wednesday) - ....Snow which began to fall early this Morning and continued the whole of the Day, but the Frost set in, more severe than before, in the Evening and the Roads became very slippery and Dangerous Some petty Robberies have been committed in Furness & Walney the beginning of this Week.

22nd (Thursday) - Continuation of severe Frost and the Roads so glazed over as to be dangerous, some Dislocations and fractured Bones have happened from Falls: the Wind blowing cold from the North East.

23rd (Friday) - The Frost continues: the Canal at Ulverston is frozen up and people skating upon it. The Wind remains at East.

24th (Saturday) - Which is Christmas Eve; there were very few people at the Market at Ulverston this Day, but great plenty of Butchers' Meat etc. the Wind blowing cold from the East.

The Band of the Ulverston Volunteers, paraded the Town and played till about Midnight, but desisted prudently before the Commencement of the Sabbath. The Roman catholics at Ulverston lighted up their Chapel early in the Evening and continued it till late in the Night.

25th (Sunday) - Christmas Day very Dull and gloomy with some little Snow and the Wind from the South East

Knott & Co. have hired some Workmen from Shiffield *[Sheffield]* and are begun the cutlery Business, chiefly cast Steel, at their Furnace at Newland.

27th (Tuesday) - Mrs. H & Mifs B. dined with us & spent the Day at Ulverston . -

29th (Thursday) - ….the Market this Day was thinly attended and little Grain there, but Abundance of Beef and Mutton from 5 ½ to 7d per pound. Agnes Carter went to Pennington.

30th (Friday) - Mr. Nicholson and self began to collect the first Half yearly payment of the property Tax in pennington.

31st (Saturday) - There was no Market at Ulverston this Day as used to be on New Year Eve ever since I can remember; the Small *[Word missing but probably 'pox']*, which are not yet exterminated by the Cowpox , have for sometime raged in Lancaster and Kendall, the Measles too have made their Appearance, but neither of them have proved fatal in any great Degree perhaps from the coldness of the Weather, this Evening the Band of the Ulverston Volunteers were up and played through the Streets till the Expiration of the Year 1808.

[Thus ends our first journey with William Fleming, leaving the year 1808 in the very capable hands of the forerunner of the Ulverston Town Band]

APPENDICES

WILLIAM FLEMING (Birth , Marriage and Death)

Born: 11th June 1770 .
Marriage: 28th April 1805, St Mary's Church,Ulverston, Lancs.
Wm. Fleming - Schoolmaster
Sarah Hodgson - Spinster
Witness: Elizth. Feetham; Geo. Coward; Elizth. Hodgson
Married by Licence
Source: LDS Film 1040491

Burial: 8th Sep 1829 St Michael and the Holy Angels,
Pennington in Furness, Lancs.
William Fleming - Age: 59
Abode: Rowe, Pennington
Buried by: Wm. Ashburner, Offg. Minr.
Register: Burials 1814 - 1870 from the Bishop's Transcripts, Page 11,
Entry 87
Source: LDS Films 1040309 and 1040491

SARAH FLEMING (Hodgson)

Marriage: 28th April 1805, St Mary's Church, Ulverston, Lancs.
Wm. Fleming - Schoolmaster
Sarah Hodgson - Spinster
Witness: Elizth. Feetham; Geo. Coward; Elizth. Hodgson
Married by Licence
Source: LDS Film 1040491

Burial: 2nd March 1830 St Michael and the Holy Angels,
Pennington in Furness, Lancs.
Age: 45
Abode: Rowe
Buried by: J. Sunderland, Vicar
Register: Burials 1814 - 1870 from the Bishop's Transcripts, Page 11 & 12,
Entry 88
Source: LDS Films 1040309 and 1040491

CHILDREN : John, Richard, William, Mary and Sarah Fleming

WILL:
Fleming, William
Address: Rowe Hall, Pennington, Furness, Lancashire.
Occupation: Gent
Date: Sep 22nd 1829
Held by the Lancashire Archives

WILLIAM FLEMING
A JOURNAL AND COMMON – PLACE BOOK

Twelve volumes in all. (Volume 1 still missing)
Vol 2 – 1800 - 1802 Vol 3 – 1802 - 1805 Vol 4 – 1805 - 1807
Vol 5 – 1807 - 1808 Vol 6 – 1808 - 1809 Vol 7 – 1810 - 1812
Vol 8 – 1813 Vol 9 – 1815 Vol 10 – 1819
Vol 11 - Transcription of Pennington Manor Court Book - 1696 - 1801
Vol 12 - Manuscript Notes & Population Survey - 1812

FACTS, HISTORY AND OTHER OBSERVATIONS

A Selection featured in Fleming's Journals

Chucha : a liquor used in South America.

Hackney Coaches first licensed 1693.

Kaviar is the prepared Roes of Sturgeons, cleanses, salted and pressed into Casks in Russia.

Lightning consists of Electric Matter, as Dr Franklin first discovered, and passes through the walls of Houses, Trunks of trees, or through moist bodies of animals: of consequence a person is safer from the effects of it, if in a room or about 4 ft distance from the wall; if in the fields, at some distance from any tree or mettallic body, and more so if he lay flat upon the ground – the distance may be computed by observing the Time betwiset [betwixt?] the Flash and the Clap, allowing a mile for every 4 and a half seconds or therabouts . A tall rod or pole set upright with a wire fixed by the side of, or round it and rising above it, the lower end fixed into a glass bottle will collect the Ariel Electricity from the passing clouds, as may be proved by receiving the sparks from it by one's finger.

Mobie, a small fruit of South America.

Snow is frozen Clouds: and clouds consist of condensed vapours the particles of which are too small separately to overcome the Tenacity of the Air, so cannot descend: but if in this state a cloud becomes frozen, it is torn to pieces by the friction of the Air in its descent and falls in flakes of snow; and if the Electric fluid which hinders the particles of which the cloud is composed, from uniting is withdrawn it will fall in a shower.

Will O 'the Wisp, or Ignis Tatuus, is generally supposed to originate from the inflammable air rising from the Brgs *[Bogs?]* and Mosses.

Zebra, or African Cow and ye Siberian or Grunting Cow are varieties of the Bison.

Archbishops of Canterbury listed from AD 569 (St. Augustin) - VOL 3. P751.

Bastille in France taken 14th July 1789.

Battle of Tewkesbury 4th May 1471.

Battles By Sea – listed Vol 4 P1086.

Bishops – listed Vol. 4 P1097.

Cathedral, Salisbury erected about 1258.

Canal, Lancaster begun 1792.

Dalton Castle – not the present one – built by Agricola AD 79.

Farmers subdued by Agricola, who raised a Forters *[fortress?]* at Dalton AD 79.

Kings of Aegypt listed VOL 3 P729.

Kings of Babylon listed VOL 3 P727.

Kings of Scotland listed VOL 2 - P260 -262.

Kings of Wales listed VOL 3 – P724.

Mungo Park, set out on his travels into the interior of Africa 22nd May 1795.

Orders of Knighthood listed – VOL 3 P 908.

Poets Laureat listed – VOL 3 P918.

Popes of Rome listed – VOL 3 P 756.

Rome besieged by Vitiges, King of the Goths, 536.

Ulverston, its charter granted the 9th – Edwd 1st for a weekly Market and Fruit [!?]

FOOD AND DRINK RECIPES

To Make Turnip Bread

Take the skin from your turnips and boil them till soft: bruise them well and press out the juice: add an equal weight of wheat flour, and knead them up with sufficient quantity of salt and bake them. (The great scarcity of wheat flour, Oatmeal, Potatoes and their consequent high prices induced many Families to make their bread according to this reciept *[recipe]* in 1800.)

To Make Currant Wine

To 8 Quarts of ripe Currants well crushed put 8 Quarts of Water, let it stand a Day or two, then prefs *[press]* out the Juice and to every Gallon of Liquor add 4lbs. of Sugar; let it stand for 10 days stirring it every Day, then put it in the Cask but do not close it up for a Week. It will be fit to bottle about Christmas *[This recipe was written in August]*

To Make Bread of Potatoes

Grate 8lbs of good and raw Potatoes with a Bread Grater into cold water: stir it well and then let the Starch subside; mix this Starch with 8 lbs of boiled potatoes crushed small and make it into Bread.

To Make Yeast

Bruize a Teacup full of peas (if split the better) and pour on them a pint of boiling Water: set it all night near the Fire and when the Froth rises to the Top is good Yeast; and sufficient for a shilling Loaf . -

INSCRIPTIONS UPON THE TOMBSTONES IN THE CHURCHYARD AT ULVERSTON

[As Recorded by William Fleming. Note by Fleming himself - These inscriptions are inserted without paying any regard to their Order, or Regularity of their Dates.
Also, the word ' Obs ' after some inscriptions are Fleming's own observations and remarks about the deceaseds' lives. The inscriptions are exactly as Fleming has written them]

February 5th 1808

No.1 - Here Lies the Body of John Gawith, younger, of Brownhow in Blawith who departed this Life on the 2nd Day of March in the 23rd Year of his Age, Anno 1761. Parents' Mourn not for me tho' I your all and only Son. Man is born to die, this is our fatal Doom' On the Right Hand lies Eliz.th Gaweth Mother of the above John Gaweth who died on the 1st of June 1772 Aged 56 years.

No.2 - John Stainton erected this Tomb in Memory of his Father Thomas Stainton of Lond in this parish, who was an ingenious and useful Member of Society, a good Christian and sincere Friend; he lived beloved and died lamented May 29th 1740, aged 62 years.

Near this place was buried his Wife and several of his

Children. Also near this place lieth the Remains of Isabel Stainton Daughter of the above Thos. Stainton who departed this Life January the 21st 1799 aged 78 years.

February 6th 1808

No.3 - To the Memory of George Lowry late of Ulverston, Merchant, who died the 27 Day of May 1805, Aged 47 years.

No.4 - To the Memory of Samuel Stephenson of nether Seathwaite who died the 1st. Day of December 1788, aged 69 years. Also Agnes his Wife who only survived him 14 Days, aged 63 years.

No. 5 - Sacred to the deposited Remains of Mary the Wife of Brigadier General, the honourable William Lumley and the second daughter of Thomas Sunderland Esq. who died at Ulverstone the 19 Day of July 1807 aged 34

[An inscription is added by William Lumley at a later date. See Main diary]

February 10th 1808

No.6 - To the Memory of Betty the Daughter of John and Elizabeth Sanderson of Ulverston who died the 10th Day of July 1794 aged 34 years. Capt John Sanderson the Father of the above Betty Sanderson was castaway in this Channel on board his Vefsel , on the 23rd Day of October 1766 aged 42 years. William Sanderson Son of the above John & Elizabeth Sanderson died at the Island of Dominica on the 28 of September 1793 aged 27 Years.

John Sanderson Son of the above John and Elizabeth Sanderson died at Ulverston the 26th of October 1767 aged 5 years -------

February 13th 1808

No.7 - Here lies inter'd the Body of James Fell of Trinkelt who departed this life the 30th Day of July 1776 in the 61st Year of his Age. Also Agnes Wife of James Fell who departed this Life the 9th Day of August 1783 in the 63rd Year of her Age. Likewise George their Son who departed this Life in the year 1757 in the 15th Year of his Age. Also Samuel who died an Infant.

March 8th 1808

No.8 - To the Memory of Bella Fox Daughter of William and Margaret Fox who died April the 12th 1769 Aged 2 Years.

To the Memory of Capt. James Fell who died January the 3rd 1765 aged 34 John Fell died January the 26th 1759 aged 22.

No.9 - To the Memory of Bella Stephenson Daughter of Thomas and Margaret Stephenson who died December the 26th aged 3 Years - Also Ann Stephenson Daughter of Thomas and Margaret Stephenson who died April the 6th 1781 aged 11 Years.

No.10 -Here lies the Body of Arthur Studart who departed this Life December the 15th. 1777 in the 77th Year of his Age.

No.11 -In Remembarance that Here lies the Body of Elizabeth Glover the Wife of Joseph Glover of Ulverston who died October the 14th Day 1769 in the 34th Year of her Age.

No.12 - To the Memory of Sarah Wife of William Burnthwaite of Ulverston who died the 9th Day of September 1780 Aged 44 Years

No.13 - Here lies the Remains of John Bellman of

Hollowmire and of Mary his Wife. He dioed 14th September 1785 aged 69 Years. She the 3rd of May 1768 Aged 41 Years .

No.14 -Josephus Wilson - Mortalis esse desiit Anno Christe 1792 Aetates 67 -

Monday 4th April 1808

No.15 - Mary Birket departed this Life the 12 Day of June 1781 in the 11th Year of her Age. Catrine Birket departed this Life the 13th. Day of June 1781 in the 14th Year of her Age. The two Daughters of Wm . And Mary Birket.

No.16 - Here lieth interred the Body of Thomas Green of Ulverston who departed this Life the 3rd Day of April 1779 in the 50th . Year of his Age.

No. 17 - Here lieth the Body of James Black Son of John and Margaret Black of Ulverston who died the 14th. Day of March 1769 in the 9th Year of his Age. To the Memory of William Black who departed this life February the 26th. 1773 in the 11th. Year of his Age. On the South Side of this Stone lies the Body of Margaret Black the Mother of the above James and William Black who departed this Life the 23rd. of February 1778 in the 56 Year of her Age.

Tuesday April the 5th 1808

No.18 - In Memory of Thomas the Son of John and Margaret Tyson died May the 13th. 1779 Aged 1 Year and 9 months Margaret the Wife of John Tyson died August the 27th. 1784 aged 44 years.

No.19 - Here rest the Remains of Jane Wife of Thomas Procter of Ulverston, Mercer, who departed this Life on the 10th. Day of February in the Year 1782, in the 20th

Year of her age. Thomas Son of the above Thomas and Jane Procter died an Infant on the 4th. Day of December in the year 1780. Elizabeth their Daughter died on the 3rd. Day April in the year 1781 Aged 5 years.

Wednesday April 6th 1808

No. 20 - Ann the Wife of Dennes Melling departed this Life the 23rd. Of June in the 27th. Year of her Age. Also Edward their son Son died July the 3rd. 1772 aged 1 Year. Dennes Melling of Ulverston who died on the 8th. Day of May 1792 in the 51st Year of his Age and lies interred here.

No. 21 - Sacred to the Memory of Capt. James Collinson who departed this Life July the 2nd. 1790 Aged 70 Years. Also of Elizabeth , Relict of the said James Collinson who died the 25th. Day of July 1790 aged 72 Years.

No.22 - To the Memory of James Collinson Junr. Late of Liverpool who departed this Life October the 20th. 1806 aged 59 Years.

Wednesday April 13th 1808

No.23 - Here lies the Body of Elisabeth the Wife of John Dodson of Ulverston who departed this Life the 7th Day of May 1778 aged 47 Years. Also the Body of John Dodson who departed this Life the 23rd. Day of May 1782 aged 68 Years.

No.24 – Jno. *[John]* Frowster *[Forster?]* Burying place of Scales park 1788.

No.25 - Sacred to the Memory of John Sawrey late of Mansriggs who departed this Life the 10th. Day of January 1805 in the 43rd. Year of his Age.

No.26 - Sacred to the Memory of George Kendal Son of

John and Ellen Kendal of Ulverston who died Decemb.
1789 aged 12 Years. 'Sweet Flow'r tho level'd with
the plain yet thou shalt rise to blow again.' Also John
Kendal Father of the above George Kendal died the 10th
of May 1807 aged 56 Years - Obs: the above John Kendal
for many years kept the Sun Inn at Ulverston and acted
as bye post from Lancaster to Ulverston before a regular
post was established.

No.27 - To the Memory of Thomas Daws who died the
9th. Of October 1787 aged 53 Years. Obs: Thomas Daws
was a Shoemaker and kept the Pack Horse public house
at the Head of the Market place at Ulverston for some
time.

No.28 - In Memory of Elizh. Taylor who died November
18th. 1804 aged 68 Years.

No.29 - M.S. Of John Turner aged 9 Years & Thomas
Ashburner Turner aged 8 the Sons of Capn. Henry and
Ann Turner who both died in one month viz the older
on the 5th. And the younger on the 13th. of Aug. 1803.
Also of Margt. Ashburner who died the 28th of Oct.
1803 aged 77.

Thursday April 14th 1808

No.30 - To the Memory of Mrs. Frances Jackson who
departed this Life on the 15th. Day of May 1793 in the
25th. Year of her Age. Also of Richd. Jackson, Surgeon
her Husband who departed this Life the 6th. Day of
January 1797 in the 32nd Year of his Age.

No.31 - To the Memory of Sarah Mackereth, Relict of the
Revd. Gawin Mackereth late of Grassmer [*Grasmere?*]
who died the 12th. Day of Decemr. 1803 Aged 83.

No.32 - Sacred to the Memory of Robert Town Son of
Rob; S.E. Town died Jan.Y the 5th. 1794 in the 5th. Year

of his Age. Also Robert Hull Town died March the 6th. 1796 in the 1st. Year of his Age.

No.33 - HENRY KENDALE

No.34 - Beneath this Stone lyeth the Remains of Mr. Willm. Machell youngest Son of James Machell Esq late of Hollow Oak who died the 11th. Day of June 1791 in the 38th. Year of his Age.

No.35 - Isabella Macartney Daughr. of James Sewart late of Edinb. Esq. and Widow of the late gallant Captain Macartney of the Princess Amelia who was killed in the Action off the Dogger Bank August the 5th. 1781 and whose Death she survived only 15 months, she died November the 20th. 1782 and was buried by her own Desire on this spot. To perpetuate her Memory this Monument was erected at the Desire of her 5 children by their Guardians.

[To be continued in future books]

MEDICAL MATTERS

Cure For The Bite Of A Mad Dog

Gather the Anagallis arvensis – commonly known as red (scarlet) pimpernel or red Chickweed, in full Bloom and dry it in the Shade, then reduce it to powder and give a table spoon full to a full grown person mixed in Beer, Honey or Molases [Molasses], the Weight whereof shou'd be one Dram and one Scruple [a measurement]; the same Quantity must be given to a child, but divided into 3 equal Doses and given in the Course of a Day. A Decotion (?) of the Herb shou'd be used to wash the Wound and a poultice of the Herb, be kept constantly upon it:

If the Wound be healed apply a Blister before the Herb be used externally------

OVERSEERS OF THE POOR

A selection from the Journals of William Fleming

1802 - November 1st - Assessed for Thomas Nicholson Constable the Sum of 19...19...3....

1803 - June 29th - Assessed for Thomas Nicholson Constable the Sum of 19...19...3....

1805 - April 15th - Elected Church Wardens for the ensuing Year:

Thomas Fell of Holebigrow

John Hartley, farmer Holebigrow

Overseers of the Poor – George Briggs of Crossmoor.

Robt. Gorill of Upper Greaves.

Poor children appointed by the Sidesmen to be educated at the Parish

School out of the poor Stock left for that purpose.

Two children of Joseph Nicholson farmer, Greaves.

Two children of Wm. Jacques, farmer, Whinfield.

1806 – January 3rd - Assessed for the Disbursements of Thos. Nicholson the Constable the Sum of £19 -19s –3d. The said Constable also received at different Times the several following Sums, viz ; Of the Servant Elijah Salthouse of Ulverston for Bastardy the Sum of 15...0...0

Of Richd. Ashburner of Gamswell for an illegitimate child fathered on his Son; the sum of 27...6...0 -

Of Samuel Robinson for an illegitimate child fathered on his Brother the Sum of 27...6...0 -

The Sum total of Money received by the said Constable amounts to £ 189 ...7s...9d.

1806 - April 6th - Easter Monday. Elected Churchwardens for the ensuing Year:

Thomas Fell of Holebigrow.

John Hartley, Farmer Holebigrow.

Overseers of the Poor:

John Robinson, Farmer, Castlehaw.

John Wilson, Farmer, Midrow.

Poor children appointed by the Sidesmen to be educated at the public School of the parish out of the poor Stock left for that purpose.

1808 - February 24th - At a Vestry Meeting examined the Acts of Thomas Nicholson of Channon House the Constable and find the following Sums were assessed and collected by the said Constable.

- April 18th - Poor children appointed to be educated the ensuing year at the parish School out of the poor Stock left for that purpose - Nobody apply'd ...

WEATHER
Examples from Various Journals

1800
NOVEMBER
22nd - Rainy 26th – Snow & Hail
28th – Severe frost. Wind NE.

DECEMBER
4th – Snow. Wind NE.
17th – Foggy. 19th – Extremely Wet. Wind S.

1801
JANUARY
2nd - Rain
25th – Snow

APRIL
1st - 2nd – Hot
3rd – Exceptionally Hot.

JUNE
18th - 20th – Hot
21st – Extremely Hot
26th – Excessive Hot.

1802
MAY
13th – Rain – Wind SE.

1803
JUNE
27th – Extremely hot
28th – Sultry
29th – Scorching.

JULY
1st – Extremely hot.

1805
APRIL
21st – Very Hot & Sultry
28th – Severe Frost, the Ground covered with Snow

JULY
16th – Very sultry
17th – Exceeding hot

DECEMBER
31st – Rain – Extremely Cold.

1806
JANUARY
1st – Rain
9th -Thunder & much lightening

JUNE
1st – Very hot & Dry
9th - Very sultry
23rd - 29th – Fine and either very dry, moderate showers or rain in the evening.

AUGUST
21st – Sultry, Thunder & Rain .

1807
FEBRUARY
4th- Snow – Three Inches

JULY
9th – A continuance of hot and dry weather
10th – Exceeding hot and dry.

DECEMBER
20th – Fog very thick in the Evening and extremely cold.

1808
JANUARY
2nd – Hills are covered with Snow apparantly very Deep.

JUNE
3rd - We have heard very little Thunder this Year ; Some distance Claps were heard this Evening to the South.

JULY
13th - Hot & Sultry in the extreme

BIBLIOGRAPHY

An Account of the Trigonometrical Survey, Carried on by Order of the Master-General of His Majesty's, Ordnance in the Years 1800-1809: William Mudge and Thomas Colby – 1811

Barrow-in-Furness Civic and Local History Society:
Dr. Bill Rollinson

Chronological History of the West Indies by C.T. Southey: Annual Register 1800 – Captain Watkin's Dispatches

Cumberland and Westmorland Antiquarian and Archaeological Society: Harriot Mellon, (1777 -1837), *Duchess of St. Albans, and the Ulverston Theatre* by Alfred Fell

Cumbria Archive and Local Studies Centre, Ramsden Square , Barrow-in-Furness: *Biography of William Close of Dalton, surgeon 1775-1813* by Alice Leach (Reference BDX/ 725/8)

The Diaries and Common Place Books of William Fleming (Reference BDX 584)

A Pennington Pepys 1770 -1829, the story of William Fleming, lecture notes by Dr William Rollinson (1977-1979) (Reference BDB 26 / Box 14 – Renaissance Theatre Trust Co. Ltd. David Marcus Productions Correspondence)

Dalton Book Club :
Website : www.daltonbookclub.org

Encyclopaedia Britannica: Biographies/Sarah Siddons - History/Treaty Of Amiens

The Epochs of Nature: George-Louis Leclerc, Comte de Buffon

The Herball of General Historie of Plants: John Gerard (1597)

The Historic Society of Lancashire and Cheshire: *John Bolton, A Liverpool Merchant – 1756-1837* by GW Mathews FSA

Internct Archive: Trial of Lieutenant General John Whitelocke Commander In Chief Of The Expedition Against Buenos Ayres

The Journal Of Antiquities : Priapus Stone, Great Urswick, Cumbria

Lancashire Online Parish Clerk Project : Burials at St. Mary in the Parish of Ulverston (1760-1812)

Burials at St. Michael and the Holy Angels Church in the Parish of Pennington (1689-1813) and (1814-1870)

Memoirs: Dr. Patrick Everard - Father Allan, Priest at Ulverston (1887-1907)

Newspapers: The Lancaster Gazette / The London Gazette

Old Lakeland: South Cumbrian Social History by J.D. Marshall

Oxford Dictionary Of National Biography: Julia Betterton or Butterton Glover

Sir William Lumley by H.M. Chichester. Revised by R.T. Stearn

The Paradise Of Furness: Sarah Elizabeth Holmes (Handstand Press)

ACKNOWLEDGEMENTS

Thanks to Cumbria Archive Service for a grant from the Kirby Archive Trust.

There are also several people I would like to acknowledge in the making of this book.

Firstly, Dr. Paul Hindle, executor of Dr. Bill Rollinson's estate for allowing me to use the title of the book.

Susan Benson, Selena Kendall and Paul Moore for their assistance over the last four years at the Cumbria Archives and Local Studies Centre, Ramsden Square, Barrow-in-Furness. Particularly Susan in helping me identify any words in Fleming's handwriting I could not!

Also, to William Fleming himself for fooling both of us - some of the time.

To Edward Fell and Philip Shipman for their translation of *Ranz des Vaches* in Chapter Five.

Finally, to Dan Elsworth of Greenlane Archaeology and Susan Teper for encouragement and initial proof reading.

All photographs by the editor, unless otherwise stated.

ABOUT THE EDITOR

Artist Biography – John Graeme Livingstone. From *The Encyclopedia of Popular Music* by Colin Larkin.

b. 21 February 1951, Nelson, Lancashire, England. Livingstone is a singer-songwriter mostly working around his home in the Lake District. *Wings Of Fire* was a powerful single, influenced by his love of John Stewart. *Ship Of The Sky* is about the courage of the Archbishop of Canterbury's envoy, Terry Waite.

A new album, *Innocent Bystanders*, featuring Wes McGhee and Cathryn Craig, was set for release in 1997. Livingstone also completed a series of songs about soldiers fighting Napoleon's forces in Spain, *Just A Little War*.

The Editor with US singer-songwriter, Dave Mallett
at BBC Radio Merseyside - Photo by Spencer Leigh

Livingstone owns Stillwater Records and Fair Oaks Entertainments. He has brought singer-songwriter Dave Mallett and Don-Oja Dunaway to the UK as well as promoting concerts by Bill Zorn, now with The Limeliters.

Lightning Source UK Ltd.
Milton Keynes UK
UKHW020950260919

350504UK00009B/320/P